THE
PRESCRIPTION
for FINANCIAL
HEALTH:

AN AUTHORITATIVE GUIDE
FOR PHYSICIANS

SECOND EDITION

Joel M. Blau, CFP™
Ronald J. Paprocki, JD, CFP,™ CHBC

EDITED BY:
Karen K. Brask
Kathy Ricker

MEDIQUS Asset Advisors, Inc.
200 N. LaSalle Street, Suite 2300
Chicago, Illinois 60601
800-883-8555
www.mediqus.com

American Association for
PHYSICIAN
LEADERSHIP

Published by **American Association for Physician Leadership, Inc.**
PO Box 96503 | BMB 97493 | Washington, DC 20090-6503

Website: www.physicianleaders.org

AAPL books are available at special quantity discounts to use as premiums and sales promotions, or for use in corporate training programs. For more information, please write to Special Sales at journal@physicianleaders.org

This publication is designed to provide general information and is sold with the understanding that neither the author nor the publisher is engaged in rendering legal, accounting, ethical, or clinical advice. If legal or other expert advice is required, the services of a competent professional person should be sought.

13   8 7 6 5 4 3 2 1

Copyedited, typeset, indexed, and printed in the United States of America

PUBLISHER
Nancy Collins

EDITORIAL ASSISTANT
Jennifer Weiss

DESIGN & LAYOUT
Carter Publishing Studio

INDEX
Robert Saigh

COPYEDITOR
Pat George

Table of Contents

Dedication and Acknowledgements

Joel Blau:
I lovingly dedicate this book to the memory of my father Sam and my younger brother Neal, who both fought long and courageous battles with cancer. Through their journeys I saw firsthand the power of the human spirit and the passion that physicians bring to their craft and their patients. My hope is that this book will make the financial aspects of physician's lives easier so they can concentrate their time and talents on providing quality care to others. I thank my wife Susie and our children, Jamie, Jason, and Diana, for their ongoing support. My love for them is all the motivation I need.

Ronald Paprocki:
I am grateful for so many of the individuals who influenced my life and allowed me to contribute to this project. In particular, I would like to offer a special thank you to my family: to my wife, Joyce, for putting up with my "attitudes" and seemingly always-changing schedules, and to my sons, Jon and Matt, for providing regular reminders to me about the importance of their lives to mine. I love you all!

Joint Acknowledgement:
We also would like to thank Kathy Ricker and Karen Brask for their editing expertise, as well as the entire MEDIQUS team for all of their valuable input and contributions to this project.

We also want to express our appreciation for the support provided by Julie Khazan and Jeff Witz. They contributed countless hours of research to his project

About the Authors

Joel M. Blau, CFP™ is president of MEDIQUS Asset Advisors, Inc. Prior to co-founding the firm, Mr. Blau was vice president and senior financial counselor for AMA Investment Advisers, L.P., an affiliate of the American Medical Association. Mr. Blau is responsible for the Institutional Services provided by MEDIQUS and has extensive experience in the analysis and design of financial plans and strategies for health care professionals and medical organizations. His areas of expertise include not-for-profit investment management, wealth preservation through estate tax planning, retirement, investment, and insurance planning.

A Certified Financial Planner™ certificant, Mr. Blau earned his bachelor's degree in business from Drake University, with a major in finance and a specialization in investments. His monthly financial articles appear in national, state, and county medical specialty society publications as well as several health care industry magazines. He is also co-author of *The Prescription for Financial Health: An Authoritative Guide for Physicians*, published in the fall of 2005, and *Medical Practice Divorce*, published by AMA Press in 2002.

In addition to frequent presentations at Board or Finance Committee meetings for our Institutional clients, Mr. Blau is a well-respected public speaker and delivers financial seminars for professional medical associations, hospitals, and clinics across the country. He is a member of the Financial Planning Association and holds various securities, insurance and professional licenses.

A life-long resident of the Chicago area, he currently resides in the northern suburbs of Chicago with his wife.

Ronald J. Paprocki, J.D., CFP,™ CHBC is the Chief Executive Officer of MEDIQUS Asset Advisors, Inc., a national financial and investment advisory firm that specializes in assisting and advising physicians and health care professionals. Before co-founding MEDIQUS in 1996, Ron was the Vice President of AMA Investment Advisers, L.P., an affiliate of the American Medical Association.

Mr. Paprocki has been responsible for the analysis and design of individual financial situations for health care professionals, closely held business owners and high level executives. His approach in assisting health care professionals has led to the development of The MEDIQUS Way,℠ a planning method that utilizes a consistent and dependable process of analytical systems and investment strategies to help clients accomplish their objectives. Specifically, Mr. Paprocki's areas of expertise include retirement, investment, and estate planning.

A Certified Financial Planner,™ Certified Healthcare Business Consultant, and Registered Securities Principal, Mr. Paprocki earned his law degree from DePaul University College of Law and his bachelor's degree from Knox College. In addition, he holds other various securities, insurance and professional licenses. Ron is a regular contributor to *Medical Economics* magazine, which recently recognized MEDIQUS as one of the top financial planners for physicians. Mr. Paprocki is frequently quoted in the *Chicago Tribune* and has appeared on CNBC. Mr. Paprocki is also the co-author of a book published by the AMA titled, *Medical Practice Divorce*.

Introduction

Historically, society has viewed you, the physician, as one of its most educated and prestigious professionals. As a student, you attended the finest universities for the greatest number of years. You achieved the highest undergraduate grades in order to move on to medical school where you studied day and night to acquire your skills. Only after seemingly endless years were you finally ready to enter the work force. Even at this point, some of you chose to continue your education and training in a specialty field.

When the time finally came for you to begin your career, you found yourself heavily in debt. Maybe you had student loans beginning to come due; maybe you had spent your savings, grants, and parents' money in order to reach your current state: temporarily unemployed!

However, you knew that once your professional career began, you could look forward to being one of the highest-paid professionals in your community and in the country. Almost before you knew it, you were receiving paychecks that you certainly would not want your office staff to see. These paychecks may have been in addition to quarterly practice bonuses sufficient to buy a new car or even help with a down payment on a new home.

As your practice of medicine continued, you found that you were able to save money on a regular basis. What would you do with those extra funds? What *should* you do with those funds to ensure your family's well-being in the event you were unable to continue working?

If these were questions of a medical nature, you would no doubt have the answers or know where to find them. You could refer to a class or specific textbook that would address your inquiry. You could contact colleagues and bounce the questions off of them. Maybe the answers were in a book in your office. Wherever the answers might be found, you could find them.

But these are not medical questions. They are financial planning questions, and when it comes to making financial decisions, how educated are you? How many courses did you take in business administration? Did you attend the lectures in Finance 101 or the class on basic investments? How many hours did you take in personal risk management and estate tax planning? The fact is, you couldn't take these classes because you were too busy concentrating on your medical degree.

The problem with this lack of financial education is that it makes you vulnerable to the financial salespeople who always seem to catch you at a bad time. Promises of doubling your original investment, tax write-offs, and lower life and disability insurance premiums fill your ears as you juggle patients and run to surgery. What should a responsible physician do? The financial salesperson is right. You do have some extra money that you should invest. Of course you want to have the right amount of life insurance, and you certainly want to pay lower taxes. You also have a responsibility to your family today as well as in the future. Unfortunately, when you are forced to make a quick decision about a financial product, it is often the wrong decision. These are decisions that can affect you for the rest of your life.

The key to building a successful financial foundation and future is a good education. Unfortunately, you probably just don't have the time to devote to that education. We conduct educational lectures for groups of physicians all around the country. After such an event, we are often asked to recommend a book that will provide a "good" financial education. We are asked about "get rich quick by beating the market" schemes. We are asked about seminars, software programs, smart phone apps, and financial planning textbooks that promise to provide answers to all of your questions and solve all of your problems in a matter of hours.

The reality is that these schemes, seminars, software programs, smart phone apps, and textbooks can't address the specific needs of today's medical professionals and the problems they face. They don't address the liability issues that are often unique to physicians. They don't address the time demands placed on physicians that impact their professional and personal lives. Physicians' incomes are not increasing as they have in the past. Many are seeing decreases in net income due to managed care and increasing overhead.

The Future's No Longer Guaranteed

These are among the many reasons you must get a handle on personal financial planning strategies that will allow you to continue doing what you do best: practice medicine.

Golf courses, tennis courts, biking trails, coffee shops, and the doctors' lounge are popular places to gain unsolicited (and usually inappropriate) financial advice. Every day you hear about a hot stock that was bought and then doubled within a month. Your colleague tells you he bought a great life insurance policy with unbelievably low rates. You can't understand how your friends have the time and the financial savvy to be so involved in their own financial plans. It seems you are hearing one success story after another.

What you never seem to hear are the financial horror stories: the stock that plummeted the week after your neighbor bought on a "hot" tip; the bond that was supposed to pay much higher-than-average interest, but in fact never did because the company declared bankruptcy. There are more stories of lost money and dreams than there are success stories, but you probably won't hear too many of these being touted in the lounge. Who among us wants to look foolish?

You can't just buy a mutual fund or stock because your colleague bought it. His or her long-term goals and objectives may be, and probably are, very different from yours. The key is to control your own destiny through a comprehensive understanding of financial strategies and techniques. Only by understanding these strategies and techniques will you be able to make the best decisions for yourself and your family.

You don't have to go it alone. You can hire advisors who will lay out your options, but you must remain the boss and be responsible for your own decisions.

This guide outlines a foundation for a successful financial future. It begins with a general overview of the financial planning process and how it relates to today's economy. Taxes and inflation will never go away, but finding a good method for managing their devastating effects will minimize the impact on your investment dollars. Although each individual's goals and objectives are different, there are some common denominators during different periods of the life cycle.

Once you learn the basics, you can focus on investment planning. This section will provide you with a better understanding of the advantages and disadvantages of various investment vehicles. We will illustrate methods used by the largest pension plans and bank trust companies to achieve their investment planning goals. By incorporating similar strategies, you can create your own portfolio in a manner that will save you time and aggravation, as well as commissions and other costs.

The Strategic Planning section discusses techniques for saving to accomplish long-term goals. We consult with physicians on a daily basis, and often find ourselves the bearers of bad news. We frequently have to tell physicians coming into our office that they will not be able to retire at their desired age and income level. Please do not shoot the messenger! We are simply attempting to analyze the situation realistically and quantitatively in an effort to avoid any potential pitfalls.

Proper planning today will enable you to avoid these bad news meetings. The answer is neither to spend all your money today nor save everything for the future. The answer lies somewhere in between, and by quantifying the savings amount required, you will indeed be able to strike a financial balance in your life.

To achieve true financial independence, you need to do three things. First, define your objectives in a manner that can balance your present needs and future goals. Next, lay out a game plan that will enable you to reach your goals. Finally, practice the discipline required to follow your plan and monitor your progress, adjusting your plan as needed. Whatever your objectives are, the time to start is NOW. Procrastination will only make your goals seem impossible to reach.

What about using insurance products to manage life's risks? Do you have the right coverage? Are your premiums higher than they have to be? If these questions sound familiar to you, it's probably because an insurance salesperson has proposed them to you. Physicians don't *buy* life, disability, and long-term care insurance; it is *sold* to them.

The Risk Management Section will look at different types of policies available in the marketplace today. We will also review the steps you can take to determine the amount of coverage you need. This is the only way you can be a savvy insurance buyer who doesn't waste valuable time listening to sales pitches.

College costs have been skyrocketing, with no leveling off expected in the near future. Historically, college tuition, along with room and board expenses, has been increasing at rates higher than the average increases in inflation. There is no question that the expense of educating children has become one of the greatest financial burdens facing parents today. The Education Planning chapter will provide proactive planning methods to enable today's parents and grandparents to save money in the most tax-efficient manner while still maintaining a level of necessary control.

Unfortunately, physicians now more than ever before have to be proactive to ensure the protection of their assets. Malpractice insurance premiums continue to rise and lawsuits continue to be filed, placing your hard-earned assets in jeopardy. The Asset Protection Planning section will describe the current environment of liability exposure facing medical practitioners today, and explore in detail effective and practical solutions to protect your assets now as well as in the future.

The Estate Planning Section will look at estate tax-planning strategies and techniques. You will work too long to allow the government to take over half of your estate at death. We know we have federal budget deficit problems, but why should the burden of excessive taxes be on you? What if your spouse remarries after your death? Will your beneficiaries be protected?

If you have spent time with a lawyer and have created various trusts, you may still be at risk. We have reviewed trusts prepared by some of the top law firms in the country, and unless your estate plan is coordinated with the titling of your assets, you have wasted the money and effort to have the plan prepared.

This final section of this guide lays out the framework for an efficient estate plan based on the size of your asset base. You will learn how to coordinate qualified retirement plans with your estate plan. We will also discuss how you can pay your ultimate estate tax for pennies on the dollar or use charitable gifting techniques that allow you to direct the distribution of assets toward a charity of choice and away from the government. This section will provide you with the knowledge you need before you walk into an attorney's office, and arm you with the questions that must be asked to ensure efficiency.

Your greatest asset as you plan for your financial future is *knowledge*. As you gain a better understanding of the important elements of financial planning, investment options, and portfolio structure, you will be able to formulate a successful strategy for accomplishing your long- and short-term goals and objectives.

We are pleased that you decided to use our book as a guide for your financial future. We welcome your comments, questions, and observations.

CHAPTER 1

Designing an Efficient Financial Plan

When constructing a financial plan, many physicians complain about the overwhelming (and often conflicting) amount of available information. The wealth of information combined with numerous strategies suggested by a variety of professionals often produces a paralysis that results in nothing being accomplished.

We find that the best way to avoid this paralysis is to break down the plan into small steps that are easily accomplished. The first step is to determine the appropriate process for building your financial plan—a plan for the plan!

Picture the pyramids of Egypt. Pyramids are built on a solid large base. As they rise into the sky, they begin to narrow until reaching the apex. This basic design has allowed the Egyptian pyramids to withstand the test of time. Would the Egyptians have had the same results if they had started with the apex at the bottom and ended up with the broad base on top? Of course not, but this appears to be the investment architecture many physicians use every day. Think of the pyramid as your financial plan.

Hazard Protection: Protecting Your Most Important Asset

The base of the pyramid serves as the financial foundation on which everything else is built. Consider the base to be the fundamental strategy of your financial plan and the apex to be the strategy you will consider only after all of the previous strategies have been completed successfully. The key is to build a strong foundation that will serve as your pyramid's base. This base should address the most basic of all your financial concerns and should focus on your most important asset.

We routinely meet physicians who have a difficult time identifying their most important asset. Many assume that their home, pension plan, or investment portfolio is the most important asset they own. However, the most important asset for most physicians is the ability to work in their profession. After all, you could lose many of your financial assets and be able to replace them simply because you can continue to earn an income from the practice of medicine. Thus, the foundation of your financial plan will address this most important asset. Let's call this section of the pyramid "hazard protection."

When you completed your residency, who was the first financial advisor to contact you? Was it a stockbroker or maybe a municipal bond broker? We would guess not. Why? Because at that point in your career you hadn't accumulated enough excess investment dollars to generate commissions for these financial salespeople. The odds are your first contact was with an insurance agent. The agent probably talked about the effect your premature death or disability would have on your family. He or she likely explained that your most important asset was your ability to earn income and that you must insure against that loss.

This does make a great deal of sense. Physicians have an excellent economic life value, meaning that the present value of your expected earnings in the future is quite high. For example, assuming a 3% discount rate, the economic life value of a physician expected to earn only $150,000 per year for 35 years is approximately $3,319,775.

What can impact this most important asset? As far as we have seen, only two uncontrollable situations: death or disability.

What if you die? Physicians, particularly new physicians, may be deeply in debt due to student loans or the mortgage on a first home or office. If you are married and are the main income earner,

Economic Life Values @ 3%

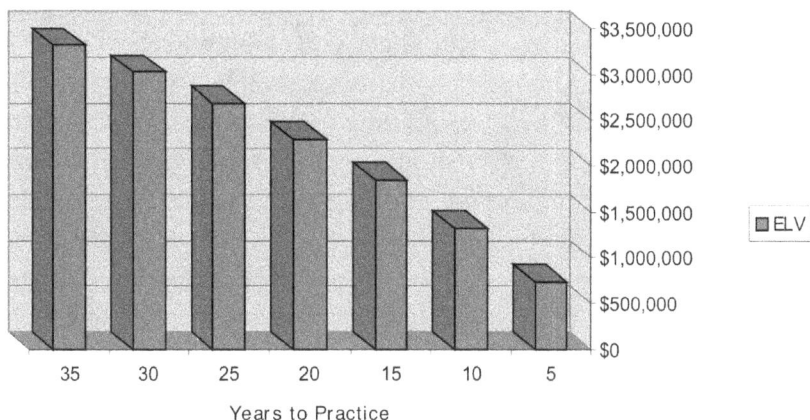

you may need a life insurance policy. The life insurance proceeds would allow your spouse to pay off debt or fund your children's education, as well as create some sort of regular income for the surviving family.

But what if you couldn't work due to disability? There would be no lump-sum payment to support your family as there is with a death benefit. The problem is that, unlike death, in disability you are still a consumer, but a consumer without an income. Did you know that the odds of incurring a disability during our working years are much greater than the odds of dying?

The chances of being disabled for more than 90 days before age 65:

At Age	Number Per 1,000 Disabled at Least 90 Days	At Age	Number Per 1,000 Disabled at Least 90 Days
25	600 — 3 out of 5	45	408 — 2 out of 5
30	558 — 5 out of 9	50	343 — 1 out of 3
35	512 — 1 out of 2	55	216 — 1 out of 4
40	463 — 4 out of 9	60	152 — 1 out of 7

(1985 Commissioner's Disability A-Table)

These statistics illustrate why it is so important to have the correct risk management plan in place. It is the only way to manage those uncontrollable situations. Protecting your most important asset—your ability to practice medicine—is critical to your financial plan.

Estate planning is another aspect of hazard protection. Regardless of your current income or the size of your estate, you must make decisions today that will affect your family in the future. If you have children, you need to name guardians (those who will care for children or other dependents) and trustees (those who will manage property). You should put your postmortem desires in writing with regard to who should receive particular assets at your death and how.

You are probably beginning to realize that a solid foundation is not the exciting entry into financial planning you may have imagined. Let's face it, who wants to think about hazards such as disability and death as their bright career is just beginning or is in full swing? Because this can be a stressful and somewhat time-consuming task, many physicians simply ignore the base and head straight for the apex—those speculative investments that promise spectacular returns and tax write-offs. By the time these individuals understand why the pyramid is not built inversely it often is too late.

Emergency Funds

After building a sound foundation, you should build a layer of cash reserves. Cash reserves include those assets that do not fluctuate in principal value—funds that are available on a daily basis. You simply walk into the bank, visit the local ATM machine, or write a check. This category includes checking and savings accounts, money market accounts, and short-term certificates of deposit (CDs). Cash reserves provide us with necessary emergency funds. The risk/reward tradeoff for cash reserves is that these vehicles usually provide the lowest interest rates and thus do not offer any meaningful growth potential. You want to have cash available in case the car breaks down, the roof needs a repair, or you simply experience a month when expenses exceed income. The amount to keep in an emergency fund depends on your personal situation.

A fully funded emergency reserve is necessary because we all know that the worst time to sell any investment, be it a stock, bond, or real estate, is when you must. To determine an appropriate funding level, you should take a close look at your average monthly living expenses. You can do this by simply adding up the amount of the checks you wrote and the online payments you made during a one-month period. Using two or three months will give you a better idea of your average monthly expenses. Don't forget to include a portion of your large bills such as insurance premiums, property taxes, and home improvements that may be paid annually. Your total average monthly expense is also known as your standard of living.

Although everyone's standard of living is different, the guidelines are similar. Financial planning practitioners recommend that an emergency fund should equal approximately three to six times your monthly living expenses, plus the expected major expenses you plan to incur within six months. Three months of living expenses may be an adequate amount assuming that your income is predictable and consistent. If, on the other hand, you are a sole practitioner and your monthly income is more erratic, you may want to have as much as six times your average monthly total living expenses allocated to cash equivalents. After all, forcing the sale of an investment at an inopportune time can be extremely expensive and may force you to suffer a loss you did not expect.

Since cash equivalents earn relatively low rates of return, many physicians have chosen another alternative that frees up more of their cash for investments. Homeowners can establish an equity line of credit against the value of their home. This alternative allows you to write checks against your home equity while paying interest only on the actual amount used. In addition, the interest paid on the loan is generally deductible on a personal tax return. This strategy works if you have the necessary equity available in your home. However, even though the interest is deductible, you still must ultimately repay the loan, and you incur an interest expense. Since another objective of an emergency fund is peace of mind, it is important that you choose the method you are most comfortable with based on your lifestyle.

Another key funding determinant relates to your disability insurance policy's waiting period. Most disability benefits begin only after satisfying a waiting period that can range from one to six months. You need to know the length of your waiting period before you can determine the amount that should be set aside for your personal emergency fund. If you are employed by a hospital or work in a large group practice, short-term disability plans are often included as part of the benefits package. If you have not supplemented your coverage with a short-term disability policy, you will need your emergency fund to pay bills until your benefits begin.

Keep in mind that, just as an under-funded reserve can force you to dip into longer-term savings vehicles, an over-funded reserve reduces your ability to invest in other assets that may offer potentially greater returns over the long term.

Liquid Investments

As you continue to climb the financial planning pyramid, you will reach the level of liquid investments. Liquid investments are those that can be sold and converted to cash within 3 to 10 days. Liquid investments will incur some level of principal fluctuation; thus, at the time of sale, the value of a liquid investment can be more or less than the original investment. However, even though the return of principal is not guaranteed, you can receive the proceeds in a timely fashion. Examples of liquid investments are stocks, bonds, and mutual funds. Also included could be the cash values of variable life insurance policies, but in some cases these can take much longer than 7 to 10 days to liquidate.

Unlike cash reserves, liquid investments have the advantage of higher potential returns over time, but this potential for higher returns comes at the cost of possible fluctuation or risk. There is nothing wrong with taking on increased risk, as long as you have an adequate emergency fund to provide the needed protection.

Nonliquid Investments

Continuing your ascent of the financial planning pyramid, you reach the level of nonliquid investments. These investments are classified in two basic categories: tax- qualified plans and tax-advantaged investments. Included in the first category are qualified retirement plans, including pension and profit-sharing plans. The investments within these plans may be in cash equivalents, stocks, bonds, mutual funds, or other types of investments. As a general rule, these funds are somewhat illiquid until you are age 59½. Withdrawals from these plans, as well as individual retirement accounts (IRAs), before age 59½ are typically assessed a 10% IRS penalty and are considered taxable income in the year received. There are exceptions to these rules, and we will cover them more specifically in the Retirement Planning chapter.

The second category includes annuities and real estate. With annuities, there can be substantial penalties for early withdrawal. Penalties notwithstanding, there are a number of advantages to a nonliquid investment that cannot be duplicated in other types of investments. Real estate offers tax-deferred growth and possible tax benefits such as depreciation. In the case of qualified plans and annuities, interest, dividends, and capital gains grow on a tax-deferred basis. SEPs and IRAs have the added advantage of tax-deductible contributions, which can save you tax dollars during your peak earning years.

Tax Shelters

Near the top of the pyramid lie tax shelters. Tax shelters were popular with physicians in the early 1980s. These investments were originally sold as a way to lower income tax liability while providing growth or income potential. Vehicles used within the shelters included real estate, equipment leasing, movie production, and even jojoba fields. While these investments are very illiquid in nature, many physicians bought into these programs not only because of the tax benefits, but also because of the EXPECTED viability of the actual investment.

However, the tax law changed in 1986, taking away many of these tax advantages. In addition, many of the underlying investment vehicles did not perform up to expectations. Tax shelters and limited partnerships are still available in the market today, but the emphasis has shifted from tax benefits to the economic soundness of the investment itself. Tax shelters must make good economic sense before you make a long- term commitment.

Apex

The apex of the financial planning pyramid is reserved for the highest risk investments. These investments typically have high return potential as well as high loss potential. Included in this category are commodity trading and venture capital opportunities. Commodity trading involves the use of leverage to buy or sell futures contracts in precious metals, grains, meats, currencies, and stock and bond market indices. Leverage and the use of margin accounts have created a situation in which losses can well exceed the original investment.

Venture capital is used to finance a new or expanding business. This category includes money you may lend to a relative or friend to start a business. On the surface these investments may appear to be viable, but in the majority of cases you will lose not only your money, but also your friend. Lending money to a relative can create an even worse situation because you are still related when the investment fails.

Remember that you generally don't get something worthwhile for nothing. There is really no perfect investment that will give you high guaranteed returns without incurring any risks. Along with this basic understanding, you should also realize that each individual's pyramid will be structured differently based on individual risk tolerance and long-term objectives.

An analysis of many physicians' portfolios shows an overwhelming amount of apex-type investments. Interestingly, underperforming investments are not usually the reason many physicians are not financially independent. The most common reason is pure and simple procrastination. The fact is that most Americans are financial planning procrastinators, and physicians are no exception. The most frustrating part of our job is telling a 50-year-old physician who makes $200,000 per year that he needs to save $225,000 annually in order to accomplish his newly defined retirement goals. This is a common problem with a simple solution. The key element in long-term savings is TIME. The sooner you begin to set aside funds for any long-term goal, be it retirement, college education, or a new home, the easier it is to accomplish that goal.

Consider the goal of funding a college education. With tuition rates on the rise, it is not uncommon for annual college costs today to run between $25,000 and $55,000. When no dollars have been set aside for college, many physicians take out home equity loans or dip into personal savings. Some take it from cash flow at the expense of not making a retirement plan contribution for a particular year or period of time. A less stressful and more cost-efficient method would be to begin an annual savings plan while the child is young. In this way, the annual savings required for a one-year-old may be only $1,000 to $2,000, depending on the rate of return.

The same holds true for retirement savings. The earlier you begin, the less painful and noticeable the earmarked savings plan will be. Let's look at a simple example. Assume two individuals, Bill and Jane, are each at the tender age of 21. Each receives a modest gift of $5,000 each year. They have the option of saving the money or spending it. Jane decides she will save the gift and does so for the first nine years, thus saving a total of $45,000. During this same time period, Bill has other plans that require he spend the gift. Things like car payments, stereo systems, and entertainment are pretty important to him! Thus, during the first nine years he saves nothing. After the ninth year, Bill and Jane experience a reversal of their saving or spending habits. Jane can no longer save the $5,000 she receives each year, and Bill begins to save every penny. This goes on until they reach age 65. Over the entire period Jane has saved $45,000 and Bill has saved $170,000 ($5,000 per year for 34 years). Assuming they each earned an average rate of return of 9% per year during the time period, who would have more money when they reach age 65—Jane, who started early but was able to save only $45,000, or Bill, who started a little later but saved a total of $170,000? Just for fun, we have placed the answer (and a bit more detail) at the end of the chapter.

Unfortunately, many physicians feel invincible when it comes to their financial future. Their optimistic view is that income will continue to increase and thus there will always be an opportunity to save later. The optimists believe that in view of their current income, this is the time to spend and enjoy life to the fullest. We are beginning to realize that this view can no longer be pragmatically supported. Physician compensation is decreasing as the practice of medicine is changing. Now is the time to evaluate your current situation and lay out a game plan so there won't be any disappointments down the road. Now is not the time to procrastinate; it is the time to take action in order to control your financial destiny.

```
┌─────────────────────────────────────┐
│             Speculative             │
└─────────────────────────────────────┘
┌───────────────────────────────────────┐
│              Tax Shelters             │
└───────────────────────────────────────┘
┌───────────────────────────────────────────┐
│          Non-Liquid Investments           │
│ (tax qualified plans, tax advantaged investments) │
└───────────────────────────────────────────┘
┌─────────────────────────────────────────────┐
│            Liquid Investments               │
│         (easily converted to cash)          │
└─────────────────────────────────────────────┘
┌───────────────────────────────────────────────┐
│              Emergency Funds                  │
│       (3-6 months after tax expenses)         │
└───────────────────────────────────────────────┘
┌─────────────────────────────────────────────────┐
│              Hazard Protection                  │
│        (lawsuits, disability, death)            │
└─────────────────────────────────────────────────┘
```

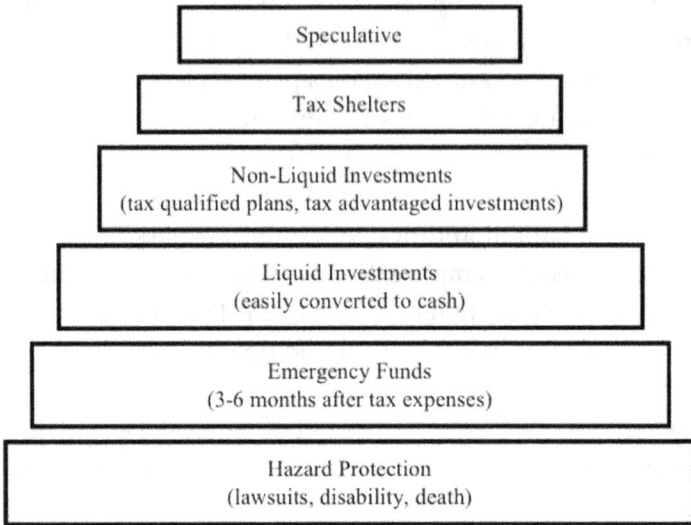

Now for the answer to the Bill and Jane question. Although she saved only $45,000, Jane has more money at age 65 than Bill who started late but saved a total of $170,000. In fact, she has over $230,000 more than Bill as the following table illustrates:

	Starting Early	**Starting Late**
Total Invested	$45,000	$170,000
Value at age 65 (at 9 percent)	$1,219,316	$984,912

This is a hypothetical illustration only, and its performance is not indicative of any particular investment. Investments with potential for higher returns carry greater risk of loss.

CHAPTER 2

Strategic Planning

Compound Interest

I n addition to understanding risk and how it relates to your financial plan, you must also have a grasp of a very basic but important concept that can affect your assets: the concept of compound interest.

Many investment vehicles have an income component. Income can be derived from interest (bank savings accounts, certificates of deposit, and bonds), dividends (common stock and mutual funds), or capital gains distributions (mutual funds). In the case of bank accounts and mutual funds, you have the option of getting the income in the form of a check every month (or whenever distributed), or reinvesting the income back into the original investment. The latter is referred to as compounding.

If you are in need of current income, you have no choice but to receive an income distribution. On the other hand, if you do not currently need the income, you should consider compounding. Compounding can impact your actual returns in a very positive way. Consider for a moment a $100,000 bank CD paying an annual interest rate of 3%. Do you remember when CDs paid as much as 3%? If you choose to take the income as a monthly distribution, you will receive $3,000 per year ($100,000 × 3%), or $250 per month. If, on the other hand, you choose to compound each month (interest is left in the investment), you will earn $3,041.60. This in effect represents a yield of 3.042%. At the end of 10 years (ignoring taxes for the moment), this CD would be worth $134,392.

Interestingly, if you were to double the rate of return to 6%, taken as a distribution, the income would be $6,000. If the amount were left to compound monthly, the actual dollar return would be $6,167.78—an effective yield of 6.167%. However, the value of the CD after 10 years would be approximately $179,085.

As you can see, there is an exponential relationship relative to compounding. Let's look at the impact over a 10-year period. If the 3% compounded rate is doubled to 6%, the interest earned increases from $34,392 (ending value at 3% of $134,392 minus original deposit of $100,000) to $79,085 (ending value at 6% of $179,085 minus original deposit of $100,000). Thus, while the interest rate doubled from 3% to 6%, the earnings more than doubled from $34,392 to $79,085. That's because interest is building on the interest. Compounding allows your investment dollars to work for you instead of you working to save even more. As a general rule, if you don't need the current income generated by your investments, don't take it—let it compound.

Picture your investments as a tank of water. As you reinvest, the tank gets more and more full. There is also a faucet attached to the tank. Turning on the faucet gives you the immediate benefit of the income. If you are not in need of current income, you simply turn the faucet off and let the compounding continue.

Unfortunately, many physicians forget the importance of compounding in their retirement years. During their working years they compound simply because earned income satisfies their spending needs. At retirement they contact their brokers and investment managers and instruct them to open the faucet wide and let the income flow. But what if there is more income than the retiree needs? This extra money is no longer affected by the exponential relationship of compounding. The key is to remove only that income which is needed.

Inflation and Taxes

In determining future income needs, you must be cognizant of the factors that work to erode hard-earned capital. Inflation, coupled with taxation, can have a devastating effect on long-term objectives. To illustrate the effect of inflation on your long-term goals, consider its effect on your desired monthly retirement income. The following illustration shows what today's 45-year-old physician can expect when retiring at age 60. To produce $1,000 of purchasing power as measured in today's standards, the following would be required, assuming a 5% rate of inflation:

**Requirement to Produce $1,000 of Purchasing Power
(5% inflation rate)**

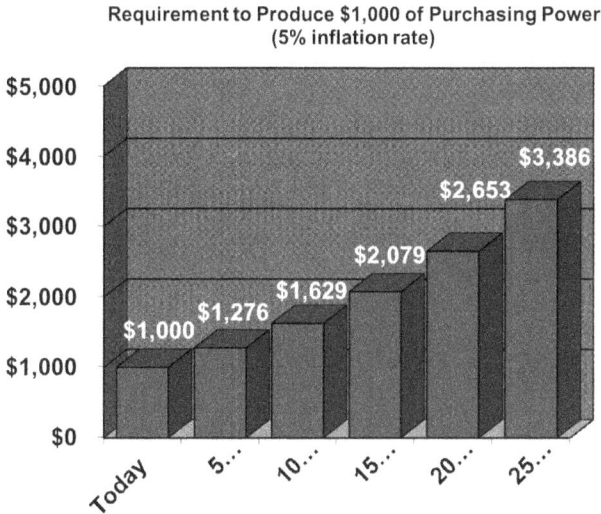

The future value of $1,000 in 15 years at 5% inflation is $2,079. Thus, $2,079 will be required to purchase the same basket of goods that $1,000 purchased today.

Many individuals find these numbers hard to believe! Will you have enough investment assets to generate this type of income? If these amounts seem unrealistic, think back 20 years and consider the cost of a new car, house, and groceries. Or better yet, remember the price of your first home. Now think back to the last automobile you bought. Was it more expensive than your first home? For a great many of us, this is definitely true! Costs have increased dramatically over the years due to inflation. Of course, over the same 20 years incomes have also increased. Twenty years ago an annual income of $150,000 was earned only by top-level executives and professionals. Today, $150,000 is the annual starting pay for physicians in many parts of the country.

During our working years, we justify the negative effect of inflation by relying on the fact that our incomes will rise at levels consistent with or above inflation. Unfortunately, many of today's physicians are experiencing the opposite. Incomes are dropping at a rather dramatic rate. It is not uncommon for clients to tell us that their income has peaked and their best financial years are behind them. That is why more physicians than ever before are concerned about their financial future. The days of working and letting your income and retirement plans automatically take care of themselves are over. Planning is now more important than ever, and planning for retirement income must take inflation into account. Failing to do so will be an expensive mistake. Just remember that, if you fail to take inflation into account, you will experience the only guarantee we can make in the financial planning business: a continually decreasing standard of living.

Taxation

No discussion of capital erosion can occur without mentioning income taxation. Tax rates change, sometimes increasing, sometimes decreasing. Therefore, you should incorporate tax planning strategies into any overall financial plan.

Income may be taxable, tax-deferred or tax-free, depending on the specific investment. Taxable income is reported on your IRS form 1040. Earned income and interest is taxed at your marginal rate. Based on the American Taxpayer Relief Act of 2012, capital gains for investment assets held for more than 12 months will be taxed at 0% for those in the lowest tax brackets, 15% for individuals earning less than $400,000, and 20% for individuals earning more than $400,000.

Deferral of investment income taxation is most commonly accomplished through qualified retirement plans. The same is true for fixed and variable annuities, appreciating securities, and real estate. The goal is to defer the taxation of the investment income to a time in the future, such as retirement. Taxes are then paid as the funds are withdrawn, possibly at a lower rate. When combined with compounding, tax deferral can have a dramatically positive effect on your portfolio. Qualified plans have the added advantage of a tax-deductible contribution. The unknown variable is what tax rates will be in the future. If you have a hefty retirement income goal, you may find yourself paying taxes at the same rate as when you were working.

Tax-free investment income is limited primarily to interest generated from municipal bonds. The investor receives this income free of federal taxes. Many states also exempt municipal bond income from state taxes, further enhancing the attractiveness of the bonds. Keep in mind the risk/reward tradeoff. Because of their relative low risk and tax-free status, municipal bond interest rates are lower than interest rates for comparable corporate bonds. The determining factor will be your specific tax rate.

Although everyone wants to pay less in taxes, what really matters is how much of your investment income you actually keep after taxes. Very often the taxable investment proves to be the better alternative. Whenever someone suggests you purchase a municipal bond, you should determine what the comparable taxable bond is yielding before making a decision. Oftentimes retired physicians buy municipal bonds because of their personal aversion to paying income taxes, while the taxable bond may be providing a higher, after-tax yield. An added concern for retirees is that a high level of municipal bond income can result in additional taxation of Social Security benefits.

Many physicians tell us they are extremely conservative. They think that if the principal value of an investment fluctuates, it carries more risk than they are willing to assume. They enjoy the peace of mind that comes from knowing that their money is being held on deposit in a simple savings account or a certificate of deposit, which allows locking in an interest rate for a specified amount of time.

Consider for a moment the effects of inflation and taxation on this "safe, risk-free" vehicle. If the CD guarantees a rate of 3%, regardless of whether or not income is taken or compounded, a 1099 form will be issued making the owner liable for taxes on the interest earned. This alone can amount to an after-tax decrease of up to 40%, depending on the level of your federal and state income tax. Now subtract the effects of long-term inflation. That pre-tax 3% rate becomes 1.8% after taxes, and likely will result in a negative return after allowing for an average inflation factor. If we were to assume 3% inflation, there is an actual loss of 1.2% per year. This "safe" strategy is known as a guaranteed method for losing money after taxes and inflation. The benefit to the investor is knowing what is going to happen to the investment, as opposed to other investment vehicles that do not offer guarantees. The key is to achieve a comfortable level of growth and/or income on an after-tax and after-inflation basis.

In order to differentiate rates of return, the financial industry uses the term *real rate of return*. The real rate of return refers to the after-inflation rate of return of any given investment. It's a reminder that you can't ignore the potential erosion of your capital. Keeping the real rate of return in mind allows you to compare investments on an even playing field.

As the following table illustrates, the impact of taxes and inflation can often produce a negative result on the return of taxable investments, especially for certificates of deposits.

HISTORY OF THE REAL AFTER-TAX RATE OF RETURN FOR CERTIFICATES OF DEPOSIT (PART 1)

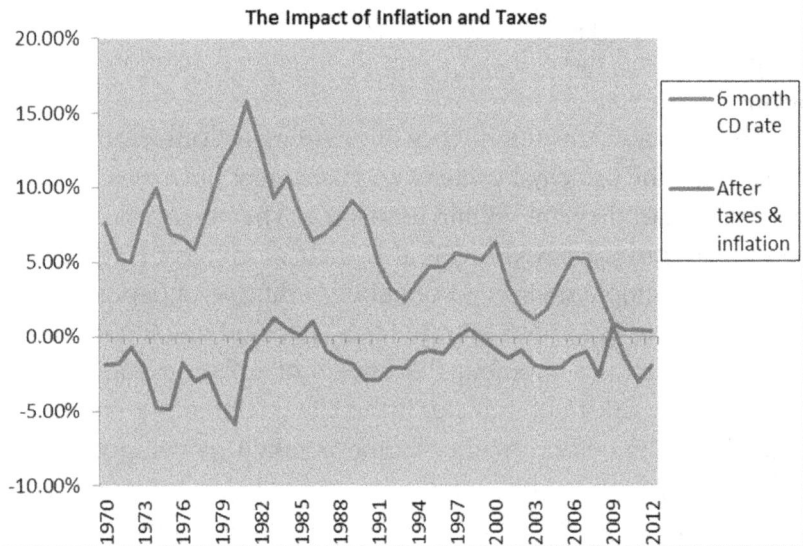

The Impact of Inflation and Taxes

HISTORY OF THE REAL AFTER-TAX RATE OF RETURN
FOR CERTIFICATES OF DEPOSIT (PART 2)

Year	6-Month CD Rates*	Less Taxes**	Less Inflation***	Return After Taxes & Inflation
1970	7.65%	50.0%	5.7%	−1.875%
1971	5.21%	50.0%	4.4%	−1.795%
1972	5.02%	50.0%	3.2%	−0.69%
1973	8.31%	50.0%	6.2%	−2.045%
1974	9.98%	62.0%	11.0%	−4.812%
1975	6.89%	62.0%	9.1%	−4.828%
1976	6.62%	62.0%	5.8%	−1.696%
1977	5.92%	60.0%	6.5%	−2.948%
1978	8.61%	60.0%	7.6%	−2.434%
1979	11.44%	59.0%	11.3%	−4.550%
1980	12.99%	59.0%	13.5%	−5.836%
1981	15.77%	59.0%	10.3%	−0.996%
1982	12.57%	50.0%	6.2%	+0.085%
1983	9.27%	48.0%	3.2%	+1.250%
1984	10.68%	45.0%	4.3%	+0.506%
1985	8.25%	45.0%	3.6%	+0.113%
1986	6.50%	45.0%	1.9%	+1.025%
1987	7.01%	38.0%	3.6%	−0.936%
1988	7.85%	33.0%	4.1%	−1.510%
1989	9.08%	33.0%	4.8%	−1.804%
1990	8.17%	31.0%	5.4%	−2.867%
1991	4.89%	31.0%	4.2%	−2.864%
1992	3.24%	31.0%	3.0%	−1.996%
1993	2.38%	39.6%	3.0%	−2.058%
1994	3.67%	39.6%	2.6%	−1.147%
1995	4.65%	39.6%	2.8%	−0.959%
1996	4.69%	39.6%	3.0%	−1.143%
1997	5.57%	39.6%	2.3%	−0.094%
1998	5.37%	39.6%	1.6%	+0.527%
1999	5.15%	39.6%	2.2%	−0.161%
2000	6.33%	39.6%	3.4%	−0.893%
2001	3.49%	39.1%	2.8%	−1.435%
2002	1.80%	38.6%	1.6%	−0.905%
2003	1.18%	35.0%	2.3%	−1.887%
2004	1.80%	35.0%	2.7%	−2.070%
2005	3.73%	35.0%	3.4%	−2.095%
2006	5.24%	35.0%	3.2%	−1.366%
2007	5.23%	35.0%	2.8%	−0.970%
2008	3.14%	35.0%	3.8%	−2.701%
2009	0.87%	35.0%	−0.04%	+0.705%
2010	0.44%	35.0%	1.6%	−1.446%
2011	0.42%	35.0%	3.2%	−3.053%
2012	0.41%	35.0%	2.1%	−1.957%
			Cumulative	−68.431%
			Annualized	−1.583%

*Annualized Average Monthly Rates Bank Monitor; Federal Reserve
**Highest marginal tax bracket for year.
***U.S. Department of Commerce—CPI; Bureau of Labor Statistics

CHAPTER 3

Investment Vehicles

Owning or Loaning

We are now ready to start a discussion of the myriad investment vehicles available in the financial marketplace today. Throughout this section we will refer to investment categories as asset classes. Asset classes can be defined as categories of investments that possess similar characteristics and have performed in a similar manner over time. The guiding principle of risk/reward is that you can't get something worthwhile for nothing. With specific asset classes, higher returns can also mean greater fluctuation of values or inherent risk. So, consider these generic vehicles as part of asset class selection options.

Before we introduce the various asset classes, it is appropriate to touch upon the distinction between loanership assets and ownership assets. Loanership assets can best be thought of as loans you have made to an entity in exchange for the promise of a certain interest rate and the promise of repayment of principal after a certain period of time. Examples of these types of assets are savings accounts, interest-bearing checking accounts, certificates of deposit, government, corporate and municipal bonds.

On the other hand, ownership assets represent actual ownership of part of an enterprise or asset. The value of your ownership is directly tied to the value of the enterprise, rising or falling with the enterprise itself. Examples of this type of asset would be shares of stock, mutual funds investing in stocks, real estate, and "hard assets" such as gold coins, stamps, etc.

As you will see, either type of asset can be perfect for your needs—depending on what your needs are! However, just as certain assets can be perfect for some purposes, the same assets could be terrible for others.

Cash Equivalents

As we stated earlier, cash equivalents are those assets that do not fluctuate in principal value because of their quality and short-term nature. These are the investment vehicles that fund your immediate liquidity needs. Because these investments have a relatively low level of risk, cash equivalents provide a very low after-inflation rate of return. As a general rule, assets in this category can be converted to cash within just one day. Simple examples include checking and savings accounts as well as certificates of deposit (CDs). A CD allows you to withdraw your money within a day; however, unlike other cash equivalent accounts, you will incur a penalty (typically three months' interest) if the funds are withdrawn before maturity. Also included are money market accounts offered through banks and mutual fund companies. These funds are available immediately simply by writing a check against the account. Since there are no maturity dates on money market accounts, no penalties are assessed for withdrawals. Bank money market accounts are generally FDIC-insured and offer a higher rate of interest when compared to checking or savings accounts. Mutual fund money markets offer shares that have a market price of $1 per share, but are not insured by the FDIC. As a general rule, the yield on mutual fund money markets is higher than the yield on bank money markets because of the lack of insurance and the inherent built-in cost of that protection.

Most mutual fund companies offer three options for money market accounts: taxable (these produce taxable income for federal and state income tax purposes); federal tax-free (these are usually subject to state income taxes); and government securities. Fund companies' money market accounts are not insured, and although mutual fund companies offer check-writing privileges, a check minimum of $250 to $500 is usually required.

Also included in this asset class are fixed annuities and the cash value of traditional life insurance policies. Each of these investments provides fixed rates of interest declared by the insurance company, and the added advantage of tax-deferred appreciation. Unlike the previously mentioned assets, cash values and annuities usually require more than a day or two to convert to cash. Please reference the chapter on annuities for additional details about these unique products.

Bonds

Bonds, as an asset class, represent debt of a government, municipality, or corporation. The credit worthiness of the issuing entity, as well as the length of time to maturity, will dictate the interest rate of the specific bond. As a general rule, the lower the credit worthiness of the issuer, the higher the interest rate will be. This is due to the risk/reward ratio. If an investor is going to be assuming more risk in the event of the possible default of a bond, he must be compensated with higher interest rates.

It is important to note that all bonds possess interest rate risk, and as a result, there is an inverse relationship between interest rates and the value of bonds. As interest rates rise, bond prices fall. When general interest rates are lowered, bonds increase in principal value. The longer the maturity of the bond, the greater the bond's volatility to market interest rate changes. Most bonds are issued in $1,000 units, with varied maturities and interest rates. Bonds can be bought at par ($1,000), at discount (less than $1,000), or at a premium (more than $1,000).

As an example, consider a $1,000 bond, due in 10 years, with an interest rate of 6%. If you paid $1,000 for the bond, you bought at par. For the next 10 years you will receive 6%, or $60 per year, paid semi-annually. At the end of the 10-year period, the issuer will repay your loan of $1000. If the bond is held to maturity, the only effect interest rate changes will have is that the bond's interest rate may no longer be competitive in the current market environment.

Using the previous example, what would happen if interest rates increased and you could buy a similar bond, at par, with an interest rate of 8%? You may not want to hold your old bond to maturity since it will be earning 2% less than the newer bond. One alternative is to sell the 6% bond and use the proceeds to buy the 8% bond. But what will you receive when you sell your bond in the market—the very efficient bond market? Would other investors be willing to pay $1,000 for a 6% bond when they can buy a similar maturity and credit bond at 8%? Of course not. But they will buy your bond for an amount less than $1,000 because even though they are earning below market interest rates, in 10 years the bond will mature at $1,000. If someone buys your bond for $900, that investor will receive 6% interest on the face value ($1,000) each year, as well as the full $1,000 at maturity. This is a principal gain of $100. In the marketplace, this is known as buying a bond at a discount.

On the other hand, again using the previous example, what happens if the interest rate on similar bonds decreases to 4%? Holding the bond to maturity still guarantees the 6% rate of return. What happens if the investor decides to sell? As opposed to a 4% bond which can be bought at par ($1,000), in order to buy a 6% bond, an investor would have to pay an amount above par. The investor would buy the bond at a premium. An investor may pay $1,100 for the 6% bond, but at maturity he receives only the $1,000 face amount.

In addition to interest rate risk, the relative safety of an individual bond is reliant on the issuing entity's ability to repay the debt at a certain point in the future. Independent rating agencies such as Moody's, Standard and Poor's, and Duff and Phelps offer letter ratings and opinions on a variety of issuers. The highest quality bonds are known as investment grade. The lowest ratings are assigned to companies whose repayment ability is questionable, and are referred to as high-yield or junk bonds. For these bonds, the issuer must promise above-market interest in order for investors to justify their purchase. Ratings on bonds are available from brokers and can also be obtained at libraries that carry rating agency publications.

Taxable bonds, such as corporate bonds, should be analyzed on an after-tax basis, since the interest can be taxed at a federal rate as high as 39.6%. Corporate bond income is also subject to state taxes, bringing the combined taxable rate even higher. Alternatively, municipal bond interest income is received tax-free at the federal level, although in some cases may be subject to the alternative minimum tax.

Speaking of which, let's take a quick look at the very complex alternative minimum tax. The alternative minimum tax (AMT) is designed to prevent taxpayers with substantial income from avoiding or deferring all tax liability through the use of deductions, exemptions, and credits. The rules add substantial complexity to the tax system. (See IRC Sec. 55 and IRS Form 6251 and its instructions.) Regular taxable income is adjusted to reflect different treatment of certain items by the AMT rules. We encourage you to discuss this tax in more detail with your tax professional.

When searching for an investment to hold outside of a retirement plan, municipal bonds can provide exposure to another asset class that alternatively focuses on generating federal tax-free income.

State and local governments, or municipalities, issue municipal bonds to finance public projects such as schools, sewer systems, and roads. Municipal bonds can be categorized as general obligation or revenue bonds. General obligation bonds are backed by the full faith, credit, and taxing power of the municipality. In contrast, revenue bonds are used to finance tunnels, bridges, hospitals, and other public works, and are backed by the expected income from these projects.

With either type of bond, you as the investor lend money to the municipality, which "promises" to pay you a predetermined amount of interest, typically on a semi-annual basis, and return your principal to you on a specified maturity date. As an investor, you can choose to hold the bond until maturity or sell it prior to maturity through the municipal bond marketplace and receive proceeds based on the bond's current value. This is known as interest rate risk. Again, keep in mind that as interest rates rise, the value of an existing bond decreases, since it pays a fixed rate of interest lower than what is being offered in the market.

If interest rate risk is an issue for you, focus on shorter-term bonds that will pay a lower rate of interest. If current interest is not a factor and you can afford to forgo the semi-annual income, an alternative would be zero-coupon municipal bonds. These bonds are bought at a discount of the face amount, pay no interest, but mature at the higher stated maturity value.

As is the case with corporate bonds, municipal bonds also carry credit risk, which rating agencies define as the ability of the issuer to pay back interest as well as principal. With higher risk, a greater amount of interest would be promised as opposed to municipalities with a high credit rating, which pay a lower amount of interest to their investors. Beyond interest rate and credit risk, there is also the risk that the issuer will "call" the bond prior to maturity at a pre-stated value. This typically happens as interest rates fall and the issuer can refinance or offer new bonds at a lower rate.

Keep in mind that municipal bonds are not for everyone, since tax brackets will dictate their effectiveness. Prior to investing in municipal bonds, be sure to gain a thorough understanding of the nuances and appropriateness of this asset class by speaking with your tax and investment advisors.

In review, bond interest may be fully taxable, partially taxable, or completely tax- free. Corporate bond interest is fully taxable to the bond holder. Government debt is generally taxable, although some issues may be exempt from state tax. Interest on municipal bonds is exempt from federal taxes. Some states offer their residents interest that is federally and state tax-free. Regardless of the tax status of the bond, the interest rate will still depend on the quality and maturity of the bond.

The difficulty with adding bonds to a portfolio in order to reduce overall inherent risk is the possibility that you'll lose principal within the bond portfolio if interest rates increase, thus defeating the objective of risk reduction. Hence, the questions become: how do fixed-income investors achieve a respectable rate of return without experiencing the higher risk associated with interest rate fluctuation? What is the adequate offset of higher risk for higher return?

VARYING MATURITIES

In an effort to minimize the impact of interest rate changes, investors may wish to diversify their bond portfolios based on varying maturities. The shorter the maturity of the bond, the less sensitive it is to changing interest rates, but it also typically pays a lower interest rate. The key lies in structuring a bond portfolio that generates higher current income, but offers greater downside protection than simply purchasing longer-term bonds.

A reasonable strategy may be bond laddering. Laddering involves building a portfolio of bonds with staggered maturities so that a portion of the portfolio will mature each year, or some other specified time period. Laddering can be accomplished by purchasing individual bonds or bond mutual funds, since the mutual funds may invest in bonds with varying maturities, or within a specific time frame, such as short-term, intermediate-term, or long-term. By spreading out the maturities, you are investing at different interest rates, with the shorter-term bonds paying a lower rate compared to the longer-term bonds. At the same time, you are spreading out the risk of principal fluctuation.

The practice of laddering a bond portfolio provides a very attractive method of diversification. If current income is not an objective, bond mutual funds offer the advantage of income reinvestment, allowing you to purchase additional fund shares at current price levels.

Municipalities pay lower rates on bonds since they offer tax-free attributes that are not found elsewhere. This makes it less expensive for the municipality to borrow. To determine if a municipal bond should be used in your portfolio, you need to compare the after-tax return of taxable bonds of comparable quality and maturity. The important point here is that what you EARN is not as important as what you KEEP after taxation. The following chart illustrates the difference between tax-free and taxable yields based on different tax rates.

	Municipal Bond Return			
	4%	5%	6%	7%
Marginal Tax Rate	**Equivalent Taxable Rate of Return**			
15.0%	4.7%	5.9%	7.1%	8.2%
25.0%	5.3%	6.7%	8.0%	9.3%
28.0%	5.6%	6.9%	8.3%	9.7%
33.0%	6.0%	7.5%	9.0%	10.5%
35.0%	6.2%	7.7%	9.2%	10.8%
39.6%	6.62%	8.28%	9.93%	11.59%

2013 Tax Rates

Government bonds are backed by the full faith and credit of the U.S. government. Because of this safety feature, you can expect interest rates to be lower than rates on other types of bonds. Municipal bonds are not backed by the government and thus credit ratings will vary. An added measure of safety can be realized when municipalities obtain insurance on their obligations, but the cost of this insurance will be reflected in lower interest rates on the bonds.

TREASURY INFLATION-PROTECTED SECURITIES (TIPS)

With interest rates near historical lows, fixed-income investments that carry a high degree of safety, such as U.S. government bonds, continue to attract investors' dollars. One type of government bond in particular, Treasury Inflation-Protected Securities (TIPS), have caused physicians to take a closer look at bonds as a viable alternative or complement to their equity based portfolio holdings.

TIPS, also known as inflation-indexed Treasuries, differ from conventional treasury bonds, which offer fixed semi-annual interest payments as well as a fixed guaranteed principal payment at maturity. Unfortunately for bondholders, the impact of inflation may ultimately cause the rates of return to be negative. In contrast, TIPS are guaranteed to provide the investor a positive after-inflation real rate of return. The principal value is linked to the constantly changing U. S. Consumer Price Index (CPI).

For example, if the CPI rises by 3% over the course of a year, the principal value of a TIPS bond will be adjusted upward by the same amount. On the other hand, if we enter a period of deflation, the principal would be adjusted downward, although you are still guaranteed the return of your principal. Due to this variable adjustment, it's impossible for an investor to know the final maturity value of a TIPS bond. Although, what the investor gains is the certainty that the principal will keep pace with inflation.

TIPS are guaranteed against default by the U.S. government (the U.S. Treasury is the largest issuer of debt securities in the world) with regard to the payment of principal and interest. However, TIPS are also marketable securities, meaning they can be bought and sold in the open market after they are issued. If the bond is sold before it matures, the investor may receive more or less than originally paid, due to fluctuations in market value. The secondary market performance of TIPS has been much different than other government bond issues. Bond prices, in general, tend to rise and fall in response to changes in both expected and real inflation rates. Thus their prices and their yields tend to be relatively unstable. This is in contrast to TIPS prices, which are influenced primarily by changes in real interest rates. Changes in inflation expectations have very little effect on TIPS because investors know that the securities will adjust themselves to the future inflation rate.

Because market prices of TIPS do not react to changes in expected inflation, their returns have very low correlations with stocks and other bonds. Correlation (the degree to which returns from two investments move in the same direction) is a key element of constructing a well-diversified portfolio. This is because investors enhance their portfolio diversification by mixing assets not closely correlated with each other.

TIPS are issued with 10- and 30-year maturities. Current income is paid on a semi-annual basis through the use of inflation-adjusted coupons. From an income tax standpoint, income generated is free from state income taxes but taxable at the federal level. The federal tax also applies to the positive inflation adjustments. Even though the investor doesn't benefit from the principal adjustments until the bond matures, the inflation adjustments are still considered to be income, and federal taxes are due each year an adjustment is made. To avoid exposure to the TIPS inherent tax inefficiency, TIPS can be placed in tax-deferred vehicles such as qualified retirement plans or IRAs.

TIPS, like other government bonds, can be purchased directly from the government, through its Treasury Direct program, or on the Internet at http://www.treasurydirect.gov without commissions or fees.

Interest payments on a traditional treasury bond are fixed and the principal fluctuates only with the movements of interest rates. During times of low inflation, bond yields are generally low and rise when inflation and general interest rates rise. With Inflation-Adjusted Bonds, the principal, not the interest rate, moves with inflation every six months, as measured by the CPI. You receive the original fixed rate, but on a higher principal value. Principal adjust-ments are made three months after the CPI is released. Other than the three-month lag, it is safe to say that as long as the bonds are held to maturity, your bonds will beat inflation on a pre-tax basis.

However, when the bonds are held in a taxable account, you incur a tax liability each time your principal is adjusted upward. Principal increases are considered ordinary income, not capital gains, and are taxed year by year. Taxpayers in a high tax bracket may prefer to own the new bonds within a qualified retirement plan or IRA in order to take advantage of tax deferral.

As with any investment, there is always a risk/reward tradeoff. You pay for the greater certainty of inflation resistance by accept-ing a lower comparable yield when you purchase the new bonds. Traditional bond yields are priced to include compensation for the uncertainty of future inflation. Since Inflation-Adjusted Bonds eliminate this risk, the yields are usually lower. This is not to say that they are risk-free. As is the case with traditional bonds, the value of the new bonds fluctuates based on interest rate changes. Fluctuation should be less when compared to traditional bonds because if interest rates rise, it is probably a function of a higher CPI, and a higher CPI would cause a principal adjustment within the new bond.

With all government bonds you are only guaranteed the repay-ment of your principal at maturity. If you sell your bond prior to maturity, you will receive the current market price of the bond in the secondary market. This price may be higher or lower than your original purchase price.

Inflation-Adjusted Bonds appear to be a viable investment option as part of an overall bond portfolio, but more so in a tax-deferred account if the investor is in a high tax bracket. Rates must be compared to other government obligations to determine the real price of long-term inflation projection.

When a single corporate or municipal bond is purchased, interest is received twice a year. When held within a brokerage ac-count, the interest is generally deposited into the brokerage account money market for current access or future investment. An exception to this is a zero-coupon bond. These bonds can be government, corporate, or municipal, and they are purchased at a deep discount from their maturity value. Zero-coupon bonds provide no current income; however, interest accrues within the bond until maturity. This gives the investor who doesn't need current income the advantage of having the interest compound within the bond. Regular bonds cannot compound since the maturity value is fixed at par.

UNIT INVESTMENT TRUSTS (UITS)

Bonds can be purchased on an individual basis, within a unit investment trust, or through a mutual fund. The disadvantage of individual bonds, assuming that only a few bonds are held, is the simple lack of diversification. In order to provide diversification, thus reducing risk of default, many firms offer unit investment trust, also known as UITs. The portfolio manager assembles a variety of bonds with similar maturities that can be categorized as short, medium, or long-term to form a UIT. Most UITs purchase bonds from 20 to 30 issuers, thus allowing the investor to spread his risk by buying a piece of all of the bonds within the portfolio. As the individual bonds within the trust mature, the proceeds are paid to the investor. Since the trust has a finite life, bonds cannot be added to the portfolio. Just as in an individual purchase of a bond, the risk associated with the portfolio is dependent on the credit ratings of the bonds within the trust. In the case of municipal UITs, insurance can be placed on the trust, or the bonds within the trust, to protect the investor from potential defaults. The biggest disadvantage of a UIT is that interest cannot be compounded within the trust. Interest is usually paid on a monthly, quarterly, or semi-annual basis. It can be paid out directly or invested in other vehicles. The main advantages are the promise of repayment of principal at some time in the future, and the use of diversification and professional selection of the bond portfolio to help reduce risk of default.

If reinvesting of dividends is important to you, you can also buy bonds in a mutual fund. Just as the UIT allows you to invest in several different types of bonds, in a mutual fund you buy a piece of a larger portfolio that has been professionally selected. In general, a mutual fund will have many more holdings than a UIT. A bond mutual fund is an open-ended investment that never matures since, as the bonds within the fund mature, more bonds are purchased. The mutual fund manager also has the ability to trade bonds before they mature. This allows the manager to make changes within the portfolio based on market conditions such as interest rate changes. Because of the ability to trade and add bonds, the repayment of your principal is never guaranteed. The advantage is that as dividends are paid, they can be reinvested and more shares of the bond fund can be purchased. Most bond mutual funds also allow the cross reinvestment of dividends into other types of mutual funds. Dividends can also be deposited directly into a checking, savings, or money market account.

Real Estate

Real estate purchases, the same as bond purchases, can be made on an individual basis or in a diversified form through partnerships or Real Estate Investment Trusts (REITs). A single purchase of a medical office building, rental house, or apartment building carries the risk of lack of diversification. You are limiting yourself to the economic climate for real estate in the particular geographic area where you buy. Additionally, you become a landlord, dealing with the day-to-day nuances and nuisances of property ownership. You may not be familiar with the specific area and the unique rental opportunities/problems that exist. The main advantage of single ownership is one of ultimate control. You make all the decisions.

Many of the tax benefits of real estate investing disappeared with the Tax Reform Act of 1986, although some still exist, particularly in individual or active ownership as opposed to partnerships. Avoid letting the tax benefit be the driving force for investment decisions. The purchase must first make sense from a long-term investment point of view. Tax benefits should be secondary to the economics of the purchase.

Your home can also provide tax benefits. Mortgage interest is generally deductible, as is your property tax payment. Depending on your long-term objectives relative to your home, you may be able to consider your home part of your overall investment portfolio. However, as a general rule, a home is not considered a retirement asset.

Even if your goal is to sell at retirement, you will probably buy another home in which to live. The new home may carry a similar value to your current home, thus you are simply exchanging homes, albeit possibly in a different part of the country. An alternative is to sell your home at retirement and buy a much less-expensive home for your retirement years. In this case, the proceeds of the sale, minus the cost of the new home, could be added to your portfolio in order to generate additional retirement income.

Keep in mind that there can be some income tax consequences inherent in the sale of your principal residence. Previous tax law allowed the deferral of gains on the sale of the primary residence if a new residence of equal or greater value was purchased. The problem is that in retirement, many people move to a smaller home that costs substantially less than their current home. Normally the individual is liable for the taxable gain on the sale of the home since he or she is not "buying up" in value.

The government recognized this dilemma and created a tax break for those who purchased a lower-cost residence for their retirement years. Tax law previously allowed an exclusion of up to $125,000 in primary residence gains if you were at least 55 years of age and had lived in the house for three of the previous five years. Additionally, this exclusion was only allowed once in a lifetime. Any gain on the sale of a home relative to the basis, which had been carried over from the sale of previous homes and on which the gain had been deferred, was taxable.

However, the rules changed with the Taxpayer Relief Act of 1997. This law as it relates to real estate sales now replaces the once-in-a-lifetime exclusion when "buying up" and the "age 55" rule. The Taxpayer Relief Act of 1997 created a universal exclusion that benefits most homeowners and now provides an exclusion for gains of up to $250,000 to individuals filing singly. If a joint return is filed for the year of the sale, the exclusion applies to a maximum gain of $500,000.

To qualify for the exclusion, a taxpayer must have owned and used the property which is being sold as their principal residence for two years or more during the five-year period ending on the date of the sale. For a married couple filing a joint return, one of the spouses must meet the ownership requirement, and both spouses must meet the use requirement of the residence to qualify for the maximum exclusion.

With the U.S. stock market's inherent volatility, many investors are seeking other potentially profitable investment vehicles. One area attracting considerable attention has been investment real estate. While real estate combines the advantages of potential appreciation with rental income, the problem with buying investment property, as mentioned previously, is that you become the landlord. You are responsible if the plumbing breaks down or the heat doesn't work. Busy physicians tend to not want to deal with these situations or the responsibility of finding renters and collecting rent. A favorable alternative, therefore, is to have exposure to real estate markets without day-to-day management responsibilities.

Real Estate Investment Trusts (REITs) are publicly traded stocks that invest in office buildings, apartment complexes, industrial facilities, shopping centers, and other commercial spaces. In order to avoid paying corporate income taxes, REITs must pay out a minimum of 90% of their earnings to shareholders in the form of dividends. Investors generally receive dividend income along with the potential for stock price appreciation.

The REIT industry has been very volatile in terms of its market cycles. It enjoyed a great run up in the early 1970s only to experience an enormous downturn during the 1973–1974 recession when many REITs actually went bankrupt due to the massive overbuilding that exceeded market demand. The industry did recover and prospered until the real estate markets again became overbuilt in the late 1980s and early 1990s. Of course, the real estate markets were hit hard in the period during 2006–2009 with many single family homes seeing current values quite a bit off their pre-2007 values. Many analysts now believe that REITs are still attractively priced and have performed very well the last few years.

An alternative to individual REIT ownership is mutual funds that invest in publicly traded real estate-oriented stocks, offering a diversified portfolio of real estate sector securities, geographic diversification, and professional management. Many of these mutual funds include REITs within the portfolio to take advantage of their relatively high dividend yields. Often included in many fund portfolios are stocks of home and industrial builders as well as the suppliers to those industries. To further diversify, global real estate funds invest in real estate-related companies around the world.

As a general rule, REITs and real estate mutual funds tend to perform better as interest rates decrease and occupancy and rental rates rise. Conversely, they tend to underperform during periods of rising interest rates and when there is an oversupply of rental real estate on the market.

With this in mind, investors may wish to assume some real estate exposure beyond home ownership that can be integrated in an overall diversified portfolio to take advantage of dividend income and appreciation potential.

On the other hand, if you are considering an individual real estate purchase as an investment, have your accountant go through a cash flow and tax projection. Only in this way will you know the tax ramifications and expected returns of an investment that you will probably hold for a long period of time.

Stocks

When you purchase stock in a corporation, you become an owner along with all the other shareholders. There are basically two classes of stock available in the marketplace today: common and preferred. As a common stock shareholder you benefit from the rise of the company's stock price, which is a function of earnings and future expectations of earnings.

Many companies are profitable and able to pay dividends to their common shareholders. This creates additional value, since any dividends received will increase the total return (stock price appreciation + dividends received = total return) of your investment. Dividends on common stock are not guaranteed. On a quarterly basis, the company decides if it will pay a dividend and, if so, how much it will be per share. Many very profitable companies do not pay dividends, as these growth-oriented corporations will choose to use the money that would have been paid out as dividends to reinvest in the company. These potential dividends fund research, development, and other areas that may provide a higher long-term value for shareholders.

As a common shareholder who owns less than 50% of a company, you have a very limited voice in the operations of the company you own. You will, however, be asked to vote for the board of directors who will represent you, as well as vote on other issues where your opinions may be of interest to the company. This is done through a proxy vote. The magnitude of your vote depends on the number of shares you own in the company. Regardless of the amount of shares you own, you are entitled to attend the company's shareholder meetings.

PREFERRED STOCK

Preferred stock also represents proportionate ownership in a publicly traded company. It differs from common stock in the amount and the manner in which dividends will be received. Ownership of preferred stock carries a promise from the company to pay a specified dividend amount per share, regardless of the profitability of the company. This specified dividend must be paid to preferred stock shareholders before any dividends can be paid to common stock shareholders. Most preferred shares are considered cumulative; that is, in the event a company has a lack of earnings, dividends are not paid to any shareholders, common or preferred. At the time when the company again begins to pay dividends, preferred shareholders must receive the cumulative total of past unpaid dividends before the common shareholders receive any dividends. Preferred stock is particularly advantageous for investors who want a more predictable and higher income flow than would be generated by the same company's common stock.

There is a clause in the tax code that may make preferred stock unattractive for individual investors. Based on current law, corporations are able to exclude up to 80% of the dividend income received from their taxable income. This dividend exclusion makes it attractive for corporations to purchase dividend-paying stocks rather than money market accounts or CDs. Since issuers of preferred stock are aware that many of the purchasers of the stock have this tax advantage, the issuers set the dividend rate lower than they might otherwise.

Individuals do not have the same tax advantage as the corporate purchaser and must pay income taxes on all the dividends received. For this reason we often suggest that our clients look at alternative investments rather than preferred stocks.

INDICES

When evaluating investment portfolio performance, a popular approach among news and print media is to make comparisons to a market index. The confusion occurs when the specific components of your portfolio are not a mirror image of those comprising the index being used as the basis of comparison. Adequately diversified portfolios may be tracked by a different index for each major investment objective. Understanding the different index components can be helpful in making comparisons, as well as in explaining why your portfolio as a whole doesn't match up to one specific index.

The Dow Jones Industrial Average (DJIA) focuses on the 30 largest New York stock exchange-traded U.S. corporations. As industries and companies change, so can the 30 stocks comprising the index. Due to its limited holdings of the largest domestic corporations, the index excludes many sectors of the market and is not an adequate basis of comparison for the overall market.

The S&P 500 (Standard and Poor's composite index of 500 stocks) is often used as a comparison for the overall market, even though it includes only 500 of the largest U.S. companies.

The NASDAQ (National Association of Securities Dealers Automated Quotation System) Index measures the performance of all 3200 domestic and foreign companies available through the NASDAQ trading system. A common misconception is that this index is a barometer of smaller stocks. The index is actually weighted based on market values, and is configured of companies that are leaders across all areas of business, including technology, retail, communications, financial services, transportation, media, and biotechnology.

The Russell 2000 Index is the key barometer and indicator of companies on the smaller end of the capitalization spectrum. This small-cap index is made up of 2000 smaller U.S. companies. The market value or capitalization of these companies ranges from $30 million to $3.4 billion.

The MSCI EAFE® (Europe, Australasia, and the Far East) Index consists of approximately 980 foreign stocks listed on the exchanges of 21 developed countries representing all major industry groups. The EAFE® Index serves as an appropriate benchmark for mutual funds that invest in these countries. Newer indices are now being developed for specific countries and regions, including emerging markets.

The performance of the bond market is tracked in a variety of ways. The most often quoted figure is not a composite average; rather, it is the return on a specific bond: the U.S. government's 30-year treasury bond. Most newspapers quote the current yield as well as the change in price or yield from the previous day's close. Investors watch government bond prices not only as a measure of their own bond performance, but also as an indicator of market interest rate changes because there is a direct correlation between the two.

Both the Salomon Brothers Index and the Lehman Brothers Index track publicly traded government and corporate bonds. The only way to make a valid performance comparison of your bond portfolio to a specific index is to know the average length of maturity as well as the quality of the bonds within the index.

Index tracking can be very useful in comparing the performance of your individual stocks, bonds, or mutual funds relative to a specific benchmark average. The validity of the comparison, however, depends on your ability to determine which index serves as the appropriate benchmark for your specific holdings.

Sub-Asset Classes

A further dissection of asset classes will enhance our study of investments. There are still many different ways to break down the performance of each of the asset classes we have defined. The fixed income, or bond category (debt instruments), can consist of corporate, government, municipal, and international. Each of these categories can be further broken down by their terms of maturity, i.e., short (1 day to 5 years), intermediate (5 years to 15 years) or long-term (15 years to 30 years).

For stocks, asset classes can be narrowed even further by company size and geographical location. We often refer to companies as large, mid-size, or small. In addition, stocks are further categorized as domestic or international. For example, you could purchase the stock of a large international company, the corporate bond of a small domestic company, the stock of a small international company, and so on and so forth.

It is interesting to look at the historic rates of return for the various asset classes and consider what one dollar invested at the end of 1925 would have grown to by year-end 2012. During the period 1927 through 2012, small company stocks had an average rate of return of 11.8%, and one dollar would have grown to $14,655. Large company stocks had an average rate of return of 9.8%, and a dollar invested at the beginning of 1926 would be worth $3407 at the end of 2012. From 1926, long-term corporate bonds and long-term government bonds had average rates of return of 6.1% and 5.7%, with a dollar growing to $173 and $124, respectively. From 1926, 30-day treasury bills had an average rate of 3.5%, resulting in one dollar growing to $20. Finally, inflation averaged 3%, resulting in one dollar of purchasing power in 1926 requiring $13 by end of 2012, according to Dimensional Fund Advisors.

Small-cap stocks are shares of companies with total market capitalization of less than $4 billion. Due to their size and potential for growth, small-cap stocks may offer the superior earnings you need to achieve your financial objectives. Historically, small-cap stocks have outperformed the stocks of larger companies.

Studies indicate that small-cap stocks perform solidly in cycles of between five and nine years, most often starting their upward trend in the wake of a recession. Following the 1973–1975 recession, for instance, small cap stocks embarked on a rally that lasted almost eight years. During the bear market beginning in early 2000, small cap stocks easily outperformed large-cap stocks. Unfortunately, all stocks suffered during the 2008–2009 market period.

The success of small companies is probably due in part to their ability to adjust to economic fluctuations and changing technologies.

Small-cap companies, unlike their larger, more diversified counter-parts, are free to search out emerging opportunities and then focus all their attention and resources on dominating them.

Small-cap companies also managed to avoid much of the stag-gering debt that many large companies assumed in the 1980s, which allowed them to show more favorable balance sheets.

Small-cap stocks can be very volatile and, as compared to large cap stocks, are riskier investments since there is a greater probability of principal fluctuation. Risk adverse investors may prefer to limit their exposure to this asset class. Small company stocks are often avoided during periods of uncertain economic outlooks as many investors prefer to invest in companies perceived as more certain performers.

International Investing

Should you invest overseas? International investing has become very popular. Bearing in mind that diversification is the basic tenet of investing; diversifying overseas means you are not dependent upon the performance of any single country's economy. For example, when other countries lag behind the United States' economic cycles, their markets could be peaking when the U.S. market is dropping, and vice versa.

As you know by now, the greater the reward offered by an investment, the greater the risk, and international investments are no exception. Before investing overseas you should consider several risk factors such as political turmoil, nationalization, and currency risk. Civil wars and political upheavals can affect your investment. Nationalization may be a potential pitfall since some emerging countries are not totally committed to free enterprise. But perhaps the most significant risk factor is currency fluctuations.

Without a doubt, currency fluctuations will affect your final return. A weak U.S. dollar will bolster any gains you receive when you convert to U.S. currency. Of course, the opposite also holds true: a strong U.S. dollar will erode your earnings. An understanding of how currency exchange rates affect international investments will enable you to better position your portfolio to realize the highest potential returns.

Exchange rates essentially represent the cost of one country's currency in terms of another's. Changes in exchange rates are driven by a complicated mix of factors including inflation, interest rates, and the country's economic growth. The mechanism that causes the changes is the theory of supply and demand. Demand for a country's currency can fluctuate based on the anticipated relative strength of the currency. The stronger the perception is, the greater the likelihood of increasing demand. When demand for a country's currency from outside buyers is greater than the available supply, the price of the currency increases, and when supply exceeds demand, the price of the currency decreases. The fluctuation in currency exchange rates is often classified as "currency risk."

As an example, let's assume you own a company located in a foreign country. If the U.S. dollar rises in value relative to the foreign currency where your company is located, the value of your investment declines. A weakening U.S. dollar, on the other hand, would increase the value in the foreign investment as measured in U.S. dollars. Of course, there will also be fluctuations in the price of the security itself, based on a variety of other factors such as earnings growth, market expectations, and demand.

While you cannot eliminate currency fluctuations completely, you may be able to reduce your exposure to their potentially negative effects. For instance, you can limit your international investments to countries with stable political systems and consistently strong economies. Another way to minimize currency risk is through diversification. Single-country mutual funds take on more risk than multi-country funds, which spread the currency risk among a number of different countries. Investing in international mutual funds provides the needed diversification, professional management, and liquidity for the individual investor.

CHAPTER 4

Acquiring Assets

Individual Securities

nvestments such as stocks or bonds can be purchased individually through a broker or collectively through a mutual fund. If you feel confident and have done the research, you can place an order for a specific stock or bond with a broker. You have complete control of your portfolio when you purchase investments individually. You select the investments and make the decisions about when to buy and when to sell—transactions that can be done through a full-service broker or a discount broker.

Full-service brokers provide research on certain issues and specific recommendations for your account and are usually compensated through a commission on each transaction. This transaction-oriented compensation is often viewed by the investor as a potential conflict of interest, since it is based on activity as opposed to performance.

An alternative, if you do your own research and make all the decisions relative to your portfolio, is to use a discount broker. Although you will still pay a commission on each transaction, the amount is generally less than that charged by a full-service broker, since you are using the brokerage firm for the transaction, not for research services or market advice.

Regardless of what brokerage service you choose, gauging how far an individual common stock might fall prior to it hitting its bottom price is certainly a difficult, if not impossible task for investors. Much time is spent forecasting how high the price of a stock is "expected" to rise, but very little time or attention is spent determining the ultimate downside risk of the investment. Investors want to know "how low can we go?" and "when should I sell?"

There are several possible approaches to calculating a stock's downside potential. The five most common valuation measures for stocks are: price-to-book value, price-to-earnings ratio, price-to-sales ratio, price-to-cash flow ratio, and dividend yield. A general understanding of these measurements will shed some light on share-pricing factors.

The price-to-book value represents a company's net worth per share, computed as its assets minus its liabilities, including preferred stock. Generally, the higher this value is, the better. However, as a valuation technique, book value is most meaningful when it's compared to the stock's current share price. When looking for a potential bargain, the lower the price-to-book ratio is, the better. For example, a stock with a ratio of less than one may be viewed as relatively cheap, since it is trading for less than the value of the specific company's net assets.

Since looking only at a company's assets ignores profitably issues, investors must also evaluate the price-to-earnings (P/E) ratio. This widely used and published figure is computed by dividing the current stock price by the amount of the trailing 12-months earnings per share. This ratio quantifies how much investors are actually paying per dollar of a company's earnings. Once again, from a valuation standpoint, the lower the ratio is, the better. Unfortunately, during periods of weakness in the U.S. economy, many previously profitable companies may not have positive earnings to facilitate a meaningful P/E ratio analysis.

The price-to-sales ratio computation is done by dividing a company's current stock price by its trailing 12-month sales per share. A ratio of one implies that a company sells $1 of its product or service for every $1 of its stock price. The downside of focusing on sales per share is that it pertains to gross revenue, not the net amount of money a business actually has at its disposal for reinvesting in future growth, paying dividends, buying back stock, and reducing corporate debt.

The price-to-cash flow analysis is used to determine how much money a company is actually generating. This is accomplished by dividing the amount of cash flow generated from operations into the company's market capitalization, with the result being the amount of cash flow per share of stock. This figure tells you how much investors are paying for each dollar flowing into the business.

The amount a company generates in dividends to its shareholders is an important tool for analysis. Companies that are in financial trouble can always cut the amount of the dividends they pay, or discontinue them altogether. The dividend yield is defined as the stock price divided by the annual dividend per share and represents the percentage income return investors are realizing on their invested dollars.

While all these financial ratios are important in determining if a stock may be over- or undervalued, combining the ratios can prove very beneficial. It's also important to understand that just because the figures may indicate that a stock may be reaching its potential high or low, it's not necessarily a sign to sell. You should also take into account other factors, such as a company's fundamentals, any positive or negative events that have occurred since the last earnings report, and a stock's long-term growth potential. Valuation models provide insight for comparisons, and the knowledge of what they represent may assist in making decisions based on analytics as opposed to emotions.

Exchange Traded Funds

As their name implies, Exchange Traded Funds (ETFs) are baskets of securities traded, like individual stocks, on an exchange such as the American or New York Stock Exchange. Unlike regular open-end mutual funds, which are priced once a day at the market close based on the value of the underlying holdings, ETFs can be bought and sold throughout the trading day at the current market price. In addition, since ETFs trade like any other common stock, they can be bought on margin, thus allowing you to borrow funds and leverage your investment. Margin buying can prove very beneficial if the security price is rising, and can be quite a disadvantage if the price of the security goes down, thus necessitating a margin call from the broker. If on the other hand, you anticipate a falling security price, you can sell short (selling first, then buying back the shares in the future) your ETF shares, which is not possible with a regular mutual fund.

Investing in an ETF allows investors to invest in index-type portfolios that replicate the returns of many widely known indexes. SPDRs (Standard and Poor's Depositary Receipts or *Spiders*) track the S&P 500 index, while QQQ tracks the technology heavy Nasdaq-100 Index. Other ETFs focus on a specific global geographic region or a specific industry sector. The popularity of ETFs has increased dramatically since their introduction in 1993. Based on The Investment Company Institute data, the ETF industry has grown from just one offering in 1993 and $464 million in assets to 1,370 ETF choices representing combined assets of over $1.06 trillion. While much of the growth has been attributed to institutional investors, individuals have also participated in ETFs' expanding appeal.

For the individual investor, the advantage of ETFs over mutual funds centers around two issues: lower annual expense ratios and tax efficiency. With open-end mutual funds, regardless of whether they are purchased on a load or no-load basis, there are internal fund expenses absorbed by the shareholder. However, investors must keep in mind that, while ETFs have lower internal expenses, the investor must pay a brokerage commission for each transaction, just like with any common stock. If you are going to invest on a regular basis, as many mutual fund shareholders do, commission costs over time can negatively impact performance.

Tax efficiency is provided through the index focus of ETFs. Since they are not actively managed, securities are only bought or sold based on changes in the underlying index being replicated, which is the same as with passively managed index mutual funds. Index funds in general, whether purchased via an ETF or a mutual fund, are more tax-efficient than mutual funds whose manager makes many changes in the portfolio, causing an income tax liability to be passed through to the shareholders.

While ETFs can provide certain advantages, it is important to keep in mind that unlike regular mutual funds, ETFs' pricing in the market is subject to supply and demand of the issued shares.

Although the price of the ETF is closely tied to the value of the underlying index securities, prices may be at a premium or a discount to the actual net asset value of the portfolio. This differs from regular open-end mutual funds where the daily price is exactly that of the underlying assets. While ETFs have gained in popularity over the past 10 years, they are not for everyone and remain best-suited for investors who would like to invest in index funds but want the same trading scenario as for common stocks.

Managed Mutual Funds

An alternative to individual stock and bond selection is to hire portfolio managers to make investment selections for you. This is commonly accomplished through the use of mutual funds, since a mutual fund pools investors' money to purchase a variety of stocks or bonds.

The type and quality of the investments of the mutual fund are predetermined by the fund managers and are described in the fund's prospectus and marketing materials. A specific fund may invest only in small domestic companies; another may concentrate on large international companies; and yet another may buy only U.S. government bonds. Some funds focus on a balanced strategy, which allows the fund manager to invest in a variety of asset classes. Once again, the fund's prospectus will detail the investment parameters of the specific fund.

When you purchase shares of a mutual fund you are buying a piece of the overall portfolio. Money flows into the fund on a varying basis. One investor may contribute $5,000 while another may invest $1 million. Regardless of the size of the investment, each share of the fund represents a partial interest in all of the fund holdings. One of the key advantages of a mutual fund is diversification. The investor with $5,000 is buying a piece of possibly 500 different stock or bond issues.

Mutual fund shares can be bought at any time. The price of a mutual fund is determined at the end of each day when the total value of the fund is divided by the amount of shares outstanding, usually causing the price of a mutual fund share to change on a daily basis.

Each share of a fund purchased on a given day, regardless when the transaction occurs during the day, is bought at the same price.

Mutual fund shares can also be sold at any time. The selling price will be the net asset value of the mutual fund on that particular day. As with a stock purchase, this price can be more or less than your original purchase price.

Mutual funds provide the investor with the potential to make money in three ways. The first is through pure appreciation. If you pay $10 per share and then sell the fund at $14 per share, you will have a real gain of $4 per share.

The second potential is when a capital gain is generated by buying and selling individual issues within the fund. This occurs because the fund is actively managed by portfolio managers who buy and sell individual stocks or bonds that make up the mutual fund. If these issues are sold at a profit, a capital gain is generated and that gain is then spread among all shares of the fund and paid out to the shareholders. Mutual fund shareholders have the choice of receiving the gain in the form of a cash distribution or of reinvesting the gain within the fund.

The third money-making potential of a mutual fund is the generation of dividends and interest. Many funds own stocks and bonds that generate dividends (stocks) or interest (bonds). As with profits generated from the sale of stocks or bonds within a mutual fund portfolio, dividends and interest earned on stocks and bonds within a mutual fund are paid out proportionately to the shareholders. When dividends are generated, the shareholder has the choice of receiving those dividends and interest in cash or of reinvesting (purchasing additional shares of the fund). If your situation is such that you do not have a current need for additional income, reinvesting is generally suggested.

As with any investment, the price of the mutual fund may move up or down. Reinvesting can occur at a price that is higher than your original investment; it can also occur at a price lower than your original investment. Reinvesting allows you to accumulate additional shares as the market price fluctuates both positively and negatively. This is a form of dollar cost averaging.

Dollar cost averaging is a technique used in an effort to reduce risk. By using a dollar cost averaging strategy, investors purchase securities on a regular, systematic basis. By investing a set amount each month, the average purchase price will tend to offset market fluctuations. Dollar cost averaging does NOT, however, assure a profit or protect against market losses

With constant market volatility, an investor doesn't know whether shares are overpriced or underpriced at any given time. Using dollar cost averaging, the investor purchases shares of a fund over an extended period of time, averaging out the high and low purchases. The investor buys some shares when prices are low and other shares when prices are high. Dollar cost averaging is the investment of a fixed amount of money in a given fund at regular intervals. Using this strategy, losses during market declines are limited while the ability to participate in bull market movements is maintained.

Let's look at an example. Assume you have the choice of investing $6,000 at one time in a particular mutual fund, or $500 per month in the same fund for one year. If you invested on a monthly basis, you would experience the following:

Month	Amount Invested	Price per Share	Shares Purchased
January	$500	$50	10.0
February	$500	$40	12.5
March	$500	$30	16.67
April	$500	$30	16.67
May	$500	$40	12.5
June	$500	$50	10.0
July	$500	$60	8.33
August	$500	$50	10.0
September	$500	$40	12.5
October	$500	$50	10.0
November	$500	$60	8.33
December	$500	$70	7.14
TOTAL SHARES			134.64
Average Market Price per Share		$47.50	
Average Cost per Share		$44.56	

Compare this with making a single investment of $6,000 in January in which you would purchase 120 shares at $50each. Based on the value at the end of December, you made a profit regardless if you invested monthly or all in January. However, because the total number of shares you purchased on a monthly basis took into account various share prices, the total number of shares is greater (134.64 shares versus 120 shares). Since the number of shares is greater, the total value is greater if you used the dollar cost averaging method (134.64 × $70 per share = $9,424.80) when compared to the January-only investment (120 × $70 per share = $8,400.00). Keep in mind that this example assumes that prices were volatile during the period. If prices simply increased and experienced no drop in value, the results would favor making the investment all at once.

While this principle applies to any fluctuating security, it is ideally suited for mutual fund investing. Mutual funds provide diversification, professional management, and controlled expenses. As a general rule, mutual funds allow additional investments to be made as often as you like. Many funds allow automatic investments to be set up from your checking account or money market fund on a monthly basis.

So often, investors let their emotions and stock market information overload guide their buying and selling decisions. They end up buying high and selling low. The automatic investment plan guarantees that feelings about the stock market are put on the sidelines as dollars buy additional shares at varying prices.

If the stock market would move in just one direction—up— then it would be better to invest in one lump sum. Unfortunately the market moves in cycles and fluctuates daily. Dollar cost averaging will not guarantee you a profit, but it is highly appropriate for long-term saving purposes such as retirement and college education funding for your children. Risk may be reduced because purchases of mutual fund shares are certain to be made at a variety of share prices.

During periods of volatility, uncertainty, and falling stock prices, the investor who utilizes dollar cost averaging has a better opportunity to accumulate a large number of shares. Over the long run, it can work to the investor's benefit. As our example showed, the longer the dollar cost averaging period, the more likely the investor is to have bought shares at a good variety of price levels, including a greater amount at lower levels and fewer at high prices.

Obviously this is not a get-rich-quick market timing strategy. It is simply an effective method for accumulating an investment portfolio at a reasonable cost.

Load Mutual Funds

Open-end mutual funds (mutual funds that issue as many shares as the public wishes) can be classified as load or no-load funds. The term *load* refers to a sales charge applicable specifically to open-end mutual funds. The sales charge for a load mutual fund generally ranges between 3% and 5.75% of the total purchase and is disclosed in the fund prospectus. This load, or sales charge, is built into the actual buy price of the fund and does not show on your statement as an additional charge or commission. The sales charge may be divided among the mutual fund company, the broker/dealer who executed your order, and the individual representative who made the recommendation, handled the paper work, and placed the order.

Sales charges are based on the total amount an individual invests in any one mutual fund family. The fund family is the management company that may offer many different funds based on varying asset classes. For example, the XYZ family of funds may offer 30 different funds while the ABC family may have only two or three.

Most large fund families offer a variety of growth and income funds. Larger fund families will also offer sub-classification or specialty funds that may invest internationally or within specific sectors such as retail or technology.

There are two ways to lower the sales charges on the purchase of mutual funds. First, you may be eligible for a quantity discount based on your total investment within the fund family, regardless of the specific fund. Referred to as rights of accumulation, these discounts generally kick in at an investment level of $50,000 and increase at higher breakpoints of $100,000, $250,000, $500,000, and $1 million. Many fund families actually eliminate the load altogether for investments greater than $1 million.

If you are investing smaller amounts on a systematic basis, you may not be able to take full advantage of a quantity discount. However, you may be able to reduce sales charges by signing a letter of intent. The letter of intent indicates that you intend to make additional investments in the fund up to a specified dollar amount over a specific period of time (usually 12 or 13 months). Your discount is based on the total amount invested over the specified time period and applies to every fund purchase.

To illustrate, a monthly investment of $4,500 in a load mutual fund would incur the maximum sales charge, even though the total investment would be $54,000 over a 12-month period. If, on the other hand, a $50,000 letter of intent had been signed with the fund family, the sales charge discount applicable to $50,000 would have been applied to the first dollar invested.

By estimating your total investment potential for the coming year, it may be possible to lower the sales charges on your mutual fund investments. If for some reason you do not meet your letter of intent commitment, your account will be adjusted for the applicable sales charge on the amount invested.

Using rights of accumulation or a letter of intent will allow an individual with more than $50,000 to invest to pay a lower sales charge than quoted in the financial magazines or papers reporting on fund performance. Keep in mind when using these strategies that most fund companies allow the investor to include investments made in their minor children's accounts, trust accounts, joint accounts, separate accounts for a spouse, and IRA accounts. Additionally, all investments within the fund family, regardless of the specific mutual fund, are included in the discount calculation.

The primary incentive for taking advantage of discounts is to increase your portfolio's rate of return, but you should never make any investment based solely on a potential discount. The funds you choose to invest in must first meet your objectives for risk and reward. It is also naive to think that any one mutual fund family offers the best funds in all asset classes even if the discounted load will increase your potential return by lowering the cost of the transaction.

In general, if a mutual fund has a sales charge at the time of purchase, there is no sales charge when selling shares. Most load fund families also allow the movement of money from one fund to another within the same fund family without incurring a new sales charge. Reinvestment of dividends and capital gains are generally handled without incurring a sales charge; however, some companies still assess a load on reinvestments.

Many fund companies also assess a 12b-1 charge to shareholders. This charge allows the fund company to pay a maximum of ¼ of 1% to the broker/dealer as ongoing compensation for maintaining and servicing accounts. This information must also be disclosed in the prospectus.

No-Load Mutual Funds

For many years, the majority of mutual funds were load funds. The load was designed not only to cover the management company's costs, but also to compensate the broker who provided research and guidance to the individual investor. Over the past 20 years, investors have begun to do more of their own research and now wish to buy mutual funds without the assistance of a broker. This can be accomplished using no-load mutual funds. As the name implies, these funds carry no built-in sales charge, thus the entire amount of your purchase is invested in the mutual fund of your choice. Funds can be purchased directly through the fund family. Since buying a no-load fund means dealing directly with a particular fund family, the client service representatives of that fund company cannot provide investment advice. They can only provide information about the available fund choices and answer questions relative to your account.

The no-load fund industry has grown dramatically as more and more investors choose to do their own research and take advantage of the savings by avoiding sales charges. All things being equal, this strategy may make sense if you don't need the assistance of a broker or financial counselor. However, in reality, all things are not equal. Just as there are high-quality mutual funds in both the load and no-load categories, both categories also have underperforming funds and fund managers.

Another cost to consider with both types of funds is the management fee. All funds, load and no-load, have internal fund management expenses. These charges are disclosed in the prospectus and are in addition to any sales charges associated with the fund. The prospectus will contain a summary of expenses that breaks out internal fund costs such as research, salaries, and the transaction costs associated with the fund portfolio. Also listed in the summary are "other expenses," which encompass shareholder services (processing and mailing of statements, and customer service telephone personnel), legal, transfer agent costs, and custodian expenses. Oftentimes marketing expenses such as advertising and brochures will also be included in this category.

When comparing expenses between load and no-load funds, you may begin to notice that some no-load funds have a higher expense ratio. Since no-load funds are sold directly to the public, they also can have higher marketing expenses. You may have noticed that there are more print and television ads for no-load funds. These added costs are shared by all shareholders within the fund.

Some no-load funds also charge a 12b-1 expense. However, this is a marketing-related expense paid to the custodian company holding the mutual funds on your behalf rather than to the broker, as is the case with load funds.

This is not to say that load funds do not market their products! Whether it is billboards, commercials, sponsorship of athletic events, or ads in the newspaper, many load and no-load funds advertise. The expense difference is in how no-load funds reach potential buyers. Their efforts are carried out by newspaper, magazine, and television advertising, and concentrated direct mail in the form of mass mailings or the mailing of a sales kit after a request for information. This can be a very expensive process for a fund company, and these expenses are covered by the overall management fee paid by all shareholders.

It is important that you, the investor, know what the total fund expenses are, since fund expenses lower fund performance. As we said before, if all funds were equal, those with higher expenses would underperform their peers whose expenses were lower. However, that isn't the case. Whether it is load or no-load, a fund with an extremely high expense ratio can be a top performer while another fund with a low expense ratio may be an underperformer.

Class B Shares

In an effort to compete with no-loads, many load mutual funds have created a class of shares known as class B shares that carry no up-front load or sales charge. Class B shares generally have a redemption charge if shares are sold within a certain period of time, usually six years. Redemption charges are known as back-end loads, and can result in charges ranging from 1% to 6% depending upon how long the fund is held. An investor can avoid the back-end load by simply holding the fund for the six-year period. Many fund companies will allow the investor to switch to other funds within the fund family without incurring a surrender charge.

At a glance, class B shares look like a win-win situation. The investor receives personal advice and service from a broker without incurring a sales charge. The broker not only is able to offer clients mutual funds without front- or back-end sales charges (depending upon how long the funds are held), but is compensated for this service by receiving a commission. If this seems too good to be true, remember the adage we have repeatedly mentioned: "you don't get something worthwhile for nothing."

You must first ask yourself, how the broker is compensated for selling a fund when the investor pays no sales charge. Across the board, class B shares carry higher internal fund expenses, often in excess of 2%, or almost a full percentage point higher than comparable up-front load A shares. The fees that a fund pays to a broker as commission are covered by higher internal costs.

Investors who work with a broker or a financial advisor should evaluate both classes of shares to determine the correct pricing structure for their particular portfolio. One way to accomplish this is to ask your broker to run projections on both funds assuming the same gross growth return over a specified amount of time. Using these comparisons, you can see the actual dilution of returns due to a fund's pricing structure.

Mutual Fund Differences

Market uncertainty has caused many physicians to closely re-examine their investment portfolios for potential changes. With mutual funds being so widely held, it is prudent to gain an understanding of fund specifics in order to make a valid basis for comparison. The universe of mutual fund options is overwhelming. An investor who takes a moment to learn the basics of how to compare mutual funds will be armed with the ability to choose wisely for themselves, or to intelligently examine the advice of their financial professional. Volumes have been written on the many characteristics that differentiate mutual funds. Understanding three fundamental concepts will help simplify the complex choices: asset class, management style, and expenses (which we've just talked about with regard to load versus no-load funds).

Asset class is often described in the title of the fund, and defines the underlying securities the fund purchases on the investor's behalf. For example, a fund can be comprised of stocks, bonds, or real estate investments, to name the largest and most common fund holdings. Among these classes are dizzying arrays of distinctions. Stock funds can be further categorized according to the location, size, and sector of companies held. Roughly the same distinctions hold true for bond funds.

The main geographic categories for mutual funds are domestic, foreign/international, and global. Domestic funds purchase shares of companies headquartered in the United States. Foreign funds purchase shares of companies operating anywhere outside of the United States. Global funds tend to invest in a combination of companies throughout the world. Of course, these categories themselves have varying distinctions.

Company size and sector are other basic asset class differentiations. Company size refers to the market capitalization, which is actually a simple calculation: multiply the total number of outstanding shares of a given company by its stock price. Mutual fund market cap distinctions are commonly divided into three categories: large-cap, mid-cap and small-cap. Large-cap typically refers to companies with a market capitalization exceeding $10 billion, mid-cap to companies in the range of $4 billion to $10 billion, and small-cap to those under $4 billion.

Sector specific funds are yet another subcategory to consider. Sector funds purchase stocks of companies in a particular sector, such as retail or finance. An energy fund, for example, may buy shares of companies that run hydro-electric power plants, build natural gas lines, or operate oil refineries. Sector funds can be broad, as in "finance," or very narrow, as in "South African precious metals." Sector funds provide exposure to a limited segment of the overall market and should be well researched and fully understood prior to taking the plunge.

Bond Funds

Investors should also be aware of the many differences and available choices in the mutual fund fixed-income arena, each of which offers varying degrees of potential risk and reward.

U.S. government bond funds invest primarily, or exclusively, in U.S. Treasury bonds, government agency obligations, and the mortgage-backed debt of Fannie Mae, Ginnie Mae, and Freddie Mac. The safety advantage of treasury bonds and direct obligations of certain federal agencies is that they carry a government guarantee relative to interest and principal repayment. But with the exception of Ginnie Mae, mortgage-backed bonds are not guaranteed by the government. While government bond funds carry the lowest credit risk among the various fund choices, they are still subject to interest rate fluctuations, which can affect their principal value.

Corporate bond funds are available with a wide variety of choices. While some invest primarily in high-quality, investment-grade bonds, others incorporate a certain percentage of below-investment-grade bonds. This is done to provide a higher income payout for the investor, but it also increases risk within the fund. Another type of corporate bond fund is known as a high-yield bond fund and focuses the portfolio entirely on the riskier lower-quality bond offerings. Along with the higher risk primarily associated with an increased possibility of default of the issuing corporation, there may also be potential for price appreciation if the issuing companies improve their financial situation in the eyes of the various credit rating agencies.

Municipal bond funds invest in bonds issued by state and local authorities, where in most cases, the interest is free from regular federal income taxes, although state and local taxes may apply. While municipal bond yields may appear lower than yields on corporate bonds, investors should focus on the after-tax yield of comparable taxable bonds, based on their specific income tax rate.

For additional fixed-income diversification, international bond funds offer the ability to invest in debt securities of non-U.S. companies and governments. If the fund invests in both international and domestic bonds, the fund is referred to as a global or world bond fund. International bonds provide investors the opportunity to take advantage of various economic and political conditions around the world, to earn a potentially higher return than they could by investing in just domestic bonds. In addition to interest rate risk, investing in international bonds includes the risk associated with fluctuations in currency exchange rates.

Individual Bonds or Bond Mutual Funds?

Clients often ask us why we recommend using bond mutual funds rather than individual bonds. Their argument goes something like, "I can just buy actual bonds and hold them to maturity, so I know exactly what I'm getting and don't have to worry about losing money." In reality, there is more to the decision, and there are some very significant benefits to using a bond mutual fund.

First, why own bonds at all? We view bonds as volatility reducers and not as income generators. In fact, we don't explicitly advocate owning any investment for the sole purpose of generating income. Instead, we advise clients to approach their portfolios from a total-return standpoint, utilizing a variety of investments. Mixing those assets can create a portfolio with the amount of potential fluctuation to better match expectations.

Some investors may be much more concerned about short-term fluctuation in value. Perhaps they have a large financial obligation coming up in the near future (down payment on a house, a new car purchase, college tuition, etc.), and they would be negatively impacted by a short-term drop in their portfolio's value. Those clients need to own assets that are unlikely to perform poorly if the stock market takes a spill, otherwise they could be in the unfortunate situation of having to sell assets from their portfolio right after suffering a big loss.

One of the big myths about owning individual bonds is that you don't have to worry about losing money or having the bonds depreciate. The truth is more complicated. Just because you own an individual bond and plan to hold it until maturity does not mean that its value doesn't fluctuate.

All bonds move in response to daily changes in interest rates, credit conditions, and a host of other variables. We understand the appeal of owning a bond to maturity: a bond owner knows the value he or she will get at the end of the period while a fund owner doesn't. But the appearance of added safety is more a function of simply not looking at the value of a bond along the way, while funds publish their prices each day. In reality, when a bond fund sees a price drop, it benefits more quickly from the higher prevailing yields that created the price drop. History shows that the chance of doing poorly in a bond fund versus owning an individual bond (or a laddered portfolio of bonds) over longer time frames is too small to outweigh the advantages of bond funds.

Do bond funds fluctuate in value? Their net asset value (NAV) changes every day in response to market conditions, but because most of these funds are highly diversified, these fluctuations are usually very small. But owning a bond is not a guarantee against losing money.

Treasury bonds and some mortgage-backed and agency bonds are explicitly or implicitly backed by the federal government, so it's a pretty good bet that they aren't going to default on either their interest payments or return of principal. Because this essentially makes them guaranteed investments, their yields tend to be lower than competing investments. In spite of these features, they are not immune to interest rate changes.

All other bonds have credit risk associated with them, including AAA-rated corporate bonds. This super-high-quality debt is very unlikely to default, but it's not guaranteed, and unless you are prepared to do the credit analysis necessary to really understand the investment, you may be taking on more risk than you realize.

Aside from diversification, one of the biggest advantages of owning a bond mutual fund is that you can benefit from low-cost professional management. Bond fund managers spend all day figuring out what the best bonds are and how best to structure a portfolio. Realistically, most individual investors are not likely to do this much work. In summary, by owning a good bond fund you get several things:

- Added value from a wider investment universe. Most diversified bond funds can own bonds of different maturities, credit qualities, and sectors.
- Better analysis. A good bond fund manager has the skill to assess uncovered opportunities and hidden risks.
- Better portfolio management. Most bond owners would be hard-pressed to know when it's best to use a barbell strategy versus a bullet portfolio versus laddered maturities, or how to exploit the roll-down of the yield curve. Yet these are just some of the portfolio management techniques bond fund managers use to add value.

If you have a known, fixed liability at some time in the relatively near future, a short-term treasury bond or CD might be a reasonable option. But for longer-term needs, we think bond mutual funds are the better choice.

Socially Conscious Funds

Socially conscious mutual funds are gaining in popularity. These funds, also known as socially responsible or ethical investment funds, have found a niche in the vast mutual fund marketplace. After all, many investors would like to invest and feel good about where their dollars are invested.

How have these socially conscious funds performed as a group? The answer is similar to the mutual fund industry as a whole. Some have achieved above-market returns while others have been perennial underperformers compared to their relative indices. Socially conscious investors seem to have greater degrees of tolerance and patience when it comes to their mutual funds; they are willing to accept marginally lower returns in exchange for the assurance that the companies in which they are investing are socially responsible. Thus, these investors achieve another personal goal beyond profitability.

Socially responsible funds typically will not invest in corporations that manufacture weapons, tobacco products, or alcohol. Many focus on environmentally friendly companies. Some funds focus on corporations that aggressively hire minority and female employees and have a history of moving them up the organizational ladder.

Some socially conscious funds concentrate on bonds as opposed to stocks. Ginnie Mae bonds, backed by the U.S. government, may be included since they provide financing for home mortgages. Municipal bonds are attractive because they create funding vehicles for libraries, parks, and schools. However, certain socially responsible mutual funds will avoid U.S. Treasuries because the funds could be used to finance government defense projects.

One of the problems managers of socially responsible mutual funds face is determining all of the types of business in which a conglomerate may be involved. It is important to read the fine print of the prospectus to determine the latitude given in selecting particular companies. The fund's prospectus will spell out the exact industries that may or may not be excluded from consideration. The fund's quarterly and annual reports are also good sources of information and will list the specific fund investments.

Chicago-based Morningstar estimates that $65 billion in assets are invested in just over 475 socially responsible mutual funds (*Morningstar Principia*, December 31, 2012 edition), although many of them are not included in newspaper mutual fund listings due to their small asset size. If they are too small to be listed, it also will be difficult to find third-party research or rankings that will allow a more detailed evaluation of the mutual fund. Some large mutual fund families are seeing this market as yet another opportunity and are joining in.

Derivatives

You should also determine whether a particular mutual fund uses derivatives. This will be disclosed in the prospectus. What is a derivative? The value of a derivative is based on the performance of other financial products or market indices. The most common forms of derivatives include futures, options, and contracts based on currencies, interest rates, and various stock market indices. In a very simple form, a home mortgage is an excellent example of the use of a derivative, since you leverage your purchasing power by borrowing funds to purchase the home.

For speculative purposes, derivatives allow investors to control a large amount of stocks or commodities without putting up much capital. This is the same leveraging technique used by options and futures traders. If the markets move in an unexpected direction, use of a derivative can be disastrous, causing losses far in excess of the original marginal investment.

A less-speculative use of derivatives is to reduce risk by hedging. For example, a mutual fund that invests in foreign stocks can minimize the currency exchange rate risk by using a form of a derivative. In this case, the derivative can provide protection from adverse currency fluctuation. On the other hand, derivatives can become a drain on returns if the fund does not experience the negative impact of currency fluctuation. The same holds true for the mutual fund manager investing in bonds who hedges against interest rate fluctuations in order to provide less volatile returns.

The key for you as an investor is to determine whether the derivative is being used as a hedge or for speculation. The prospectus and annual report will show you to what extent the fund allows the managers to engage in derivative trading. Unfortunately this information is often lost in footnotes and other balance sheet categories.

Derivatives have been around for many years and represent a major component of our complex financial marketplace. Unfortunately, derivatives, which were intended to be an effective method of hedging risk, are now being used in hopes of increasing returns. Additionally, the types and complexity of derivatives have multiplied. Many fund managers speculate with derivatives in order to beat the market and the return of competing mutual funds. This strategy can backfire, creating even greater losses.

By avoiding the use of derivatives, you may be missing an opportunity to increase returns or provide a valuable hedge for your investments. However, through some research and leg work on your part, you can quantify and control your exposure to derivatives within your overall portfolio by being aware of how they are used.

The Relevance of Fund Size

Because of the tremendous growth of the mutual fund industry, many investors now are concerned about fund size. Mutual funds range in size from a few million dollars to tens of billions of dollars. Most mutual fund research groups consider funds with assets of $250 million or less small, and large if fund assets exceed $1 billion. It is important to understand both the advantages and disadvantages of fund size.

Large funds generally have been in existence long enough to establish performance records that can be analyzed and compared to those of their peers. The relevance of these track records, however, depends on the tenure of the fund manager. High turnover of managers minimizes the significance of a fund's long-term track record.

As a fund grows, the list of companies that it invests in also grows. This can be an advantage since it creates greater stock diversification, which may reduce price fluctuations within the fund. Large funds tend to purchase larger companies for liquidity reasons. If a fund is the majority shareholder of a small company stock, it may be difficult to move in or out of the position without causing drastic price changes.

Remember that all funds start out small. A new fund has the ability to build a portfolio that reflects the manager's view of attractive investments. A new, smaller fund is not burdened by tax issues related to previously held investments.

Some small funds don't want to become large funds. To preserve this perceived investing advantage, some funds close to new investors once they have attained a certain size. Small funds tend to hold fewer stocks than large funds, resulting in a more focused portfolio—an advantage as well as a disadvantage.

As a general rule, when smaller mutual funds gain in popularity due to stellar performance, they also gain in asset size. The unknown variable is how that fund will manage its growth.

Management Style: Active versus Passive

Management style can mean many different things. Let's begin with a discussion of active and passive management. In simplest terms, passive management refers to index funds. Investors utilize passive management because it provides broad diversification and cost-effective management and implementation. Passive management is essentially a buy-and-hold strategy that results in relatively low trading costs in spite of the large number of security positions in an index portfolio. Passive investing through an index fund also provides significant diversification benefits since index portfolios hold all the stocks comprising their specific asset class universe.

On the flipside, investors select actively managed stock market funds to utilize various stock selection strategies in order to gain potentially higher rates of return in relation to market indices. Over the years, investors have made large cash inflows into the index funds that seek to replicate the S&P 500. Active managers, on the other hand, feel that as the market retreats, their funds will be in a better position to minimize losses because, they hope, they can liquidate positions before the full impact of a market correction is experienced, thus enhancing these funds' long-term performance results.

The benefits of passive investing may be more attainable in some market segments than in others. For example, large company U.S. equities are extremely liquid and easy to transact, while small company stocks often traded on the over the counter market are not. This difference results in much higher transaction costs, more difficult trading, and poorer tracking in small-cap index portfolios than in large-cap portfolios.

Active management may make sense in the small cap area since small-cap stocks are often less well-known based on limited earnings and dividend history. These less-publicized valuation projections present an opportunity for active managers to take advantage of existing stock information to evaluate specific issues. Also, since most small-cap stocks are in the early stages of corporate development, they may have additional growth potential fueled by new technology and developing business.

The merits of passive investing in the large-cap equity segment were demonstrated during the last bull market. The same generally cannot be said about the small-cap U.S. market sector at that time. Keep in mind, though, that with an actively managed fund, the challenge is to find a good manager with demonstrated skill and sound management style.

Investment Websites

With the advent of modern technology, it is easier than ever for physicians to take control of their financial situation and address these important issues. Whether you are researching investment options or performing financial planning retirement projections, the currently available online resources are abundant. The following will serve as a guide for those looking to proactively change or simply be better informed about their financial situation.

For investors, perhaps the most difficult task is keeping track of various investment portfolios. While it's obviously important to know what you own, it is equally important to know how well specific investments and the overall portfolio are doing, both on a dollar as well as percentage basis, over varying time periods. Morningstar's portfolio tracker at http://www.morningstar.com is a great tool to keep a close eye on your investments. You can enter your holdings on a screen or import the data from Quicken, Yahoo, and even many online brokerage statements. Heavy on analytics, it provides overviews and performance charts, and allows you to view a visual map and analysis using several factors, including a breakout of holdings by asset allocation percentages. Similar tracking can also be accomplished on the MSN Money website at http://money.msn.com/.

One of the best overall financial sites is Yahoo Finance at http://finance.yahoo.com. Yahoo's text-based interface makes navigating through the site simple and fast. The opening page provides up-to-the-minute market data, prices on individual stocks, and bond market commentary. From this site, you can also access respected outlets such as Briefing.com, *Financial Times*, and *Business Week*. Of particular interest is the stock research link, which takes you on a journey of exceptional research tools covering stocks, bonds, mutual funds, and options. International news is also available as well as finance-based chat rooms.

Economic data and the expectation of new data being released certainly are major factors affecting stock market movement. Moody's

Analytics economy website at http://www.economy.com provides access to raw data, general economic news—both domestic and worldwide—and a most helpful commentary to interpret it all. Use caution as you navigate through this site, as its online subsidiaries often charge various subscription rates to access various economic reports. However, one of the subsidiaries, Free Lunch, lets you search for over 900,000 items of economic and financial data without charge.

For a general financial education, spend some time with the solid tutorials on market basics with The Motley Fool at http://www. fool.com. Ease is the key here, as all of the educational information and tools are easily accessible from the website's Fool's School. Another option for general market and retirement planning education is the CNN Money website at http://www.money.cnn.com. This site, takes advantage of the long-time involvement of many experts with varied interests and specialties. Of particular interest is their section on managing the retirement nest egg. A concise dictionary of financial terms and tools and other interactive features makes it a valuable site for investment novices as well as the more seasoned physician investor.

Given that there are more mutual funds to choose from than common stocks, there is a plethora of sites dedicated to evaluating load and no-load mutual funds. The leader in the field of mutual fund research is Morningstar. Via its website, http://www.morningstar.com, visitors can obtain a one-page summary on almost any mutual fund. Included are analyst reports and the Morningstar ratings. For more indepth research, such as fund alerts, changes in fund management, and portfolio optimization tools, site visitors will need to purchase a paid subscription.

While most sites provide a variety of financial news, one of the best sites dedicated to U.S. and global events is the *Wall Street Journal* at http://www.wsj.com. Links on the home page will take you to news by region as well as topic.

If you are interested in delving into the intricate finances of America's publicly traded corporations, a couple of sights warrant your attention. Reuters at http://www.investor.reuters.com and Hoover's website at http://www.hoovers.com are sure to have enough reports and company fundamentals to keep sophisticated investors well-educated. Simply enter a company's trading symbol or name and the site will take you to abundant company information, including charts, earnings estimates, income statements, balance sheets, and cash flow reports. Of particular interest may be the reports detailing insider trading and the level of institutional ownership. Both sites also make more indepth reports available on a paid subscription basis.

If your interest lies in corporate, municipal, or government bonds, spend some time at the Yahoo Bond Center at http://bonds.yahoo.com. You will find educational information, professional commentary, current rates on bond offerings, as well as a helpful glossary of terms and financial calculators.

For those who are students of technical analysis, the site to visit is Bigchart's website at http://www.bigcharts.com, where you can easily chart individual securities and mutual funds.

There are, of course, many other sites that the do-it-yourselfer will find valuable. For one of the most comprehensive glossaries of financial terms, go to http://www.investorwords.com. For a nice overall investment site, take a look at http://www.investorguide.com. For economics-based articles, both Bloomberg at http://www.bloomberg.com and Barron's website at http://www.barrons.com offer an online alternative to their written publications. In addition, many discount stock brokerage firms offer websites that cater to investors who do it themselves.

CHAPTER 5

Annuities

Investors seeking a tax deferral strategy, or those who wish to create a retirement stream of income that they cannot outlive, often look to tax-deferred annuities. The word *annuity* comes from the Latin term meaning *annual*. It refers to any situation in which principal and interest are liquidated through a series of regular payments made over a specified period of time. A deferred annuity is an annuity in which taxation is postponed or deferred until it is actually paid out. Annuities were first created in response to investors looking for an alternative investment that had the safety of a bank-issued CD, but would allow them to defer taxes on their interest.

With this in mind, insurance companies created the annuity product. This vehicle is able to provide the tax deferral desired by investors due primarily to the life insurance coverage included in the annuity. This protection guarantees that the original investment will be available to the owner's heirs in the event of the owner's death. While this guarantee is not substantial, it is adequate to allow the annuity to be classified as an insurance product and thus eligible for special tax-deferral treatment. This special tax treatment allows all earnings in the annuity to accumulate tax deferred. Tax deferral allows an individual to earn interest on the original principal, on the interest previously credited, and also on the amount that would have been paid in income taxes. The following graph illustrates the power of tax deferral and the resulting additional income available from the use of this strategy.

Tax Deferral

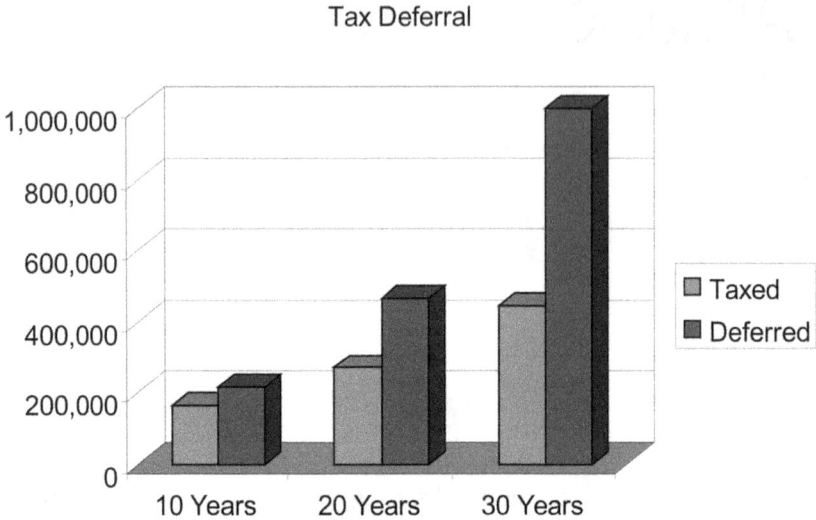

When purchasing an annuity, it is important to understand some definitions of terms as they relate to the policy. The *policy owner* is the individual who makes the investment and has all of the rights of ownership, including terminating or transferring the annuity to another insurance company, and changing beneficiaries. The *beneficiary* is the individual or entity who will receive any potential proceeds payable upon the death of the owner or the annuitant. The *annuitant* is the individual whose life is used to determine the amount of the payments made during the annuity payout periods.

Originally, annuities were policies requiring regular deposits over a specified number of years or via a lump-sum investment. As the deposits earned interest, no income tax was due. At maturity, the annuity made income distributions on a schedule selected by the annuity owner. Payments were often based on the life expectancy of the owner and provided income payments for the rest of the owner's life. Such options were referred to as "life only" payments. However, individuals soon realized that if they died soon after they began to receive these life only payments, all future income payments were lost. This provided insurance companies with a substantial profit!

To provide a more equitable form of income payment, insurance companies tied income payments to a variety of guaranteed periods of time, such as payments for life with 10 years certain or life with 20 years certain. In such arrangements, the owner was guaranteed to receive income payments for the rest of his or her life, but in the event of a premature death, payments would continue to the beneficiary for the guaranteed time period. Examples of current payout options include:

1. *Lump-sum withdrawal:* An annuity owner can actually withdraw all of the accumulated funds within the policy, without having to spread the payments over a certain amount of time. A complete lump-sum withdrawal is considered by the issuing company to be a surrender of the policy, thus terminating any remaining annuity benefits.

2. *Partial withdrawals:* In order to allow policy owners limited access to their accumulated funds without terminating the contract, many annuities allow partial withdrawals without a surrender charge or penalty. The amount allowed to be withdrawn is generally limited to just 10% to 15% of the annuity's value on an annual cumulative or absolute total basis.

3. *Life only annuity:* Regular payments are made for as long as the annuitant lives. Upon the annuitant's death, payments cease and no refund or benefits are paid to beneficiaries, even if the annuity owner has not received back his or her initial investment.

4. *Life with term certain:* To avoid the potential loss of principal associated with the life only option, the owner can select a term certain option. If the annuitant dies before the specified time certain period, typically 10, 15, or 20 years, the annuity payments continue to be paid to the beneficiary for the remainder of the term. If death does not occur within the term certain time period, annuity payments continue for as long as the annuitant lives.

5. *Joint and survivor:* This option allows for the regular annuity payments to be made over the lives of two individuals. At the death of either of the individuals, annuity payments continue to be paid to the survivor. Depending on the specific annuity, the payments may be made at the same or at a reduced level.

6. *Period certain:* Annuitants who do not wish to tie their payouts to life expectancy can choose to have regular payments made over a set period of years. Once the payout period ends, no further lifetime benefits are available. If the annuitant dies before the end of the specified period, payments continue to be paid to the named beneficiary for the remainder of the pre-selected time period.

Annuities developed further when individuals began to focus with interest on various investment products that could save income taxes. The fixed Single Premium Deferred Annuity (SPDA) was developed to compete with bank CDs. Similar to a bank CD, SPDAs allow for single sum deposits and guaranteed minimum rates of interest, and typically pay higher rates of interest than bank CDs. Fixed annuities carry a minimum interest rate, which is guaranteed by the issuing insurance company. The money contributed is placed in the insurance company's general account, and any investment risk rests entirely with the insurance company. With a fixed annuity, as is the case with a CD, the main investment objective is safety of principal and stable returns. Originally, all interest in the SPDA accumulated on a tax-deferred basis and withdrawals were made on a "first in, first out" basis. This meant that an individual could deposit $100,000 into a SPDA, allow it to grow, and later begin to take withdrawals that were income tax-free until the sum of the withdrawals equaled the original investment (basis) in the SPDA.

This advantageous tax treatment was eliminated in the TEFRA tax act of the mid-1980s. Annuities sold after the tax changes are taxed on a "last in, first out" basis. This means all withdrawals are assumed to be withdrawals of interest and are taxed until the amount of assets in the annuity is equal to the original investment.

Fixed annuities offering a guaranteed fixed rate of return and tax deferral on earnings, as well as an income stream that can last a lifetime, can be an appealing money management tool for physicians with a low risk tolerance and/or as a method of further diversification of an overall portfolio. You can invest in a fixed annuity in a single lump sum, through a single premium annuity, or by making periodic payments into a flexible premium annuity.

The tax benefits of fixed annuities do come with restrictions: Payouts can begin after you reach age 59½, or earnings may be subject to a 10% federal income tax penalty. In addition, if you withdraw funds during the accumulation period, usually within the first seven years of purchasing the annuity, the issuing insurance company may levy withdrawal charges. If you decide to cash in the full value of the annuity during this accumulation phase, you may also incur substantial surrender charges. It is for this reason that fixed annuities should be viewed as a long-term investment. For those who would like to invest in an annuity and begin receiving income payouts right away, the product of choice would be a fixed immediate annuity, which doesn't have the typical withdrawal or surrender charges associated with other long-term annuities.

It is important to understand that fixed annuities are neither insured nor guaranteed by the FDIC, and that they may actually decline in value if surrendered prior to maturity due to surrender or withdrawal charges. The guarantees are actually based on the claims-paying ability of the issuing insurance company. Fixed annuity products can be excellent alternatives to the fully taxable cash asset products that are often used.

Variable Annuities

Many long-term investors also want the advantage of tax deferral combined with the long-term growth potential of equities. With this in mind, insurance companies and mutual fund companies joined forces to create the variable annuity. Variable annuities generally provide no guarantees as to investment return or future potential annuity benefits. The money invested is allocated into different variable annuity sub-accounts. Within these sub-accounts, choices are available to invest funds in a wide variety of investment vehicles. Stock sub-accounts options may include conservative growth, comprising large U.S. value or blue chip stocks; aggressive growth, which focuses on high-return/high-risk growth stocks; global or international equities; and even sector sub-accounts, which focus on a particular industry or segment of the U.S. economy. Bond sub-accounts often include choices among corporate bonds with various maturities and quality ratings, government bonds, as well as international bonds.

Also typically included is a fixed account where, like a fixed annuity, the insurance company will guarantee a specific rate of return for a set time period. Investments within the annuity can be split up among the various available sub-accounts in varying percentages. The variable annuity industry has worked with the mutual fund industry to contract with some of the top-performing mutual fund managers to manage their sub-account portfolios.

The ultimate annuity payouts for variable annuities depend on the investment results achieved within the various sub-accounts the funds were directed to. The investment risk rests solely with the annuity owner, not the issuing insurance company. Investors therefore look to variable annuities in order to achieve higher potential returns compared with fixed annuities in an effort to keep pace with inflation.

Dividends, interest, and capital gains distributions within the annuity currently are not taxable. Taxes are deferred to such time that withdrawals are made. Then all income received in excess of the original principal is taxed as ordinary income. As is the case with fixed annuities, any lump-sum payment received before the annuitant is age 59½ carries a 10% IRS penalty. However, unlike a fixed annuity, a variable annuity cannot guarantee repayment of the principal or original investment during life. This is based on the fact that stock and bond markets carry inherent risks that once again are borne by the investor, not the annuity company.

Similar to the fixed annuity, variable annuities do provide some form of guarantee. While repayment of principal cannot be guaranteed during your lifetime, there is a guarantee at death. Upon the death of the variable annuity holder, the insurance company guarantees the beneficiary will receive the amount invested, regardless of current market value. Some companies even increase the guaranteed amount at certain time periods based on the then-current market value of the separate accounts. The added benefit of a guarantee to a beneficiary comes with a price. Variable annuities carry a mortality charge, a type of life insurance cost that becomes part of the overall expense figure. This is the reason variable annuities as a whole, carry higher expenses when compared to mutual funds.

Variable annuities are considered securities and you will receive a prospectus before you make your purchase decision. The prospectus will detail all of the expenses of the annuity, including management expenses, mortality charges, and other administrative costs. Prepare yourself for annual total expenses that range from 2% to 3.5%. The generally higher expenses may make you lean towards a more aggressive portfolio in hopes of diminishing the effects of the expenses.

Although tax savings through deferral is the main advantage of a variable annuity, you are actually waiving your rights to the beneficial treatment of long-term capital gains available with other investments. Profits generated within a mutual fund or stock may be eligible for special tax treatment. Investment vehicles held for more than 12 months are not subject to capital gains for taxpayers in the lowest tax bracket, are subject to a 15% capital gains tax rate for individuals earning less than $400,000 per year, and are subject to a 20% capital gains tax for individuals earning more than $400,000. This beneficial treatment is not available for investments held within a variable annuity.

When income is paid out of a variable annuity during retirement, the gain—or appreciation—is taxed at your then-current income tax rate. The variable annuity strategy works well if you plan to be in a tax bracket lower than the maximum capital gains rate when you receive your annuity income. However, it may not be advantageous if your tax bracket remains high. Taxes and expense factors must be considered before you add a variable annuity to your overall portfolio.

Along with the benefit of tax deferral comes the price of owning a nonliquid investment. Once again, if funds are withdrawn prior to age 59½, the investor is liable for a 10% IRS early-withdrawal penalty. Annuity companies may also assess surrender charges during the first 6 to 8 years that funds are held within the annuity. Some companies even assess charges for as long as 12 years.

Equity-Indexed Annuities

A unique hybrid type of tax-deferred annuity combines some of the benefits of both fixed and variable annuities. Equity-indexed annuities' (EIA) returns are tied to one of a number of different market indices, such as the Standard & Poor's 500, the NASDAQ Composite Index, or the Russell Small Cap Index. The annuity owner is guaranteed to receive the greater of the return of chosen index, reduced by certain expenses and contract provisions, or a minimum guaranteed rate of return, typically 25 to 3%. If the chosen index appreciates dramatically in value over the specified time period, the greater return is credited to the contract owner's annuity. On the other hand, if the specific index does not go above the guaranteed threshold or declines in value, the guaranteed rate is credited to the contract. In this situation, the EIA owner is always guaranteed at least all of his principal and some type of positive return, regardless of market declines.

While this hybrid method may seem too good to be true, some nuances should be discussed. When reviewing different EIAs, be sure to compare differences relative to the participation rate. The participation rate, also known as the index rate, quantifies how much of the percentage increase of the selected index will be credited to your annuity contract. A participation rate of 80% means that you will receive 80% of the increase of the chosen index over the specified time period. For instance, if the chosen index is the S&P 500 and it increases by 10% for the year, your annuity would be credited with an 8% return (80% of 10%). The participation rate and the guaranteed rate will vary among the different EIA providers.

In addition, as is the case with variable annuities, there are administrative and internal management expenses netted out of the returns, often resulting in internal expense fees ranging from 15 to 3%. Also, some EIAs limit potential growth exposure by creating cap rates. A cap rate quantifies a maximum allowed percentage increase of any selected index. For example, if there is a 15% cap rate and the index increases by 25%, you are limited to a 15% return credited to your account.

Recent Income Alternative for Annuities

Current interest rates are at historically low levels. That impacts savers who are trying to earn something on the funds they have set aside. The broader investment markets have been fluctuating quite a bit over the past years, which can make an investor anxious over the day-to-day values of their accounts.

Insurance companies are designing products to take advantage of the uncertainties of the investment markets, which is something they have done ever since there have been insurance companies. However, current products are combining the possibility of earning stock market-like returns while also placing a "floor" underneath the initial amounts invested. Of course, all this is provided at a cost to the investor/purchaser as we will explain.

To better understand what these products do, let's quickly review a couple of definitions:

1. *Fixed annuity.* Fixed annuities pay a set rate of interest (determined by the insurance company) on deposits. Fixed annuity values are generally carried on the insurance company's books as assets of the insurance company. Withdrawals can be taken at any time, but are generally postponed until a future date (such as when the owner reaches retirement). All interest earned is tax-deferred until withdrawals are made. Withdrawals generally are taxed at ordinary income rates until withdrawals exceed the amount of interest earned. Thereafter, withdrawals are considered a return of deposit and therefore classified as tax-free. As an alternative, withdrawals can be made by annuitizing the amount in the annuity, as we explain below.

2. *Variable annuity.* Variable annuities offer the alternative of investing deposited amounts into separate accounts (which are invested in stocks, bonds, real estate, or cash) managed by typically well-known mutual fund companies. Assets in a variable annuity are not considered assets of the insurance company, as they are invested with the asset management companies. Therefore, rather than earning a rate of interest set by an insurance company (as with fixed annuities) deposits earn a gross return based on the performance of the separate account. For example, a separate account invested in an S&P 500 Index fund earns approximately the same amount as the index. Like the fixed annuity, all growth or interest earned is tax deferred until withdrawals are made. Withdrawals are also taxed at ordinary income rates until withdrawals exceed the amount of total growth/interest earned.

Thereafter, withdrawals are considered a return of deposit and therefore classified as tax-free. Annuitizing is also available.

3. *Annuitizing.* This is a process in which the insurance company converts the value of an annuity into income payments to be paid for a set time period, such as 10 years, 20 years, or for as long as the owner lives. A part of each income payment is considered gain (and thus taxable), the balance as a return of deposit (and thus tax-free). The possible appeal of annuitizing is the creation of an income source that can last for the rest of the owner's life.

These definitions are important because each concept plays a role in understanding the potential benefits of current annuity products. In a sense, insurance companies are combining the elements of each product in an attempt to create an investment that offers a fixed rate of interest and the possibility to earn rates close to what's happening in a more diversified investment world.

Let's take a closer look at the particulars of current products that tend to combine these elements.

1. *Income base and variable account.* When an investor purchases an annuity, the insurance company credits the deposit into an income base account. This account is credited a fixed rate of interest, like the fixed annuity. In addition, the deposit is also credited into a variable account, invested into whatever separate accounts the owner selects, which earns investment market returns like the variable annuity.

2. *Income base interest credits or adjustments.* Some companies apply the interest to the income base at simple interest, others compound interest payments. Most companies determine the value of the income base by applying the greater of the fixed rate or actual investment experience of the variable account. This valuation can be done at different time periods, depending on the company. Some companies do the valuation at the end of each year, some at the end of each quarter a few do so monthly.

3. *Income production from the annuity.* If the variable account investments do well, the insurance company will use the variable value and offer the alternative to annuitize for payments based on the age of the owner at the time income payments begin. On the other hand, if the investment markets do poorly,

the insurance company will use the income base for income production. Income payments received reduce the value of the income base and variable account values of the annuity.

4. *Surrender values.* If an annuity owner wishes to close or surrender the annuity and receive any value of the annuity, all companies determine the amount paid to the owner based on the variable value, not the income value. In addition, surrender charges can apply.

Based on this information, these products can provide an interesting opportunity: earn market rates if the market does well; earn the fixed rates if the market does poorly. However, additional factors should be considered:

1. *Costs.* All such annuities have the following expenses:
   • Internal management fees charged in the separate accounts.
   • Mortality expenses assessed by the insurance company.
   • Additional costs for the establishment of the income base.
   The actual amount of expense depends on the company selected.

2. *Financial stability.* We believe it is important to evaluate the financial strength of the insurance company. Keep in mind that the value of the income base of the annuity and the promise to make annuitized income payments is based on the promise of the underlying insurance company. If they cease to exist, your assets or income can be jeopardized. In this regard, we carefully screen any company we might recommend to our clients to offer those with extremely high financial ratings.

3. *Flexibility.* One appealing aspect of these products is the production of income during retirement years. One drawback is the limitations an owner has in tapping into the account for more substantial withdrawals. Withdrawals that exceed the amounts credited to the certain account can have a major impact on future account valuations, so much so that the annuity can run out of funds in later years. While this potential can be mitigated if other assets are appropriately managed, it is something to consider.

4. *Investment alternatives.* The last item to compare is the selection of available separate accounts in the annuity. If the separate accounts are not decent, the expenses associated with the product will further reduce the owner's expected returns.

These recent developments could create an opportunity for an annuity product to provide a base for retirement income needs. Be diligent in examining the potential benefits and drawbacks to these types of products.

CHAPTER 6

Investment Objectives

During the past several years we have spoken with thousands of physicians around the country about their investment plans. Many common threads emerge from our discussions, but what strikes us as most significant is the growing number of physicians who are handling their portfolios themselves as opposed to working with a broker. When asked why, the answer is always the same, "Why should I pay commissions to a broker when I can do my own research and end up with better results?"

As we've already pointed out, research data is easily accessible through newspapers, magazines, and market research companies. Additionally, online computer users can access stock, bond, and mutual fund information through various services and discuss specifics with other investors on the Internet. Physicians are among the first to subscribe to financial publications or online services that provide economic information as well as expert opinions on market direction. Unfortunately, simply having the information doesn't guarantee success.

So much of the information we receive on a day-to-day basis comes from media sources that may "occasionally" sensationalize the news in an attempt to attract our attention. The financial press is no exception. How often have you read headlines such as, "The Best Mutual Funds to Own," "Financial Strategies to Guarantee Success," or "Mutual Funds That Can Beat the Market"? These headlines *do* attract our attention. How much useful information the articles contain is questionable, making it difficult to sift through the vast amount of financial advice bombarding us daily and determine which advice is sound.

Investor Profiles

Whether you are an investment do-it-yourselfer, or work with a professional advisor, the goals of your investment plan must be well-defined. To better match investors' goals with investment products, the financial industry uses general guidelines known as investor profiles. You will see these investor profiles in mutual fund literature as well as in material provided to you by professional money managers and brokers. By working within a profile, you can ensure that a prospective investment vehicle or portfolio mix meets your personal risk and reward parameters.

The *income investor* has a very conservative bias and/or who requires income. Income investors want minimal volatility coupled with a low probability of substantial capital losses. Such portfolios would include only a modest amount of equities and have a high concentration of fixed income vehicles such as bonds. The income investor's focus on income results in a substantial reduction in long-term growth potential, but such an approach should provide minimal short-term fluctuation in value.

The *income and growth investor* places considerable emphasis on a stable income stream with portfolio appreciation a secondary (but important) objective. This investor understands that stocks and bonds can be volatile assets and seeks to limit the prospect of capital losses to a specified amount, such as a loss ranging from 3% to 5% within a 12-month period. Quality, income-producing assets lessen capital loss over the long run, but at the cost of a significant reduction in long-term growth.

The *growth investor* is a total return investor primarily interested in capital appreciation. This investor is willing to accept volatility in order to achieve long-term growth. Current income is clearly a secondary objective. To build wealth over time, the growth investor must invest in assets with the potential, during unfavorable markets, to show a capital loss over a 12-month period ranging from 5% to 10%.

The *aggressive investor* strives to build significant appreciation over time. This investor focuses on investments that offer the greatest potential for high returns despite the possibility of substantial capital losses during market downturns. As potential rewards are high, so also is the potential for capital losses over the short run, which can be substantial. Aggressive investors should understand that during an unfavorable market environment, such as the bear market of the 1960s and the most recent down market activity that began in 2000 and 2008, capital losses and high volatility can last 5 to 10 years.

Being able to identify your own investor profile allows you to focus your time and attention on investment vehicles that meet your specific goals, objectives, and risk/reward parameters. Having described the generic attributes of various investment vehicles and investor profiles, we can now begin to look at investment strategies and portfolio construction.

Economic Indicators

Economists and market research analysts use various economic indicators to help them get a pulse on economic trends. There is much debate about which indicators are actually relevant, and some economists claim that certain indicators are more important than others during certain points in the economic cycle and less important at other times. Despite the ongoing debate, economic indicators certainly can impact investment decisions and the financial markets. The key is to understand the differences among the indicators that can ultimately affect potential investment decisions.

Gross Domestic Product (GDP) measures the value of all goods and services produced in the United States. It encompasses all major sectors of the economy, including consumer spending on goods and services, business investment in equipment and inventories, exports, imports, and government spending on everything from the military to local budgets. GDP figures are released by the U.S. Department of Commerce's Bureau of Economic Analysis in three phases. The advance estimate is reported late in the first month after the end of the calendar quarter. Two further revisions, the preliminary and final report, are released over the subsequent two months.

The Consumer Price Index (CPI) measures the price changes of items Americans use on a daily basis. The monthly measurement focuses on the change in prices of a fixed market basket of various goods and services assembled from eight major groups: housing, food and beverages, transportation, medical care, apparel, recreation, education and communication, and other miscellaneous goods and services. The U.S. Department of Labor's Bureau of Labor Statistics releases the CPI every month. The Bureau reports how much the market basket of goods and services costs each month and then compares that figure to the price of the same goods and services in a prior period. Since the CPI provides the most accurate gauge on inflation, the federal government uses it as a guide in setting monetary policy. Inflation affects bond yields as well as the cost of living, both of which can have an impact on economic growth. If inflation rises quickly, interest rates may rise sharply. Wages don't always keep pace with inflation, causing a reduction in purchasing power, which ultimately can slow the economy. Many economists feel that seasonal factors can cause extreme price fluctuations, particularly with food and energy. They contend that it is more important to focus on the core CPI, which excludes these two volatile components.

The Producer Price Index (PPI) consists of a group of indices that measure the average change in selling prices received by U.S. producers of goods and services. It includes price movements for almost every goods-producing sector: agriculture, forestry, fisheries, mining, scrap, and manufacturing. It recently added a category of non-goods-producing sectors such as transportation, real estate, and legal services. The figures are released by the Bureau of Labor Statistics during the second week of each month, making it the first measure of inflation every month. While most economists look at producer prices to help them forecast what will happen to consumer prices, the relationship between the PPI and the CPI is not always that simple. While the PPI can sometimes provide an early read on the CPI, producer price increases are not always passed on to the consumer. Again, many economists prefer to focus on the core PPI data, removing the volatile and seasonal impact of the food and energy components.

An understanding of key economic indicators can certainly help you become a more knowledgeable investor. Information on release dates of the various indicators are found in most daily business publications, as well as on the U.S. government's website. When evaluating the various economic indicators, it is also important to understand that while indicators can help provide insight into future economic trends, they are just a few of the many factors that impact investment decisions and the movement of the overall stock market.

Key Determinants of Performance

Think for a moment about how you allocate time to develop and monitor the performance of your portfolio. Then think of the overall performance of that portfolio over the past five years. Studies conducted by economists and market analysts have shown that three distinct determinants affect the performance of the portfolio: security selection, market timing, and portfolio construction.

The first determinant, security selection, refers to the specific stock, bond, or mutual fund choice you make. This will undoubtedly have an impact on your rate of return. You have probably made security selections based on information or research that you learned through publications or other public information sources. If your experience is similar to many physicians, you have probably received your fair share of "tips" regarding high potential opportunities.

The second determinant, market timing, means executing the purchase or sale of an investment based on various technical indicators. Graphs and trend lines are used to determine various points in time for purchases and sales. Market timers hope to buy before prices increase and sell before prices decline.

The third determinant, portfolio construction, refers to asset class selection—how much of the portfolio is invested in U.S. stocks, international stocks, bonds, or cash. Stock can be subcategorized into large company versus small company; bonds can have long-, medium- or short-term maturities, high quality or high yield (lower quality).

The sum of these three determinants—security selection, market timing, and portfolio construction—will equal 100% of your portfolio's return. Which of these three components takes the greatest amount of your time? If you are like most physicians, the majority of time is spent on security selection. You may get ideas or suggestions for specific stocks or mutual funds from friends or other members of your practice. Security selection is the focus of publications and television stock market programs. Everyone seems to have an opinion on security selection—what's hot and what's not.

The same can be said about market timing. Investment newsletters and brokerage firms declare various buy and sell signals relative to individual issues or the market as a whole.

What does it really take to structure a successful investment portfolio? Several studies have been conducted over varying time periods to quantify the importance of security selection, market timing, and asset class selection on a portfolio's overall return. The results of these studies can provide us with a sense of direction as we focus on each of the three segments of portfolio building.

The most widespread study was conducted by Brinson, Singer, and Beebower and published in the May-June 1991 issue of the *Financial Analysts Journal*. This study looked at institutional money management for large retirement plans and bank trust companies over two different 10-year periods. It was determined that security selection accounted for only 4% of the portfolio's return. Market timing, defined as making decisions based on technical indicators or other forecasting techniques, accounted for 2% of the portfolio's return.

Researchers found that 94% of the portfolio's total return was a function of asset allocation. While most investors spend nearly 100% of their time focusing on market timing or security selection, the studies illustrate that asset allocation is the key to constructing a successful and efficient portfolio.

If you are like most people, you are spending the majority of your time on security selection, and possibly a significant amount of time on market timing, while completely discounting the importance of asset class selection. When your broker calls in the middle of a hectic day, is the call to discuss your allocation in the different asset class categories? Odds are it is not. Odds are the call is about a specific stock or bond (security selection) that needs to be purchased right away because of market timing. Think about the calls you receive at night from brokers you don't even know. Once again, the focus is on security selection and timing. It is likely that, regardless of your own personal goals and risk tolerance, you are receiving the same recommendation as everyone else the broker is calling.

The financial media also focuses on these two relatively un-important determinants. It is simply human nature to want to do better than the market and take advantage of short- and long-term opportunities. Unfortunately, due to the efficiencies of the market, this is very difficult, if not impossible.

The inherent danger of market timing is missing the market's upswings. By timing the market you may be lucky enough to get out before the downside run of the market, but you may not be in the market in time to take advantage of the market's upside. We remember the physician who was explaining with pride the fact that he had sold a substantial amount of the stocks in his re-tirement plan a few weeks before the 1987 correction. He was so pleased that he had avoided such a dramatic market loss! As we were speaking, it became evident that although he had been lucky enough to sell his securities before the correction, he had not taken the necessary steps to reinvest in the same types of investments he had abandoned in October 1987. Our conversation was held in 1995. In the meantime, he had missed all the appreciation that such investments had experienced.

In another example, a physician reacted to what the markets were doing in 2008–2009 by selling out ("because the markets will drop further!!!") in March 2009. This happened to be the end of the rout and the beginning of the recovery. Remaining "safely" invested in cash helped her sleep for a few days, but she soon realized she was cursed with the inability to resume a long-term investment plan while the investment world made substantial gains.

Often the market timer doesn't get into the market until the market has reached new highs. You may sell before your stock or mutual fund slides, but you may also be buying when prices are high.

After meeting with physicians and discussing portfolio performance, we discovered that those who have concentrated on security selection and market timing at the prompting of a broker or on the advice of a newsletter, financial advisor, or friend ultimately confess that their system just hasn't worked. If there were a foolproof, winning system, why would brokers need commissions or financial newsletters need subscribers?

Consider for a moment the large number of mutual funds available in the market. Let's narrow it down to mutual funds that invest in large U.S. companies that are part of the S&P 500. Do most of the mutual funds outperform the S&P 500 relative index? Absolutely not. Most large company stock funds underperform the market. The same is true for small company stock funds and international equity funds. The reason for the general underperformance is that these fund managers are trying to beat the odds. Since these types of mutual funds are asset class specific, the managers have no choice but to concentrate on security selection and market timing. That is why so many investors are turning to index funds as opposed to active management.

A number of funds have beaten the odds and have outperformed the index during varying time periods. So if you can select an outstanding manager, it may be possible to enhance your portfolio's return. But never forget that the main determinant of performance is asset class selection.

When we earlier discussed the various asset classes, we looked at the historical returns associated with a specific class. On the surface it would seem that creating a high-return portfolio is as simple as buying international and small company U.S. stocks since, historically, they have provided the highest returns. Unfortunately, it is not that easy. Each asset class has a corresponding element of risk. You may not be comfortable assuming the level of risk associated with some asset classes.

What is the appropriate blueprint for building a portfolio? The key in investment planning is to minimize short-term risk while maximizing long-term gain. We most often see portfolios that contain an unnecessary amount of risk given the expected rate of return. The important question to answer is, "How much short-term risk are you willing to endure for the long-term benefit of your investment portfolio?" The risk/reward ratio implies that in order to achieve a higher rate of return, you must assume a higher level of risk. However, this is not necessarily the case.

Let's look again at the various asset classes and their possible range of returns within a 12-month period. As you may imagine, the range of return for ownership assets is much greater than for loanership assets. Small company stocks have experienced a range from as low as -58% to as high as 142.9%. The stocks of large companies were a little less volatile, with a low of -43.3% and a high of 54%. Moving to loanership assets, corporate bond returns have ranged from as low as -8.1% up to 43.8%, government bonds from -9.2% to 40.4%, and Treasuries from 0% to 14.7%, according to Ibbotson Associates.

As you can see, the asset classes with the highest long-term rates of return also have the highest amount of short-term risk. The best way to think of risk is in terms of fluctuation. How much will that asset fluctuate over time in order to achieve those average rates of return? How much fluctuation are you comfortable with in order to achieve your target average rate of return?

Adding Stability to Your Investment Portfolio

Asset allocation creates a balance for your portfolio by investing in a variety of asset classes, such as stocks, bonds, and money markets. Each component is designed to provide certain characteristics for your portfolio.

Stocks offer the potential to earn attractive returns, but they entail more risk than some other types of investments. Bonds are an integral part of asset allocation because they generally provide more stability than equities. By including both bonds and equities in your portfolio, you seek to balance your portfolio. Cash assets, such as money markets, offer liquidity and a convenient "parking place" for cash intended for future investment opportunities.

Within the general classes there are yet more sub-categories. For example, the equity class of assets can be further divided into U.S. large company stocks, U.S. small company stocks, and the stocks of international companies. Fixed income can be subcategorized by length of maturity and includes both U.S. and international bonds. Over time, these asset classes will perform differently. This fact also applies to international stocks and bonds. Therefore, diversification among asset classes is important to maintain a consistent level of performance over time.

Another concept that is important to the asset allocation process is modern portfolio theory. The 1990 Nobel Prize for Economics was awarded to three economists for their work in developing modern portfolio theory. This theory is important to the efficient management of an investment portfolio. Three basic premises of modern portfolio theory are worthwhile considering in detail.

First, markets are efficient. Over time, it is very difficult for an individual investor to consistently "beat the market." Technology has created an environment that makes information instantly available to a potentially limitless number of investors.

Second, attention should be focused on the investment portfolio as a whole rather than on individual investments that make up the portfolio. As previously discussed, studies have shown that over 90% of the impact of an investment portfolio is a result of the selection of asset classes rather than the selection of a particular security or market timing, according to Brinson, Singer, and Beebower in the May–June 1991 issue of the *Financial Analysts Journal*. Therefore, much of the energy spent trying to pick or time the purchase of the "best" stock, bond, or mutual fund is wasted. Individual investors would be much better off deciding on and monitoring a specific asset class selection among domestic and international asset classes.

Third, at any given level of risk, there is a particular combination of asset classes that will maximize return. Therefore, not only is the selection of the type of asset class important, but determining the amount to be invested in each class will help to maximize return at a given level of risk.

Reducing Risk

There are two ways to reduce the impact of risk: diversification and time. Your investment time frame may be long-term (retirement), medium-term (college funding), or short-term (purchasing a new home). The return on your investments will be more predictable the more time you devote to any given investment strategy.

If the investment time period is less than 3 to 5 years, the appropriate strategy would be to invest primarily in fixed income (bonds) and cash equivalents (money markets or treasury bills). If, however, the time period is expected to exceed 3 to 5 years, invest-ing a portion of assets in equities would be reasonable. Periods of longer than 5 years have provided a much lower level of volatility for equities (stocks).

Once you have defined your investment goals and determined a time frame, your investment strategy can be accomplished by creating a diversified portfolio. You diversify your portfolio by combining various asset classes, blending high return–high-risk asset classes with lower return–lower risk asset classes.

To reduce risk with asset allocation, we should view historical data and sample portfolios. Let's look at a typical, ultra-conservative physician's investment plan. This physician has decided to invest his entire portfolio in U.S. Government bonds. He knows that these bonds are guaranteed to return his principal at maturity as well as provide him with a guaranteed fixed yield.

Now refer back to our asset class and risk returns, and let's take a closer look at U.S. government bonds. The risk associated with this type of bond is higher than that of cash assets, but lower than all of the equity classes. If the bonds are guaranteed, where is the risk? Once a government bond is purchased, it fluctuates in value. Remember earlier we learned that bond values move inversely to interest rates. Interest rate changes cause the price of government bonds to change. Therefore, if you sell the bond prior to maturity, you may not receive your full principal. This fluctuation causes us to assign a risk level to this asset class. There is another element of risk not included in the standard deviation figure. What if the bond you bought yields 6%, rates rise, and now current bond buyers are guaranteed 9%. You are now achieving a rate of return 3% below current market yields. Regardless, this physician is content with his investment. What we can now do is take the standard deviation figure associated with government bonds and structure a diversified portfolio that has the same amount of risk.

By adding U.S. blue chip stocks as well as cash assets, we can actually provide a higher expected rate of return with the same risk level. If the physician is not happy with this blend, he can have a portfolio with the same level of return but with less risk.

By concentrating on asset class selection, you can structure a portfolio and be relatively confident of its overall risk as well as its projected long-term return. A number of computer software programs can aid in asset allocation number crunching. Many financial advisors can also assist you in the proper structure of a portfolio based on your specific risk/return parameters.

Now think about your own investment plan. Are you spending the majority of time on issues that add very little to the bottom line, such as market timing or specific stock selection? Most investors do!

Physicians buy into the "hot" tip, because it is being promoted as a money-making sure thing. They do this without a thought to its place in their portfolio. If you need to buy this hot stock or take advantage of a tip, do it with a limited amount of funds you have set aside for such risk taking. But do it only after having set up a truly diversified, well-funded portfolio, not at the expense of a diversified investment plan.

Unfortunately this is not how most physicians structure their portfolios. The stock market continues to be the main topic of discussion just as it was during the day of the technology boom, which saw inexperienced investors earn double-digit returns in the late 1990s. Euphoria was rampant as many felt these returns were expected and the chance of loss seemingly slim. Disappointment settled in the minds of those who earned 23% during one year, while their neighbors earned 29%. What we do know, is that of the previous 22 major declines since 1925 (average one every 3½ years), the market has always come back to make new highs.

Interestingly, highly respected economists are varied as to their market forecasts, as are the top stock analysts working at the country's largest brokerage firms. What is known for certain is that there are three indisputable elements of stock market activity.

No one can predict consistently when market declines or rallies will occur. (It's easy to do so in hindsight, however.)

Once you have focused on the most important determinant of a portfolio's performance—asset class selection—you can structure a portfolio that will meet your specific needs. After deciding how your portfolio should be allocated among the various asset classes, you can begin funding your investment plan.

A Systematic and Proven Process Can Keep You on Track

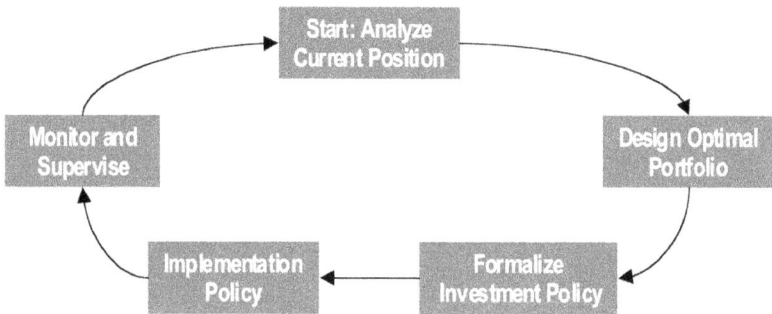

Not surprisingly, we believe there is a process that you should follow to begin implementing your investment plan. First, you need to determine the length of time that your investments will be dedicated to the specific portfolio. For example, are you setting aside assets you will need in two months or in 20 years? For needs that are short-term, you should be looking more towards the loanership types of assets we have discussed. Long-term needs are more likely to require ownership assets.

The next step would be to determine what asset classes should be considered for the portfolio. Should you include small domestic companies, international or emerging markets? You will then need to determine what amount you feel comfortable having invested in the asset class. After all, there is little benefit in selecting an asset class, but being uncomfortable with the amount of funds you have invested in the category.

The next step is to decide what management styles should be considered. Growth or value may be the likely choices. Growth managers search for those companies that offer the greatest potential for long-term growth, irrespective of the company's current earnings, or lack thereof. Value managers, on the other hand, search for companies that appear to be "on sale." Their analysis points to companies whose current stock price appears to be undervalued relative to current earnings and balance sheet data.

Finally, you should make the decision regarding the particular product you want to use in your portfolio. Investment product selection usually, and incorrectly, is where most physicians begin their decision-making process. Armed with the knowledge and power of asset allocation, you can remove this item from your list of high-priority items.

Earlier we described the major investment vehicles used for portfolio funding. At this point you must decide if you are going to use individual stocks and bonds or mutual funds. Because of the advantages of diversification and ongoing professional management, mutual funds are often used to develop an investment portfolio based on asset allocation strategies.

Personal investment portfolios that do not have the benefit of tax-favored treatment require an additional level of consideration to maximize long-term after-tax returns. For example, strategies that utilize tax deferral or that eliminate the taxation of the gains of the investment in question should be reviewed to determine how they may impact your overall investment strategy.

If you select professional active management provided by the fund's portfolio managers in an effort to outperform the indices, you must determine which funds you would like to include in your portfolio design. When looking at various funds, you should concentrate on those that have outperformed their peers as well as the relative indices over a long period of time. Any fund can have a great year by making some good stock or bond selections. This is important since the manager who attained the past superior track record may be long gone.

If you are going to use load mutual funds, your broker should be able to do the research and make specific recommendations based on your goals and objectives. To ensure you are satisfied with the recommendations, you should ask your broker his or her reasons for selecting specific funds. You will also want to know the funds' expenses, both sales charges and internal management expenses.

Working with a Registered Investment Advisor (RIA) is an alternative to using a commissioned broker. RIAs are registered with the Securities and Exchange Commission and are the only advisors legally allowed to provide investment advice while charging a fee for service. The majority of RIAs concentrate their efforts on no-load rather than load funds because they can make specific recommendations for no-load purchases and still be compensated through fees. Compensation for researching the funds and making the transactions for you, as well as maintaining portfolio allocations, is generally based on a percentage of the dollar amount under management, as opposed to commissions on transactions.

To construct a portfolio that is efficient and meets your own investment objectives, be sure to prioritize your decision-making process as follows:

- What is the length of time that your portfolio can be committed to a specific investment policy?
- What asset classes will be considered for investing?
- How much of the portfolio will be invested in each asset class?
- Within each specific asset class, what strategies or styles will be used?
- Which manager(s)/products will be selected for each specific strategy or style?

CHAPTER 7

Education Planning

The expense of educating children has become one of the greatest financial burdens facing parents today. Tuition costs have increased significantly faster than inflation, and many more students are continuing on to graduate or professional school. Along with the purchase of a home and the accumulation of a retirement fund, paying for college is one of the highest priorities—and one of the most expensive decisions—that parents will ever make. As with other financial goals, parents must determine education-funding goals for their children and set priorities According to the College Board, the average cost of tuition and fees for the 2011–2012 school year was $28,500 at private colleges, $8,244 for state residents at public colleges, and $20,770 for out-of-state residents attending public universities. The following table illustrates four years of projected college costs with an annual inflation rate of 6%:

PROJECTED COLLEGE COSTS (6% ANNUAL INFLATION RATE)

Years in School	Public	Private
2010–2014	$62,752	$164,397
2011–2015	$66,517	$174,261
2012–2016	$70,508	$184,716
2013–2017	$74,739	$195,799
2014–2018	$79,223	$207,547
2015–2019	$83,977	$220,000

PROJECTED COLLEGE COSTS (6% ANNUAL INFLATION RATE)
(continued)

Years in School	Public	Private
2016–2020	$89,015	$233,200
2017–2021	$94,356	$247,192
2018–2022	$100,018	$262,024
2019–2023	$106,019	$277,745
2020–2024	$112,380	$294,410
2021–2025	$119,123	$312,075
2022–2026	$126,270	$330,799
2023–2027	$133,846	$350,647
2024–2028	$141,877	$371,686
2025–2029	$150,390	$393,987
2026–2030	$159,413	$417,626
2027–2031	$168,978	$442,684
2028–2032	$179,116	$469,245
2029–2033	$189,863	$497,400
2030–2034	$201,255	$527,244
2031–2035	$213,331	$558,878
2032–2036	$226,131	$592,411
2033–2037	$239,698	$627,956

The array of options for physicians saving for their children's or grandchildren's college education is greater than ever before. The combination of tax benefits and the potential to lock in today's tuition rates has been both a boon for savers and a source of confusion when choices must be made. The key for today's college fund saver is to be aware of the options available and to understand the differences and advantages and disadvantages of the multitude of plans now available.

One thing is for sure: a college education is becoming more expensive and cost-prohibitive for many. Over the last 40 years, annual college costs have outpaced the annual rate of inflation by an average of 3.2%. This trend is expected to accelerate with many estimates pegging annual tuition and fees increasing an average of 7% to 8% per year over the next 10 years. For those with a newborn child or grandchild, a four-year Ivy League education is estimated to cost approximately $312,000 starting in 2021. In contrast, a public four-year college education is expected to cost over $119,000 by the time today's newborns reach college age. With college expenses the second largest expense for many physicians (the first being their homes, typically financed with a mortgage), proper proactive planning is crucial. The starting point is to gain an understanding of the various savings vehicles that can help you reach your college education-funding objectives.

Among the various choices, the focus now seems to rest on the Section 529 plan. Founded in 1996 but not made federally tax-free until 2002, the Section 529 plan has sparked a dramatic increase in college savings by parents and grandparents. Investors are drawn to the high limits of contribution as well as the tax-free growth and the more liberal withdrawal provisions. The benefit to grandparents with substantial estates is that they can transfer money out of their estate to open the account for their grandchildren, while still maintaining control of the assets while they are alive. Section 529 plans do not offer a guarantee that the funds accumulated will be sufficient to pay future education costs. Whatever the fund grows to is what will be available. The various state plans offer many investment options based on the amount of risk an investor wants to take. Many states also offer plans designed around the child's age, typically becoming more conservative as the child approaches college age. While many savings incentive plans typically limit participation based on annual earnings, the Section 529 plan is available to all taxpayers regardless of their income. The investor receives the advantages of tax-free buildup and withdrawal, limited control over the funds invested, and no restrictions as to the school attended, as long as the money is used for higher education.

Almost all states offer their own Section 529 plan, which is managed by an investment management company chosen by each state. While the IRS permits tax-free buildup as well as withdrawals, a state can add its own perks, such as state tax deductions on deposits. However, if funds are not withdrawn to pay higher education expenses, the taxpayer must pay tax on the gains in addition to a 10% IRS penalty. This can be avoided by using the remaining funds for siblings under the same criteria. While the basic features of Section 529 plans are mighty attractive, physicians may realize substantial benefits that have nothing to do with saving for college education costs. With traditional custodial accounts, such as the Uniform Gifts to Minors Accounts (UGMA/UTMA), gifts can be made tax-free through use of annual exclusion gifts, currently $14,000. From an estate tax standpoint, these irrevocable gifts are usually considered as removed from the donor's estate, as long as the donor is not the custodian of the account.

The Section 529 plan takes it a step further by allowing a taxpayer to make five years' of excluded gifts in one year, without taxation, for a maximum gift of $70,000 from each donor. While on the surface it appears to be a great way to remove assets from a grandparent's or parent's estate, be aware that if the donor dies during that five-year period, gifts attributed to future years will return to the donor's estate for purposes of calculating their estate tax.

Also worth considering is the use of Section 529 plans as an asset-protection strategy. As these accounts grow in value, asset protection will become a higher priority, especially in light of judgments that go beyond malpractice insurance coverage limits. What we do know is that the ability of judgment creditors to reach Section 529 assets varies from state to state. This is especially important since donors are not mandated to use the plan offered through their own state. The restrictions do vary, with some states offering limited levels of protection. States with statutes restricting access by the donor's creditors obviously offer a greater level of asset protection.

When you are evaluating and comparing Section 529 plans, you must carefully weigh many issues prior to implementation. Unfortunately, most of the information available in the press and on the Internet comparing the various state plans tends to focus on the investment managers the states have selected rather than on estate tax-planning and asset-protection issues.

Prepaid tuition plans, in contrast to Section 529 plans, offer the advantage of locking in today's tuition rate for tomorrow's college education. Most prepaid plans offer various options designed to fit different needs—from tuition-only plans, to those which include room and board—but only at state institutions. This is because most prepaid tuition plans require students to attend in-state universities. This changed in 2004, as private schools also became able to offer prepaid college tuition plans.

The previously popular Educational IRA now has a new name as well as new limits. The new account is known as a Coverdell

Education Savings Account (ESA), named after the late Georgia senator, Paul Coverdell, who pushed for educational savings reform. ESAs have an annual contribution limit of $2,000 as compared to the original limit of $500. In addition, the account can be used not only for college, but also private school tuition for those in kindergarten through 12th grade.

In contrast, the Uniform Gifts to Minors Act (UGMA) and the Uniform Transfer to Minors Act (UTMA) accounts allow a custodian (typically a parent or grandparent) to save for a minor but not specifically for college education. The beneficiary actually gains control of the funds at the age of majority. These accounts offer the benefit of favorable income tax treatment based on the child's age and the amount of taxable income generated. For children under age 14, the first $1,000 in earnings is tax-free; the next $1,000 is taxed at the child's federal rate; and any earnings over $2,000 are taxed at the custodian's (usually the parents) federal tax rate. For children over age 14, the first $1,000 in earnings is tax-free and all earnings after that are taxed at the child's tax rate.

Section 529 Plan Advantages

Section 529 plans are very flexible. The money in a Section 529 investment plan can be used for college expenses at any accredited college in any state. By contrast, prepaid tuition plans work best with in-state schools because most plans do not credit a large cash-value buildup to these accounts. Also Section529 plan assets can easily be transferred between family beneficiaries. If one child does not use the money for college, you can easily designate another recipient—a cousin, niece, or nephew. Grandparents who set up the plans can switch the money between grandchildren. Or you could set up your own plan and later transfer the assets to your child.

Section 529 plans offer control. Parents who save for college using Uniform Gifts to Minors Act (UGMA) accounts lose control over the money when the child reaches the age of majority (age 18 in most states, 21 in others). For example, you may have been saving for Princeton; she may buy a Porsche! With a Section 529 plan, the giver retains control over the assets until they are distributed to pay for college.

Section 529 plans have estate tax advantages. Although most plans will be started with small initial investments and regular contributions, the law allows one-time gifts of as much as $70,000 to a Section 529 plan without reducing their unified credit. Therefore, the giver can aggregate five years of the allowable $14,000 annual gift-tax exclusion to jump-start a Section 529 investment plan. Wealthy grandparents might consider making a large gift to get cash out of their estates—if they are not worried about needing the money for their own expenses as they age. Because the donor retains control over the gift, it can be taken back at any time after paying a federally mandated 10% penalty. Even with this control, 529 assets are not included in the estate of the donor.

Section 529 plans have financial-aid advantages. Assets in these plans are not considered a student asset in the formulas used to determine financial aid. By contrast, assets held in UGMA custodial accounts *are* considered student assets—and are counted seven times more heavily in the financial-aid formula when you fill out the dreaded Free Application for Federal Student Aid (FAFSA). Until the 2001 legislation, withdrawals from a Section 529 plan might have been considered income to the student. But now that withdrawals can be made tax-free and no 1099 form is sent out, withdrawals have no effect on a student's assets. Moreover, if the grandparents have established the plan, it may not need to appear even as a parental asset on the FAFSA form (this varies from state to state).

Section 529 plans have no limit on parental income. Many other college savings plans limit the amount of contributions each year or place restrictions on parental income. Section 529 plans have very high limits—a one-time $70,000 contribution per donor, and state-imposed maximum total contribution limits that range as high as $341,000. And the contributor does not have to be a parent, grandparent, or even a relative. You can make a contribution for any living beneficiary who plans to attend college. If you're an adult and plan to attend law or medical school, you can contribute your own savings to a Section 529 plan. If you don't use the money, one of your children can. And if a child is awarded funds from an accident or medical settlement, some of that money could be deposited to grow tax-free in a Section 529 plan, as long as the settlement allows.

Some Comparisons

Section 529 versus custodial accounts. The case for using a Section 529 plan is so compelling now that many parents may consider closing their custodial (Uniform Gifts to Minors Act) accounts, paying taxes on any gains, and transferring the cash to a new Section 529 account—where it will grow tax-free. In UGMA accounts, taxes on income or gains are paid at the parents' rate for children under age 14, and thereafter at the child's rate. Be aware that Section 529 assets have more limitations than in a custodial account. Section 529 plans require you to spend the tax-free money only on a student's tuition, room, and board (whether on or off campus—to the limits established by the school as for cost of attendance purposes), fees, books, and supplies. Money taken from a Section 529 plan and spent for other purposes is subject to a 10% penalty. Custodial accounts have a broader definition of allowed expenditures.

Section 529 versus Education IRA. The 2001 tax law expanded the Education IRA annual contribution from $500 to $2,000. It also increased the phase-out income limit for joint filers who contribute to such an account to $190,000 to $220,000—double the limit for single filers.

Also, the old tax law did not allow students to use the Hope Scholarship Credit or the Lifetime Learning Credit in the same year they withdrew money from an Education IRA. The two credits were created under 1997 tax legislation. Now, the law also allows you to contribute to an Education IRA and a Section 529 plan in the same year. Still, it appears that there are only two advantages to an Education IRA—and they may not be advantages for everyone. With an Education IRA, you can self-direct the investments, much as you would in any other IRA. Section 529 investment plans are limited to mutual-fund accounts offered by the plans. And the new law provides that money saved in an Education IRA can be used for private and religious elementary and secondary schools, while Section 529 assets can only be used to pay for expenses at an approved institution of higher education (see table on next page).

Type of Account	Income Limits	Contribution Limits	Tax Treatment	Control Flexibility	Investment Flexibility
529 savings plan	No limits. Anyone can contribute.	Contribution limits vary from approximately $100,000 to $340,000 or more.	Earnings can grow free from federal tax, and withdrawals for qualified higher education expenses are free from federal tax.	Owner (parent or grandparent for example) maintains control of the assets, decides when withdrawals will be made, and can change the beneficiary.	Owner can move assets among funds once each calendar year or when there is a change in beneficiaries
Coverdell Education Savings Account	Ability to contribute is phased out for individuals with incomes between $95,000 and $110,000 and for couples with incomes between $190,000 and $220,000.	$2,000 per year per beneficiary.[1] (child must be under 18)	Earnings can grow free from federal tax, and withdrawals for elementary, secondary, and qualified higher education expenses are free from federal tax.	Beneficiary may assume control at age of majority, 18 or 21 in most states.	Owner can move assets as often as desired.
UGMA/UTMA	None. (up to $14,000 per donor for each donee federal gift tax free)	None.	For children under 14, the first $1,000 of earnings are tax-free. Earnings between $1,000 and $2,000 are taxed at the child's rate; earnings above $2,000 are taxed at the parents' rate. All earnings for children 14 and older are taxed at the child's rate.	Beneficiary assumes control at age of majority, 18 or 21 in most states.	Owner can move assets as often as desired, but each transfer usually involves a taxable event.
Parents' Investment Account	None.	None.	Dividends and interest are taxed to parents at ordinary income rates, and capital gains are taxed at capital gains rates.	Owner maintains control of the assets and decides when withdrawals will be made.	Owner can move assets as often as desired, but each transfer usually involves a taxable event.

The selection of the best college savings plan involves many different considerations specific to each family's situation. Many websites are available that can provide additional information on college savings. These resources include http://www.savingforcollege.com, http://www.collegesavings.org, and http://www.princetonreview.com.

CHAPTER 8

Retirement Planning

M any physicians find themselves unprepared for retirement, financially as well as emotionally. From the financial standpoint, unfortunately, the majority of physicians fail to reach their own financial objectives. As the saying goes: people don't plan to fail; they fail to plan.

The main reason is that as a whole, physicians start saving too late and are unable to make up the shortfall during their peak earning years. Procrastination and poor planning can result in the need to continue working in some manner during retirement or reduce the income desired during the retirement years. Successful retirement planning requires three key elements:

1. Setting clear goals
2. Maximizing tax benefits
3. Exercising discipline.

When setting a clear retirement goal, give thought to the age that you would like to achieve financial independence. Consider financial independence to be the point when you do not have to earn an income to support yourself. There is no better feeling than continuing to work, on a full-time or part-time basis because you want to—not because you have to. So first give some thought to the age you would like to achieve true financial independence. Once you determine the age goal, you will need to quantify the amount of income needed to maintain a comfortable standard of living. Many retirement planners suggest an annual income need of approximately 70% to 75% of your current standard of living. A more specific and personalized method of determination would be to review your expenses over the last 12 months by going through your checkbook. While doing this, consider which expenses you won't have or that will be less during retirement, and also think about categories of expenses that may increase, such as travel and other leisure activities. To assist in this project, we have included a personal budget planner at the end of this chapter. Next, take an inventory of your investment assets, including your retirement plans. What types of rates of return have you been earning and what can you expect in the future? Is your rate of inflation assumption realistic?

From an income tax-planning standpoint, you need to realize that there are three distinct phases of an investment:

1. The deposit or purchase phase: Do you invest with after-tax or pre-tax dollars?
2. The accumulation or growth phase: Is the growth taxable, tax-free, or tax-deferred?
3. The liquidation phase: Will you receive the income on a taxable or tax-free basis?

Based on current tax law, the government allows, at best, a tax benefit to be available in two of the three periods. Proper proactive planning ensures that you will receive the tax benefits to which you are entitled.

Exercising discipline makes the difference between financial independence security and failure. All the retirement and tax planning strategies in the world will prove ineffective if you don't actually implement a retirement planning strategy. You not only need to gather information and determine objectives, but you need to make informal decisions and act on them. Don't put it off, as the sooner you begin, the greater the chance of enjoying a financially successful retirement.

Planning for retirement can be an enjoyable experience. Use the following checklist for a successful retirement as a starting point.

CHECKLIST FOR A SUCCESSFUL RETIREMENT

❏ Have your financial planner prepare a retirement income projection to ensure there are adequate assets to support your retirement standard of living.

❏ Anticipate and prepare for non-financial changes. After being with patients and colleagues for so long, many physicians miss the social aspect of medicine. One way around this is to work on a limited basis with shorter hours and no call. If you're interested in this kind of arrangement, explore the possibilities.

❏ While working a full schedule, have a business valuation conducted on your practice. This should provide a starting point for discussions about selling your share of the practice. Selling a practice may take upwards of two years.

❏ Determine liability coverage options and other asset-protection strategies to be used during retirement.

❏ Map out a strategy to coordinate the tax treatment of income generated from the rollover of qualified retirement plan assets.

❏ Decide who will assist you in managing your rollover portfolio during your retirement years.

The earlier you begin, the greater the chance you will enjoy a financially successful retirement. Remember, it's important to plan, but critical to act! Sometimes the goal of financial independence can seem deceptively easy to attain. Many times physicians give us the following optimistic scenario as their objective: "If we can save $1 million by retirement, we will be able to live off the interest without ever touching the principal." Let's take a closer look at this rationale:

$1,000,000 × 7% (current rate of interest) = $70,000 per year
Result: Principal remains constant at $1,000,000
Annual income remains constant at $70,000

Have you ever sat down and tried to figure out how much you will actually need, incorporating both inflation and taxation? If you have, then you know that as the illustration shows, $1 million won't be enough. If $1 million were to be invested to generate a 7% annual income stream, exclusive of Social Security payments, the income would be $70,000. Unfortunately, due to inflation, that

$70,000 will feel like less and less each year. The reality is that at retirement, most physicians are not able to generate their ideal annual income. (See figure on page 19, Chapter 2)

To maintain a yearly income equal to or greater than an inflation-adjusted $70,000 per year, you would need to do one of two things. You could either increase your principal amount or you could increase the amount you earn per year on that investment. If you couldn't increase your principal, you would want to increase your rate of return. Now you need to find a way to increase your rate of return without increasing your risk. As we have learned, this may be accomplished using modern portfolio theory.

How Can You Guarantee a Successful Retirement?

The most common reason for not enjoying a financially secure retirement is poor planning and procrastination. There never seems to be a good time to begin to plan. "Maybe next year when the house is paid off; only two more years until the kids are through with school; after my daughter's wedding, then I'll be able to save for retirement." And on it goes; the excuses are endless, but the reality is that you must begin today!

What benefits can you expect from your retirement plans? Should you count on Social Security? As you continue to pay into the Social Security system, you should be aware of the realities that face the future of the program.

Fifty years ago there were approximately 42 workers contributing to the Social Security system for every retiree collecting a benefit. Today there are only 4 workers for every beneficiary. Projections indicate that by the year 2025 the ratio will have dropped to 2.2 workers per retiree. While legislators discuss various options to save the system, we can almost be assured that the outcome will involve higher taxes on working Americans, changes in accepted retirement ages, and lower benefits for at least some retirees.

In the past, when financial planning discussions turned to Social Security benefits, physicians with incomes in excess of $200,000 and million-dollar qualified retirement plans often discounted the need for Social Security benefits. The consensus was that with retirement plans and nonqualified savings growing exponentially, the need for government benefits was greatly reduced, if not eliminated. In addition, with retirement income goals in the six-figure range, many felt that even if Social Security benefits were available, the amount would barely make a dent in their standard of living. For physicians nearing retirement who have seen their retirement nest egg depleted by market forces, payments from Social Security play a far greater role in their annual retirement income needs.

Government figures suggest that the system will run out of money unless changes are made. When the system runs out of money, and for the years to follow, the government would have to borrow or raise taxes each and every year to pay the rising benefits. Unfortunately, many misconceptions exist about the workings of Social Security, and clarification of those points should better position you to proactively plan for your retirement income needs.

The first misconception is that the federal government saves or sets aside a portion of taxes collected to be used specifically for Social Security benefits. In reality, all of the tax dollars received by the government are spent very quickly, typically in a matter of days.

Secondly, common sense dictates that Social Security payroll taxes are earmarked for Social Security benefits. Common sense, as many of you already realize, is not the government's modus operandi. The payroll taxes collected far exceed the amount required to pay the promised benefits. But the surplus is spent on other things completely unrelated to Social Security.

A close look at the numbers today reveals a Social Security trust fund of approximately $1.2 trillion, which is expected to grow to $5 trillion by 2016. However, an even closer look reveals that the trust fund balance is a running tally of all the Social Security surplus money spent on other things over the years. That money is now gone. If, as anticipated, Social Security goes cash flow negative in a matter of years with no money in the trust fund, only IOUs, the government will need to borrow or raise taxes to redeem those IOUs and meet the anticipated shortfall.

This all leads to the premise that the Social Security trust fund contains real assets, which is certainly debatable. The reality is that the next generation may need to pay higher payroll taxes, perhaps high enough to fund half of an average retiree's benefit.

This situation does not bode well for those expecting to receive a certain Social Security retirement benefit. While discounted in the past as an amount that would barely dent their retirement needs, newly retired physicians should take a closer look at the impact of the government benefits relative to their overall income needs, and as a way to supplement income shortages during down cycles in the stock market. Younger practicing physicians may want to simply ignore the goings on of Social Security and instead save money at a greater pace and invest wisely in order to have greater control over their future financial security.

Lawmakers are weighing a number of proposals to deal with the fund's long-term solvency issues, including raising payroll taxes, increasing the amount of income subject to Social Security payroll taxes, raising the retirement age, or simply reducing future benefits.

While there are still quite a number of details and other options to be considered, it does appear extremely likely that some form of change in the Social Security system will need to take place.

Traditionally, the magic age to receive a full benefit was 65. Based on current law, for those born after 1937 but before 1960, the age of full retirement benefits is dependent on the specific year of birth. For those born in 1960 and later, full retirement benefits are payable at age 67. The benefit payable will, of course, be based on an individual's past earning record and is adjusted annually for inflation.

A reduced benefit remains available beginning at age 62. However, assuming a traditional current full retirement age (FRA) of 65, beginning benefits at age 62 reduces the monthly amount by 20%. With the new FRA, receiving an early benefit at age 62 would result in a monthly benefit reduction of approximately 30%. You can verify your full retirement age on the Retirement Age Calculator on the Social Security website (http://www.ssa.gov/pubs/ageincrease.htm).

In addition to deciding at which age to begin taking benefits, it is also important to understand how working impacts your Social Security benefits. The Senior Citizens' Freedom to Work Act of 2000 repealed an earnings limitation on Social Security benefits for individuals ages 65 to 69. Under the current law, generally you can receive full Social Security benefits, regardless of earnings, starting with the month you reach FRA. If benefits are taken prior to the FRA, only $15,120 can be earned before a reduction in your Social Security benefits. Benefits are reduced by $1 for every $2 you earn above this amount.

Once benefits begin, earnings are defined as any wages earned as an employee and any net earnings from self-employment. Wages include bonuses, commissions, fees, vacation pay, and pay in lieu of vacation. Not included as earnings is investment income, including stock dividends, interest from savings accounts and CDs, annuity income, limited partnership income, and rental income from real estate. Also excluded from the earnings definition is income from Social Security, pensions or other retirement plan income, gifts, and inheritances.

While planning a strategy to maximize your Social Security benefits, the starting point is to ensure that all of your earnings are accurately recorded, and to obtain an estimate of the amount of future benefits. The Social Security Administration (SSA) now automatically mails an annual benefit statement to each worker age 25 and older not receiving current benefits approximately one month prior to his or her birthday. You also may request the records at any other time by completing form SSA-7004, "Request for Social Security Statement." The form can be requested by calling the SSA at 1-800-772-1213 or via the SSA website at http://www.ssa.gov.

LIVING EXPENSE ESTIMATOR:
Please use the following to obtain a better understanding of your living expenses:

Living Expenses		Monthly	Annually
Children	Allowances		
	Child Day Care		
	Lessons/Tuition		
	Team Dues/Sports Registration Costs		
	Toys/Gear/Miscellaneous		
Clothing	Dry Cleaning/Laundry		
	Purchases: Children/Dependents		
	Purchases: Self		
	Purchases: Spouse		
Contributions			

Credit Card Interest			
Entertainment & Recreation	Cable & Satellite		
	Concerts/Theater		
	Country Club		
	Health Club (YMCA)		
	Hobby Expense		
	Internet Access Costs		
	Recreation/Miscellaneous		
	Sports Equipment		
	Subscriptions: Magazines & Newspaper		
	Books/CDs		
Food	Groceries/Sundries		
	Dining Out		
Health Care (unreimbursed)	Dental/Orthodontia		
	Doctors/Nurses/Hospitals		
	Hearing/Other		
	Medical Transportation		
	Medicines/Drugs		
	Vision Care/Eyeglasses		
Home	Domestic Services		
	Improvements/Furnishings		
	Lawn Service/Garden Expenses		
	Maintenance		
	Repairs		
Insurance	Disability Insurance		
	Health Insurance		
	Life Insurance		
	Long-Term Care Insurance		
	Malpractice Insurance		
	Other		
Miscellaneous	Dues/Memberships		
	Gifts/Family/Friends		
Personal Care	Hair Salon/Barber		
	Personal/Hair Care/Cosmetics/etc.		

Pet Care	Food		
	Grooming Costs		
	Miscellaneous Expenses		
	Veterinarian/Pet Medications		
Residence	Assessment/Association Fees		
	Mortgage or Rent		
	Property Taxes		
Taxes	Federal		
	FICA		
	Other		
	State		
Transportation	Fuel		
	License Costs		
	Maintenance & Repairs		
	Parking/Tolls		
	Public Transportation		
	Vehicle Insurance		
	Vehicle Lease Payments		
	Vehicle Loan Payments		
Utilities	Electricity		
	Gas/Oil		
	Telephone		
	Cell Phones		
	Waste Removal		
	Water & Sewer		
Vacations	Accommodations		
	Air Fare		
	Auto Rental		
	Food		
	Ground Transportation		
	Pet Boarding		
	Souvenirs		
Vacation Property	Assessment/Association Fees		
	Mortgage or Rent		
	Property Taxes		
Support of Other Dependents			
Other Items Not Listed Above			

TOTAL			
Systematic Savings	College Funding		
	401K Contributions		
	Payroll Deduction Saving		
	Other		
	Other		
	Other		

CHAPTER 9

Choosing an Efficient Retirement Plan

In the past, physicians planned for retirement by reviewing a potentially expansive list of income sources such as Social Security, pensions from healthcare organizations, and income from various investment portfolios. Today, planning for retirement has become much more focused on areas that the physician is able to control and to which he or she can contribute. As we just saw, it is now appropriate to question whether Social Security will be available for retirement income. It is becoming more important to plan well in advance for the income needs that will exist during retirement.

One of the greatest benefits of any business is the ability to contribute to retirement plans on a tax-deductible basis. When the business is a medical practice, the owner(s) will choose the plan that can most benefit their personal situation and create long-term incentives for their employees. As more physicians become aware of their own need to plan for retirement income security, qualified retirement plans remain the logical starting point. Qualified retirement plans are generally classified as defined benefit or defined contribution. Some plans may combine features of both types.

Defined-Benefit Plans

Defined-benefit plans tend to favor older, highly compensated employees such as a physician who is close to retirement. That is because the employer has fewer years over which to accumulate enough money to provide the promised benefit. Actuarial calculations are made to determine how much money must be contributed each year to accumulate the necessary future amount. Interest rates, investment rates of return, and the age of participants will impact the calculation. The investment risk rests solely on the employer, who is required to fund the plan adequately each year, although the annual contribution can vary based on the plan's investment results. The future benefit received may be based on a flat percentage of compensation, a percentage that increases with the length of service, a percentage that changes at certain compensation levels, or a number of other formulas.

A defined-benefit plan offers employees many advantages. First, the plan is completely funded by the employer, and neither the contributions nor earnings are taxed to the employee while in the plan. Also, the employee has peace of mind knowing he or she will receive a future benefit. Many plans even allow an employee to borrow from the plan within certain strict guidelines.

The primary disadvantage of a defined-benefit plan relates to younger plan participants. Younger employees generally receive a smaller portion of the total contribution, primarily because of the longer time period before their retirement.

From an employer's standpoint, some advantages of a defined-benefit plan are:

- Long-term employees are rewarded with a substantial retirement benefit even though they are close to retirement age.
- Forfeitures from terminating employees reduce future funding requirements for current employees.
- Plan investments are directed solely by the employer.

Although it was once the qualified retirement plan of choice for many medical practices, the defined-benefit plan has become much less popular because of the following disadvantages to the employer:

- In low-profit years, the employer is still obligated to make plan contributions.
- Investment risk rests solely with the employer.

- Administration costs are higher than for defined-contribution plans because an actuary must be retained to certify the reasonableness of the contribution and deduction.

However, recent legislation has lifted other defined-benefit obstacles, and its popularity is on the rise again. Defined-benefit plans afford significant contribution and deduction opportunities.

Defined-Contribution Plans

There are several variations of defined-contribution plans commonly used by medical practices: money purchase pension plans, profit-sharing plans, age-weighted profit-sharing plans, new comparability plans, 401(k) savings plans, and "SIMPLE" Plans.

MONEY PURCHASE PENSION PLANS

In a money purchase pension plan, the employer contributes a specified percentage of the total participating employees' salaries each year. This contribution is allocated among the participants. Up to 25% of the participants' payroll can be contributed and deducted by the employer. Plan contributions can be based on total compensation, including bonuses and overtime pay. Maximum recognized compensation for 2013 is $255,000, which is indexed for inflation in future years. As of 2013, a participant's annual account contribution may not exceed 25% of compensation or $51,000 per year, whichever is less.

Money purchase pension plans typically favor younger participants because they have a longer time period over which their accounts will grow. In many instances, they will share in plan forfeitures. Forfeitures occur when participants leave the practice before they have become 100% vested. The non-vested forfeitures are then reallocated to the remaining participants, thus benefiting employees who remain in the plan the longest.

In addition to the deductibility of the contributions, there are other advantages for the employer:

- Contributions, as well as administrative costs, are known in advance.
- Contributions will rise as compensation rises, but they are controllable both by formula and absolute dollar amounts.

- The employer can direct the investment portfolio or the employees can self- direct their own portions of the plan.

The primary disadvantage to the employer stems from mandatory contributions. The employer is obligated to make contributions, even in years when the practice loses money. The primary disadvantage to the employee is the lack of a guarantee of the amount of retirement benefit, since the investment risk rests on the employee participant regardless of who directs the investments. Money purchase pension plans have all but become extinct. Profit-sharing plans now allow for up to the same 25% of salary contributions, but on a year-by-year discretionary basis.

PROFIT-SHARING PLANS

For greater employer flexibility, a profit-sharing plan may be the defined-contribution plan of choice. Employer contributions to the plan need not be made every year. The maximum annual deduction is limited to 25% of compensation, with an individual recognized maximum compensation of $255,000 (as of January 2, 2013). Although annual contributions are generally discretionary, if there are profits, the employer is expected to make "substantial and recurring" contributions. As a rule of thumb, contributions in 3 out of 5 years or 5 out of 10 years will usually satisfy the IRS.

For employees, profit-sharing plans tend to favor younger participants. However, the down sides of a profit-sharing plan are similar to a money purchase pension plan. There are no guarantees of the amount of future retirement benefits, and the investment risk rests on the employee. In addition, there is no assurance of the frequency and amount of employer contributions. Advantages of a profit-sharing plan to the employer include:
- The plan gives an incentive to employees to be productive to maximize the profit potential of the practice.
- Contributions are totally flexible.
- Forfeitures of terminating employees are reallocated among active participants, generally with a greater percentage allocated to the highest-salaried participants such as the physicians.

While contribution limits of profit-sharing plans are set at 25% of covered payroll, this type of plan will generally not produce as large a contribution and deduction for older employees when compared to a defined-benefit plan.

AGE-WEIGHTED PROFIT-SHARING PLANS

Since defined-contribution plans tend to favor younger employees, another alternative is the age-weighted profit-sharing plan. Employer contributions in this type of plan are not necessarily based on profits. The contributions are totally flexible and at the discretion of the employer. Contributions need not be made yearly, as long as they are substantial and recurring. Employer contributions are allocated to provide an equal retirement benefit for all participants at normal retirement age. Older participants are favored from a contribution perspective since they are closer to retirement. However, all participants would receive the same projected retirement benefit percentage at age 65. Age-weighted profit-sharing plans do have some potential disadvantages for the employer:

- If the key employees are younger than other employees, they will not receive as large a proportion of employer contributions.
- Administrative costs are higher because of actuarial calculations.
- It is more difficult to explain the plan to employees.

NEW COMPARABILITY PLANS

As if the scope of retirement plan alternatives wasn't complex enough, recent IRS regulations allow businesses and professional practices to establish a hybrid type of profit-sharing plan known as a new comparability plan. This plan allows for very substantial contributions to be made to a favored and, on average, older group with much lower contributions for other employees. In certain situations, annual contributions for tax year 2012 can be as high as 100% of income, up to a maximum of $51,000, for each member of a highly compensated group of employees such as physicians and as little as 5% of pay for younger non-highly compensated employees.

This new allocation method is made possible by IRS regulations that allow employers to divide plan participants into one or more classes and, in many cases, make larger contributions for one class than for another. Section 401(a)(4) of the Internal Revenue Code states as a requirement for plan qualification that "contributions or benefits provided under the plan do not discriminate in favor of highly compensated employees."

The justification for the new comparability plan lies in the word "or" and is based on an analysis of projected benefits at retirement age showing that the benefits provided to highly compensated and non-highly compensated employees are comparable and are therefore considered to be nondiscriminatory. This is the same justification behind the very popular and widely used age-weighted profit-sharing plans which provide a greater benefit for older employees.

With the new comparability plan, the percentage of the plan's contribution going to the owners, partners, or highly compensated employees (such as physicians who are not partners) in the practice can be much higher than with a traditional age-weighted profit-sharing plan. This is due to the fact that, unlike age-based or weighted plans, new comparability plans also allow participants to be divided into classes, with one favored older class—highly compensated employees—receiving a much higher level of contribution than the other class (the non-highly compensated employees). New comparability plans are generally ideal for practices with owners or partners who:

- Are older, on average, than their other employees.
- Want the contribution flexibility of a profit-sharing plan versus the mandatory contributions of a defined-benefit pension plan.
- Want the largest share of the plan contribution allocated to their own accounts.

401(K) PLANS

Physicians can no longer be content maximizing retirement plan contributions and assuming there will be sufficient assets to create a comfortable retirement standard of living. The stock markets over the years have taken numerous prisoners, as evidenced by investors who jumped on the high-growth tech bandwagon in the late 1990s only to find that their portfolios declined in value by over 50% during the following three years of the last bear market cycle. This situation reminded many physicians approaching retirement age to reevaluate their options in order to determine if they will be forced to work longer or work at a reduced level during retirement.

Younger physicians were also impacted, as portfolio rates of return often times fall well below their initial expectations. While the market will continue to move in various cycles, negatively as well as positively, now is the time for all physicians to reevaluate their qualified retirement plans to be certain they are taking advantage of the new increased limits as well as understanding a major change impacting 401(k) plans.

Internal Revenue Code Section 401(k) retirement savings programs allow employees to contribute on their own behalf, on a pre-tax basis, with the benefit of tax-deferred compounding similar to traditional IRAs, pension, and profit-sharing plans. The maximum allowable pre-tax contribution for employees is $17,500 for 2013. Employees who are age 50 and over may be able to contribute an additional $5,500 via the catch-up deferral. In order for physicians to be able to contribute the maximum allowable amount to their 401(k) plans, there also must be participation from the lower-compensated employees in order to ensure the plan is not discriminatory.

A traditional 401(k) plan is subject to two nondiscrimination tests: the actual deferral percentage (ADP) test for employee elective deferrals and the actual contribution percentage (ACP) test for matching contributions. Now, as an alternative, an employer may adopt a safe harbor 401(k) plan, which is not subject to all nondiscrimination testing.

Under current tax law, there are two safe harbor alternatives to the ADP test. In the first, the employer makes a nonelective contribution of 3% to each eligible highly compensated and non-highly compensated employee. The other alternative offers the employer the opportunity to make matching contributions of 100% of non-highly compensated employee elective contributions up to 3% of pay, and 50% of non-highly compensated employee additional elective contributions up to 5% of pay. All matches and nonelective contributions made to satisfy the safe harbor must be immediately vested. In addition, the employer must notify employees within a reasonable period of time, prior to the plan year, of their rights and obligations under the safe harbor arrangement.

By meeting the above criteria, many highly compensated owner/ physicians will be able to accrue a greater benefit for themselves. With the objective of most qualified retirement plans being tax-advantaged growth for future income needs, obviously the greater amount allowed to be invested annually can make a dramatic difference down the road. Often acting as contribution limitations, guidelines are in place to ensure that there is not a great disparity of contributions, with highly compensated key employees receiving the lion's share. The safe harbor alternative to the traditional 401(k) plan will enable many physicians to accrue a greater retirement benefit while still conforming to IRS guidelines. Based on the history of prior employee participation, the safe harbor plan may prove to be a viable alternative for those wanting to maximize their retirement planning options.

Not surprisingly, financial independence remains a primary goal for most physicians. While the desirability of this goal hasn't changed over the years, the feasibility of attaining it has. Faced with lower incomes and longer hours, physicians will come to rely more heavily on their portfolio returns, especially within qualified retirement plans, in order to become financially independent. Whether an owner or an employee, physicians may be able to have some say-so in investment decisions to better fit their long-term personal objectives.

According to a U.S. Chamber of Commerce survey, 80% of businesses with fewer than 100 employees offer defined-contribution plans, while only 47% still sponsor some type of defined-benefit plan funded solely by the employer. With the shift toward profit sharing and 401(k) plans being the primary retirement funding vehicle, it's imperative to take advantage of its design flexibility in order to maximize benefits.

Roth IRAs have become an extremely popular option for those who prefer the unique advantage of being able to withdraw funds during their retirement years on a tax-free basis, as opposed to traditional IRAs where withdrawals are taxed as ordinary income. The only real downside to Roth IRAs is that contributions are made on an after-tax basis and are not tax-deductible like with a traditional IRA. Unfortunately, most physicians have not been able to utilize Roth IRAs due to their relatively high income levels; Roth IRA eligibility phases out between $107,000 and $122,000 for single filers and $169,000 to $179,000 for married taxpayers filing a joint tax return. However, highly compensated individuals previously unable to contribute to Roth IRAs, as well as younger workers expecting to be in higher tax brackets during their retirement years, are now able to take advantage of a new type of tax-advantaged savings plan called Roth 401(k).

As its name implies, the Roth 401(k) incorporates elements of both traditional 401(k) plans and Roth IRAs. Part of the Economic Growth and Tax Relief Reconciliation Act (EGTRRA) of 2001, the Roth 401(k) became available January 1, 2006 and allows workers to make greatly expanded Roth IRA contributions without any income restrictions impacting eligibility. Contributions to Roth IRAs are limited to a maximum of $5,000 for taxpayers under age 50, and $6,000 for those 50 and older. The Roth 401(k) maximum contribution level, on the other hand, enables workers under age 50 to contribute up to $16,500, while workers age 50 and older can contribute as much as $22,000. At that point, an employee currently contributing to a traditional 401(k) plan has the option of simply having the contributions diverted to a Roth version of the plan. That election impacts the amount of take-home salary, since the contributions are made on an after-tax basis, as opposed to pre-tax contributions made into a traditional 401(k) plan.

While all of this appears quite straightforward, there are a few nuances to consider prior to making the switch. First, matching employer contributions still must be made and invested in the traditional 401(k) account, not the Roth 401(k) account. Even if the employee makes all of his or her contributions exclusively to a Roth 401(k) account, the employee would still owe tax on retirement withdrawals from funds contributed by the employer, which were made on a tax-deductible basis, as well as the earnings on those contributions.

Second, workers should also be aware that the annual deferral limits apply to all 401(k) contributions, regardless of whether they are made on a pre-tax or after-tax basis. While employees are allowed to contribute to both types of 401(k) plans, contributions to the traditional plan may need to be reduced or discounted to comply with the over limits. Employees considering the Roth option should know that, like the traditional 401(k) but unlike the Roth IRA, they will be required to begin mandatory minimum distributions by April 1 of the year following attainment age of 70½. This may be avoided by rolling over the Roth 401(k) to a Roth IRA, thus avoiding the minimum distribution rules.

It is also important to understand that you cannot simply assume that your current 401(k) plan will be amended to allow after-tax Roth contributions. Employers should contact their plan administrators to determine feasibility of adding the Roth feature. Interested employees should inform their employers that this is an option they would like to see included in next year's retirement plan structure.

SIMPLE PLANS

The Small Business Job Protection Act of 1996 created a unique retirement plan called SIMPLE, an acronym for Savings Incentive Match Plan for Employee. SIMPLE replaces the salary-reduction version of the Simplified Employee Pension, also known as SARSEP. The SIMPLE allows small business owners to put aside money easily and inexpensively in tax-deferred accounts for themselves and their employees.

To take advantage of this new form of retirement savings, the business entity must have no more than 100 employees and cannot use any other retirement plan in the same year. Also, eligible employees must have earned at least $5,000 in the previous calendar year from the same employer and be likely to do so in the current year.

SIMPLEs are available in two forms: a SIMPLE individual retirement account and a SIMPLE 401(k). SIMPLE IRAs can be set up for each employee for a nominal fee at a bank, mutual fund company, or brokerage firm. SIMPLE 401(k) plans are more expensive mainly because of administrative costs.

SIMPLEs allow owners and employees to defer a percentage of their compensation, up to $12,000 a year, indexed for inflation, with a catch-up provision for workers age 50 and over, allowing an additional $2,500 to be contributed. Owners may contribute to employees' plans by contributing a matching contribution of 100% of the first 3% of participating workers' annual compensation deferred, up to a maximum of $12,000, or by contributing 2% of compensation up to $5,000 in 2013, for all workers, whether or not they participate in the salary-deferral portion of the plan.

Because the SIMPLE is a newer form of retirement plan, many options must be considered before implementation. On the positive side, SIMPLEs require no discrimination testing (which requires a certain relation between the amount of compensation deferred by the group of participants included in the lower level of compensation and those in the higher level of compensation), employees need not participate for a business owner to defer up to $12,000 plus the 3% match per year.

The traditional 401(k) plan limits an employer's tax deferral by the amount employees put into the plan. In addition, the employer has no fiduciary responsibility for employee investments under the SIMPLE arrangement.

The physician who wants to save more for retirement and take a bigger deduction may find the maximum contribution confining. Other qualified plans allow an employer to deduct as much as 100% of his or her salary up to $51,000 per year. Also, since SIMPLE money is fully vested from the beginning, the plan provides little incentive for employee loyalty.

The table on the following page summarizes many of the basic characteristics of qualified plan alternatives and should help you understand the differences among plans.

What Plan Offers the Right Fit?

There are many factors to consider when evaluating different types of retirement plans for a medical practice. The table on page 133 will help evaluate the benefits of each and narrow the alternatives. Of course, consulting with retirement experts before making a final decision is critical.

QUALIFIED PLANS COMPARED

Feature	Defined-Benefit Plans	Defined-Contribution Plans			
	All DB Plans	Money Purchase Pension	Profit Sharing	Age-Weighted Profit Sharing	SIMPLE
Employer contributions deductible?	Yes	Yes	Yes	Yes	Yes
Employer contributions to participant currently taxable?	No	No	No	No	No
Earnings accumulate with income tax-deferred?	Yes	Yes	Yes	Yes	Yes
Maximum annual employer contribution or deduction?	Determined by actuary	100% of compensation	100% of compensation	100% of compensation	100% match up to 3% of compensation or 2% of compensation of all eligible employees
Employer contributions required?	Yes	Yes	No	No	Yes
Employer contribution is allocated:	N/A	1. as a percentage of total covered compensation 2. integrated with Social Security	1. as a percentage of total covered compensation 2. integrated with Social Security	based on number of years before participant reaches retirement age	pro-rata by compensation
Employee contributions required?	No	No	No	No	No
Maximum participant benefits (for defined-benefit plans) or allocations (for defined-contribution plans)	Lesser of 100% of compensation or $205,000 annually	Lesser of 25% of compensation or $51,000	Lesser of 25% of compensation or $51,000	Lesser of 25% of compensation or $51,000	Lesser of 100% of compensation or $12,000
Investments can be self-directed by participants?	No	Yes	Yes	Yes	Yes
What plan participants are favored by the plan design?	Older, closer to retirement, highly compensated	Highly compensated	Highly compensated	Older, closer to retirement, highly compensated	Younger
What will participants' account value at retirement depend on?	Formula of the plan, which can be calculated based on: years before retirement, compensation, years of service	1. the amount of contributions 2. the number of years until retirement 3. investment return	1. frequency and amount of contributions 2. number of years until retirement 3. investment return	1. frequency and amount of contributions 2. number of years until retirement 3. investment return	1. frequency and amount of contributions 2. number of years until retirement 3. investment return
Who bears investment risk?	Employer	Employee	Employee	Employee	Employee

Source: Mary Jo Stvan, President, Merit Benefits, Oakbrook, IL

EVALUATING RETIREMENT PLANS

Plan Type	If you need flexibility in making deposits.	If you would be the oldest, most highly compensated, or closest to retirement of all participants	If you would be able to afford contributions that would exceed 25% of participant compensation
Defined-Benefit Plan	unlikely to consider	definitely consider	definitely consider
Money Purchase Pension Plan	may consider	consider	no impact
Profit-Sharing Plan	definitely consider	unlikely to consider	consider
Age-Weighted Profit Sharing	definitely consider	definitely consider	consider
SIMPLE Plan	definitely consider	unlikely to consider	unlikely to consider

Implementing Your Plan

To determine the feasibility of implementing a new qualified retirement plan for your own practice, be sure to analyze a number of testing models that can compare your current plan to other alternatives. Your accountant or a third-party administrator (TPA) can be a valuable resource in exploring various qualified retirement plan options. Typically, TPAs do not offer investment advice but focus exclusively on the mechanics of the various plans and assist in analyzing whether the plan options can attain the goals and objectives of the practice owners. Since we are in an environment of constantly changing tax laws, it generally makes sense to reevaluate your retirement plan options on an ongoing basis to ensure you are taking the greatest advantage of today's tax-advantaged opportunities.

Many skilled professionals are available to assist with qualified-plan implementation. A third-party administrator helps in plan design, participant information, and governmental reporting. The trustees can take responsibility for investing or can hire an investment manager. An actuary will be involved when using defined-benefit plans. Many professional financial organizations can act in multiple capacities. For smaller plans, the practice's accountants may perform the duties of plan administration, while the principal physicians act as trustees and hire investment professionals to construct and invest the portfolio. Whatever group or entity the medical practice chooses to work with, they must be aware of the goals and objectives that the practice has determined to be in its best interest.

Regardless of the type of plan chosen, care must be taken to observe the various tax and legal requirements established by the IRS and the Department of Labor. IRS regulations require the filing of the appropriate tax forms for the plan, such as Form 5500, which reports on the assets, contributions, and expenses of the plan. Your accountant or third-party administrator usually handles these matters. Department of Labor requirements include distributing required information to plan participants, making distributions to former participants in a timely fashion, and other miscellaneous items.

A separate item that falls under Department of Labor domain is the need to satisfy a variety of requirements regarding the investment of plan assets. To assist plan trustees, a series of requirements have been identified in the Employees Retirement Income Security Act (ERISA). These requirements are:

- An investment policy must be established and should be in writing (ERISA Sections 402(a)(1), 40229(b)(1) to (2), 404(a)(1)(D)).
- Plan assets must be diversified (ERISA Section 404(a)(1)(c).
- Investment decisions must be made with the skill and care of a "prudent expert" (ERISA Section 404(a)(1)(b)).
- Investment performance must be monitored (ERISA Section 405(a)).
- Investment expenses must be controlled (ERISA Section 404(a)).
- Prohibited transactions must be avoided (ERISA Section 404(a) and (b)).

These requirements make it important for qualified plan trustees to have a general understanding of investments. The allocation of the plan's investment portfolio should be based on many criteria, including the age of the participants, the plan's risk parameters, the plan's expected liabilities, and the type of plan. Many physicians act as the trustee of a defined-contribution plan and take responsibility for managing the portfolio on their own or by hiring an investment advisor. In this situation, there is a pooled fund for all employees and each owns a proportionate share. The problem with this scenario is that employees may have investment objectives based on age, risk tolerance, and required return that may conflict with those of the physician trustee. The existence of various investment objectives can create a conflict and possible liability for plan trustees.

Participant-Directed Accounts

To minimize the potential conflict due to various investment objectives, many plans now offer employees the ability, through self-direction, to manage and make investment decisions for their portion of the plan's assets. This is usually referred to as providing participant-directed accounts.

Providing participant-directed accounts can increase employee involvement in retirement plans; transfer part or all of the cost of funding the plan to the employees; and transfer investment responsibility to the employees. Based on our experience, this last item is of key importance to many physicians.

SELECTION AND MONITORING OF INVESTMENT OPTIONS

Understand that some fiduciary responsibility—and potential liability—cannot be transferred. The responsibility for selecting and monitoring the investment options—as opposed to participants choosing among a pre-selected menu of investment options—cannot be transferred to the employees. Therefore, someone other than the employees chooses the investment options offered by the plan. This "someone"—the plan trustees, the board of directors, a plan investment committee, an officer of the practice—is the responsible fiduciary. In selecting the investment options, the responsible fiduciary must act prudently and is liable for losses resulting from an imprudent decision. In addition to the initial selection of the investment options, the responsible fiduciary must monitor the options to ensure that they continue to be a prudent choice for the plan.

What is prudent? The legal requirement for prudence under ERISA is for a fiduciary to discharge its duties with, among other things, "the care, skill, prudence, and diligence under the circumstances then prevailing that a prudent man acting in a like capacity and familiar with such matters would use in the conduct of an enterprise of a like character and with like aims. . . ." (see ERISA § 404(a)(1)(B)). This is sometimes referred to as the prudent expert rule because ERISA requires that the fiduciary act not just with prudence, but with the prudence of someone "familiar with such matters."

As a practical matter, prudent in this context means selecting investment options expected to perform reasonably well relative to other similar investment products and against appropriate standard indexes. In addition, it means periodically (e.g., annually) reviewing how each investment has performed historically relative to others and to appropriate benchmarks, and making changes when reasonable.

For example, as your plan invests in mutual funds, the responsible fiduciary should review the performance of each fund at least annually against a comparable index of performance. The fiduciary should determine if each fund compares favorably to the performance of other funds of the same type and with the same investment objectives. For instance, we might use the S&P 500 Index to judge the performance of a large-cap equity fund. A small-cap equity fund could be compared with the Russell 2000 Index. The responsible fiduciary should determine whether the funds have a poor rate of return relative to other similar funds and in relation to the appropriate benchmark or index. If so, the fiduciary should consider switching funds, and at some point, a prudent fiduciary will be obligated to switch funds.

Simply conducting these comparisons is not sufficient, however. Fiduciaries must keep minutes of the meetings at which they conduct their review, ensuring that the minutes reflect the alternatives considered and why they were chosen or rejected. Copies of the materials reviewed at the meeting should be attached to the minutes.

If the fiduciary exercises prudent selection of the investment options and proper monitoring of the investments, two of the three basic steps have been taken that should avoid liability for any losses suffered by the plan participants on the investment options that the participants select.

ERISA SECTION 404(C)

To effectively transfer responsibility for selecting among the investment options, the plan must also follow specific rules. These are found in the Department of Labor Regulations under ERISA Section 404(c). Employers are typically told that they must do only three things to comply with Section 404(c): give the employees three investment options; let the employees make their own choices among the investment options; and let the employees change the investments at least every three months. But depending on how the actual requirements of the Section 404(c) Regulations are counted, there are actually 20 to 30 different conditions that must be met.

One of the most commonly overlooked condition is the need to tell participants that the plan intends to comply with Section 404(c) and that the fiduciaries will be relieved of liability for investment losses. This can be done in the summary plan description (SPD) or in another written notice to the participants from the third-party administrator. The plan document and related materials are often generic, pre-printed forms. If the plan documents do not include the right language to comply with ERISA Section 404(c), the protection is not available to the plan, the company, or the fiduciaries.

Another common error is the failure to offer confirmations to the participants when investment choices and changes are made. Some investment vendors provide these confirmations automatically, but many do not. If the plan custodian does not provide confirmations as a matter of routine, the plan fiduciaries must tell the participants that they have a right to request confirmations. Failure to advise the participants of this right will result in loss of Section 404(c) protection.

EDUCATION

There is a common misperception that investment education is required under Section 404(c) to transfer investment responsibility and liability to the employees. There is no such requirement. Although investment education is not required, employers are still providing this service to their employees. They have become increasingly aware of a tendency of their employees to invest too conservatively and of the insecurity felt by employees in making investment decisions. In addition, we have found an inverse relationship between the amount of education provided and the amount of distractions occurring in daily workplace responsibilities. The better educated the employee, the fewer the distractions. Employers have sought to address these concerns by providing the additional employee benefit of investment education and retirement planning.

Employers have also turned to a variety of investment education vehicles, including employee seminars, newsletters, and retirement counseling. Investment education was inhibited by a concern among employers that if too much (or incorrect) advice was given, the individuals providing the investment education might become a fiduciary and, as a result, assume liability for its employees' investment decisions.

The Department of Labor alleviated this concern by clarifying that investment education could be provided to employees without fiduciary liability, as long as the information was general (that is, did not specify particular investments) and the providers of the education were prudently selected and monitored. Broadly stated, investment education (as opposed to "investment advice") can cover (1) plan information; (2) general financial and investment information; (3) asset allocation models; and (4) interactive investment materials.

If you offer participant-directed accounts and adequate investment education is provided, the potential for fiduciary liability should be limited. Further, if the ERISA Section 404(c) rules are satisfied, you should have a defense to employee claims—so long as the investment options are properly selected and monitored.

To assist with this process, allow us to provide a few additional resources. Here are the basic steps required to mitigate fiduciary liability when offering participant-directed accounts.

DESCRIPTION

1. Appoint an investment committee that will act as the "responsible fiduciary" to handle specific plan issues. (The committee would most likely consist of the partners in the practice.)

2. Provide the responsible fiduciary with the process and standards for selecting or retaining funds on the list of investments offered to plan participants.

3. Provide the responsible fiduciary with a detailed analysis for the specific investments that should be offered to plan participants.

4. Provide the responsible fiduciary with the appropriate comparative and monitoring data relating to the investment alternatives that should continue to be offered to plan participants.

5. Provide the responsible fiduciary written summaries of all recommendations and the basis for such recommendations.

6. Provide an effective process for the transactions relating to the addition or replacement of an investment offered to plan participants.

7. Provide alternative asset allocations from which plan participants can select.

8. Provide each participant with a personalized Investment Policy Statement based on the model asset allocation chosen.

9. Provide all plan participants with telephone, electronic, and in-person access to investment advisor representatives.

10. Provide printed confirmations for all purchases and sales of securities in each account.

11. Provide monthly statements to all participants identifying the values of their accounts and specific investments.

12. Provide quarterly performance reports for all participants identifying the performance of the account for the past quarter, calendar year-to-date, and since-inception time periods.

13. Coordinate activities with the third-party administrator of your choice.

14. Provide educational sessions and materials for plan participants on a regular basis.

15. Provide supplemental financial planning services (retirement planning, risk management planning, estate planning) at reduced costs to plan participants.

16. Contribute to regular participant educational meetings to reinforce the benefits of the plan, plan design, plan structure, basic investment education, allocation strategy alternatives, and investment descriptions.

In addition, there are informational items that *must* be provided to plan participants. The information must be generally sufficient to enable the participant to make informed investment decisions.

INFORMATION

---

1. An explanation that the plan is intended to be a 404(c) plan.
2. An explanation that the fiduciaries may be relieved of liability.
3. A description of each investment alternative available under the plan, which can be general when the plan permits any investment, but should encourage participants to review information on the investment.
4. A general description of the investment objectives and risk and return characteristics of each designated alternative, and information regarding the type and diversification of assets in the portfolio of the designated alternative.
5. The identity of any designated investment manager.
6. An explanation of the circumstances under which participants may give investment instructions, including limitations on such instructions; restrictions on transfer; limitations on voting rights; and information on penalties or adjustments related to fund transfers.
7. A description of transaction fees and expenses chargeable against the participant's account.
8. Information on indemnification of the plan fiduciary responsible for giving information on request.
9. A copy of most recent prospectus provided to the plan if the investment is subject to the Securities Act of 1933 (this can be given immediately before or after investment).
10. After investment, plan materials related to the exercise of voting, tender, or similar rights. If there are plan provisions regarding the exercise of such rights, participants must receive a description of or reference to such provisions. While the plan is not required to pass through such rights, Section 404(c) relief is not available to the extent that plan fiduciaries exercise the rights.

Other information must be available to participants *upon request*. Most of this information can be provided by those who help you with your plan, such as the TPA or investment advisor. This material must be based on the latest information available to the plan, including:

INFORMATION

1. A narrative of the annual operating expenses of each designated investment alternative, including investment manager fees, administrative fees, and transaction costs, which reduce the rate of return to the participant. The aggregate amount of such expenses must be expressed as a percentage of average net assets of the designated investment alternative. If the information is already in the prospectus, providing the prospectus is sufficient.

2. Copies of prospectuses, financial statements and reports, and other materials related to the investment alternatives to the extent the information is provided to the plan.

3. The value of shares or units and past and current investment performance of each available alternative, net of expenses.

4. The value of the shares or units held in the particular participant's account.

Beyond satisfying the lengthy requirements for plan compliance, plan sponsors have the opportunity to select among a variety of platforms for the investment of participant accounts. It is important for you to be aware of the general arrangements (or platforms) available for investment management and the alternative methods of compensation for those who are involved. Please keep in mind, this does not comment on the qualified plan design, such as the type of profit-sharing plan or 401(k) plan, but rather on the arrangements in place regarding how investments are selected, held, and sold for the benefit of plan participants.

• *Transaction-based.* In the transaction-based model, plan assets are held in a brokerage account where the broker earns commissions from every transaction that occurs in the account. These types of arrangements may (but not always) provide a large number of investment alternatives. We believe this arrangement creates an inherent conflict of interest, since transactions may occur that benefit the broker but not necessarily the plan participants. For this and other reasons, we are seeing fewer employers utilize this model.

- *Closed platforms.* The plan assets are held in an account with a limited number of investment offerings. In addition, these offerings are often proprietary products of the platform sponsor. Once again, commissions may be paid to the representatives who have responsibility for the account. These commissions are often generated from the higher management fees associated with the investments. Examples of such plans include plans sponsored by insurance companies (offering a limited number of accounts for participants to select); wrap programs offered by brokerage firms (offering a limited number of investment managers for selection by plan participants); and proprietary mutual fund companies (usually offering a limited selection of their funds for investment by plan participants). Occasionally, providers with closed platforms may also provide administrative services. This can help control costs for smaller plans. Thus, we believe that closed platforms may be appropriate for small plans with limited assets. However, there is also a conflict of interest with the limited number of investment offerings, provider bias regarding the investment offerings, uncertain payments to financial company representatives, etc.
- *Open platform.* The plan assets are held in a brokerage account that has extensive investment alternatives, not restricted by a particular mutual fund company, brokerage firm, or insurance company. Proprietary products are usually not involved—if so, usually for index fund purposes only. Open platforms are frequently used by fee-only investment advisors who receive their only compensation from the client rather than from a particular fund company, bank, or brokerage company. Thus, the open platform provides an environment free of transaction-based conflicts and free of closed platform limitations or bias.

Given the number of platforms and compensation arrangements, it is common to find plan sponsors who are unaware of the payments being made to firms in the form of excessive expense charges or support of proprietary products. To help you develop a better sense of the differences among investment platforms, allow us to share the following comparison point spreadsheet for your use in comparing alternatives:

Impact	Questions	Plan A	Plan B
Trustee	Is it possible for the firm to act as trustee of the plan?		
Trustee	To what extent does it absolve the plan sponsor from any liability?		
Trustee	Other alternatives?		
Trustee	How does the plan sponsor determine the selection of investments available for the participant?		
Trustee	Is the participant offered guidance with choosing of funds?		
Trustee	Does the firm produce quarterly performance reports for participants and plan sponsor?		
TPA	Are TPAs restricted?		
TPA Cost	What is the base fee?		
TPA Costs	What are the one time set-up fees?		
TPA Cost	What is the compliance fee?		
TPA Costs	What is the per-participant charge?		
TPA Costs	What is the Form 5500 fee?		
Platform Costs	What is the asset management fee?		
Platform Costs	What is the average expense ratio?		
Platform	Who pays the advisor?		

There are many options to consider when comparing and ultimately implementing a qualified retirement plan for a medical practice. While the tax laws are constantly changing and evolving, they have historically been very beneficial relative to specific retirement plan funding limitations and deductions. If structured properly, a retirement plan will help you attract and retain key employees while providing you with a substantial tax-advantaged savings plan to help you reach your financial independence goals.

Qualified Plan Distributions

So you have chosen the type of plan and the investment platform. The education doesn't stop there. If you are acting as the administrator or are responsible for your qualified plan, you will need to know the steps you are required to take when an employee requests a distribution upon retirement or termination of employment.

Administrators are required to give participants about to receive a distribution a written explanation covering the following four items:

1. You must explain any special tax treatment for lump sum distributions that may be available to the participant.
2. If the employee is under age 59½, you must inform him or her of the potential 10% IRS penalty for early withdrawals.
3. You must explain the regular rollover rules.
4. You must explain the new mandatory withholding rules and the preferred alternative.

We will take a closer look at withdrawals and rollovers later. Let's first consider what retirement savings options are available to the physician who is unable to participate in a qualified retirement plan.

Individual Retirement Accounts (IRAs)

If a qualified retirement plan is not available to you, knowing the ins and outs of individual retirement accounts (IRAs) is critical to your retirement planning. Currently, there are two types of IRAs: a traditional, or regular IRA, and the Roth IRA.

If you qualify, you may be able to deduct contributions to a traditional IRA. For tax year 2013, the maximum contribution allowed for most wage earners is $5,500. An individual who is age 50 or over is also allowed to make additional catch-up contributions of $1,000. Contributions for the current tax year must be made by the tax return deadline, with no allowances for extensions. The deadline for tax year 2013 contributions is April 15, 2014.

Contributions are tax-deductible unless you are an active participant in an employer-sponsored retirement plan and your adjusted gross income exceeds the specified limits. The deduction for 2013 is phased out for joint filers with an adjusted gross income between $95,000 and $115,000; and for single filers between $59,000 and $69,000. If you are not an active participant in an employer-sponsored plan but your spouse is, the phase out occurs between $178,000 and $188,000. If you don't qualify for the tax deductions, you may still contribute to a traditional IRA, but on a nondeductible basis only.

From a distribution standpoint, withdrawals of tax-deductible contributions and earnings are taxable at ordinary income tax rates. If you withdraw funds from an IRA before age 59½, a 10% penalty tax will apply to the taxable portion of the distribution. Withdrawals and distributions prior to age 59½ are subject to a 10% penalty tax, in addition to current income tax, unless one or more of the following apply:

- A distribution is made because of the death or disability of the participant.
- A distribution is paid as an annuity over the life of the participant, or the joint lives of the participant and a designated beneficiary. The 10% penalty is triggered if the distribution schedule is modified within five years or before attainment of age 59½, if later.
- The distribution is rolled over into another IRA.
- The distribution is used to pay for medical expenses in excess of 7.5% of AGI.
- The IRA is withdrawn by an unemployed individual to pay health insurance premiums. (Only applies to certain situations.)
- The IRA distribution is used to pay for qualified higher education expenses for the individual, spouse, child, or grandchild.
- For a first-time homebuyer, there is a lifetime exception of $10,000 from the 10% penalty tax. The purchaser of the home may be the individual, spouse, child, or grandchild. A first-time homebuyer is someone (or his or her spouse) who had no ownership in a principal residence during the two years prior to the purchase of the new home.

As a general rule regarding withdrawals, you must begin taking IRA-mandated minimum distributions from the IRA by April 1 of the year following the year in which you turn age 70½.

Roth IRAs allow the same maximum contribution of $5,500 for tax year 2013 and provide the same provisions for catch-up contributions as does the traditional IRA. In addition, you can split your contribution between a traditional IRA and a Roth IRA, as long as the total does not exceed the overall $5,500 limit.

Unlike a traditional IRA, contributions to a Roth IRA are never tax-deductible. On the other hand, distributions are received on a tax-free basis if the Roth IRA has been in existence at least five years, and you have reached age 59½. In addition, certain exceptions apply to the minimum-age rule. Examples include the withdrawal of funds for a child's college education or a first-time home purchase up to a maximum of $10,000. In addition, Roth IRAs have the advantage of no lifetime mandatory distribution requirements.

Eligibility to contribute to a Roth IRA in a particular year is phased out for joint filers with an adjusted gross income between $178,000 and $188,000, and between $112,000 and $127,000 for single filers. If you already have a traditional IRA, the law allows you to convert it to a Roth IRA, but certain rules and tax issues must be considered prior to the conversion.

DISTRIBUTIONS

The IRS recently adopted final regulations relating to required distributions from retirement plans as a result of the life expectancy tables having been updated to reflect the fact that people, on average, are living longer.

The tax law requires IRA owners and pension plan participants to begin taking distributions from their retirement funds at a certain point (no later than the April 1 following the calendar year in which the participant turns 70½). The newly finalized regulations reduce the required minimum distribution (RMD).

The RMD is generally calculated using one of two tables. The Uniform Life Table, the more common of the two, is used for IRA owners. The second, the Single Life Table, is used for beneficiaries who have inherited an IRA. Because the distribution periods in the Uniform Life Table and the life expectancies in the Single Life Table have increased under the new regulations, the RMD is lowered.

Because distributions are taxed as regular income, the income tax savings for individuals who want to take the absolute lowest distribution can be significant under the new regulations.

There may be additional tax considerations depending on the relationship and ages of designated beneficiaries, including surviving spouses. In addition, the new rules make it clear that an

UNIFORM LIFE TABLE	
Age of Participant	Distribution Period
70	27.4
71	26.5
72	25.6
73	24.7
74	23.8
75	22.9
76	22.0
77	21.2
78	20.3
79	19.5
80	18.7
81	17.9
82	17.1
83	16.3
84	15.5
85	14.8
86	14.1
87	13.4
88	12.7
89	12.0
90	11.4
91	10.8
92	10.2
93	9.6
94	9.1
95	8.6
96	8.1
97	7.6
98	7.1
99	6.7
100	6.3
101	5.9
102	5.5
103	5.2
104	4.9
105	4.5
106	4.2
107	3.9
108	3.7
109	3.4
110	3.1
111	2.9
112	2.6
113	2.4
114	2.1
115	1.9

estate is not a designated beneficiary. This clarification of the law makes it critical that IRA owners and plan participants name beneficiaries and contingent beneficiaries on each and every retirement account. The new rules also give certain trusts named as IRA beneficiaries a second chance to have the oldest trust beneficiary qualify as a designated beneficiary, even though the trust did not qualify under the old rules.

Careful proactive planning may further reduce the taxable impact of the new distribution rules. Be sure to consult with your tax advisor to ensure that your beneficiary designations are properly structured in light of the new IRA final regulations.

ROLLOVERS

There are several reasons rolling over your IRA funds makes sense. You may be dissatisfied with the investment return from the IRA or are interested in pursuing other investment opportunities. One unique reason might be the need for immediate cash. If you withdraw funds from an IRA, but redeposit the funds back into an IRA within 60 days, there are no current income tax ramifications. When all of the requirements are met, IRA rollovers are tax-free and exempt from the usual 10% penalty on early withdrawals before age 59½.

However, it is important to keep in mind that there are several potential pitfalls with IRA-to-IRA rollovers:

1. *Missing the 60-day rollover period.* The rollover must be completed within 60 days after the date you receive a distribution from the old IRA. For years, the IRS has ruled the 60-day requirement could not be waived, even when the delay was not the taxpayer's fault. Recently, the IRS indicated that it's more willing to grant an exception or waiver under extenuating circumstances, but it is still best to play it safe and stay within the 60-day rollover period.

2. *Failure to roll over the same assets that were distributed.* To qualify for a tax-free rollover, the cash or other assets withdrawn from the old IRA must be transferred within 60 days. You are not allowed to substitute other property. For example, in a recent tax court case, an individual withdrew cash from his IRA and used the money to invest in common stocks. He then transferred the stocks to a new IRA within the required 60-day rollover period. The tax court ruled that the transfer was taxable, since there was a change in the distributed assets.

3. *Rolling over to the wrong IRA.* The tax-advantaged rollover is valid only if you make a timely rollover to an IRA that you personally own. If you mistakenly transfer the rollover funds to your spouse's IRA or some other account, the transfer is fully taxable.

4. *Initiating more than one rollover during the year.* You are allowed to roll over funds from one IRA to another IRA only once a year. The one-year period begins on the date you receive the distribution, not the date on which you roll over the funds into the IRA. The one-year rollover rule applies separately to each IRA that you own.

5. *Rolling over a mandatory distribution.* The law requires you to begin minimum distributions from an IRA by April 1 of the year in which you reach age 70½. You cannot avoid the minimum distribution rule by rolling over the distribution to another IRA. Mandatory distributions may be avoided if the retirement plan assets are not held within an IRA, but are kept within the plan, and you have not yet retired. This exception, however, is not available for distributions made within an IRA.

6. *Rolling over IRA assets to a Roth IRA.* In general, the rollover from a regular IRA to a Roth IRA is completely taxable, but the

funds will be able to be withdrawn tax-free after the mandatory five-year holding period.

AVOIDING THE EARLY RETIREMENT WITHDRAWAL PENALTY

As a general rule, distributions from qualified plans and IRAs are subject to a 10% penalty tax if they are withdrawn prior to the participant reaching age 59½, becoming disabled, or dying. Remember that the term *qualified plan* includes pensions, profit-sharing plans, Keoghs, and 403(b) annuities. Additionally, withdrawals are subject to ordinary income taxation. This will reduce your premature distribution even further.

When the age 59½ rule was enacted, a general assumption was made that a normal minimum retirement age would be 60 years of age. But times have changed! Corporate downsizing has forced many to begin retirement in their mid-50s. Many physicians look at healthcare reform and are considering retiring before the magic age of 59½. How can you access retirement funds without paying the 10% penalty?

Depending upon your personal situation and possible need for the funds, there are several possible exceptions to the penalty rule. If your objective is simply early retirement, the IRS will waive the 10% penalty if the distribution is part of a scheduled series of substantially equal payments. There are three different approved methods when calculating distributions:

1. *Single or Joint Life Expectancy Method.* This method spreads payments over the number of years set forth in the IRS tables based on a single life or joint life, which includes your named beneficiary.
2. *Amortization Method.* Using this method, payments are similar to the annual amount required to pay off a loan at a reasonable interest rate over your life expectancy.
3. *Annuity Method.* This method uses an annuity factor that has been determined from a reasonable mortality table using a given interest rate assumption. Once you begin annual distributions, you must continue them until age 59½ , or five years, whichever is later. Under this rule, a 55-year-old may receive fixed annual distributions to age 60. At that time, he or she can stop the

fixed amount and take out as little or as much as needed from the qualified plan at their his or her own discretion. (Internal Revenue Code Section 72t).

Even though all three methods may seem similar, they all yield different required annual distributions. If you are considering using the substantially equal payments exception, have your accountant determine each method's results in order to match your income needs and avoid additional income taxation.

BENEFICIARY DESIGNATIONS

With their individual retirement account (IRA) generally representing most physicians' largest financial asset, it only makes sense to ensure that retirement account mistakes be avoided. While many institutions provide custody services for IRA assets, the onus is on the IRA owner to make the most of the rules, while avoiding the most common traps both in the law and in those created by custodians.

The most common mistake physicians make with IRAs relates to the designation of beneficiary. As each IRA is established, whether at a bank, brokerage firm, trust company, or mutual fund, you are required to complete a beneficiary designation form. What makes this form so critical is that it, not your will or trust, will determine who will inherit this valuable asset.

Individuals who aren't quite sure frequently name their estate as their beneficiary. Consequently, at the time of their death, their entire IRA will need to be fully distributed over five years. If distributions have already begun, then the payouts will continue based on the initial projected life expectancy of the deceased.

Typically, IRA owners name a spouse as beneficiary while not naming or giving very little consideration to who the contingent beneficiary should be. Based on current and updated tax law, there are now greater advantages to naming children or grandchildren. If your spouse predeceases you or survives you but is financially comfortable enough not to need the distributions from the IRA, the children or grandchildren will be able to stretch out the distributions over their own life expectancies, thus creating a longer period of tax-deferred accumulation.

Caution does need to be exercised in the event that one of the named children dies prior to the IRA owner. In this situation, the deceased child's portion of the inheritance would go to the other living children, as opposed to the deceased child's family. This, however, may be your objective. If on the other hand, your desire is to have that child's portion pass through to his or her heirs, be sure to add the line: "to my descendants per stirpes." This specific legal jargon will ensure that if the beneficiary child dies, his or her descendants get the full share. Also keep in mind that if for any reason the IRA custodian form doesn't allow for much beneficiary designation flexibility, they will often allow you to submit an attachment that better clarifies your wishes.

With regard to minimum required distributions from an IRA over your lifetime, remember that if you have more than one IRA account, you need not withdraw money from each. Instead, you can aggregate required distributions from your IRAs (with the exception of IRAs inherited from a non-spouse) and then take the total from the account of your choosing, even if they have different custodians. To facilitate these distributions, the IRS requires custodians to send notices to IRA owners when they turn 69 1/2, although you don't have to withdraw the funds until April 1 of the year after you turn 70½. Missing a minimum required distribution subjects you to a hefty 50% penalty on the amount you should have taken.

Divorce Issues

There is no doubt that physicians are among the many Americans impacted by divorce and/or remarriage each year. When it comes to divorce, physicians may be even at a higher risk than other Americans. Various studies, including those conducted by the *New England Journal of Medicine* and Johns Hopkins, found that physician divorce rates are actually higher than the national average. In addition, certain specialties tend to have even higher rates of divorce, with psychiatrists having the highest divorce rate followed closely by surgeons. On the other hand, internists, pediatricians, and pathologists tend to have a much lower incidence of divorce. The National Center for Health Statistics puts the divorce rate for first marriages at 43%, but the rate for marriages in which at least one spouse is a physician may be up to 20% higher based on research compiled for the American Medical Association publication, *The Medical Marriage: A Couples Survival Guide.*

Again, because the most sizeable financial asset many physicians have is their practice retirement plan or IRAs, it is important to understand the economic impact of divorce and what choices are available.

In situations where one spouse has been out of the workforce during all or part of the marriage, that spouse may not have had an opportunity to save for retirement on an individual basis and thus may be entitled to a substantial share of the spouse physician's retirement benefits. In other cases, retirement plans may be used to balance a division of marital assets. An understanding of the nuances associated with dividing retirement plan assets is critical for today's physicians in order to avoid surprises down the road.

Retirement assets, categorized into qualified retirement plans (defined-benefit plans and defined-contribution plans) or individual retirement accounts (IRAs), can be divided like any other part of the marital estate. But in order to divide a qualified retirement plan, you will need to obtain a Qualified Domestic Relations Order (QDRO). A QDRO is a judgment, decree, or court order issued to give a spouse, former spouse, child, or dependent of a participant in a retirement plan the right to receive all or part of the benefits. Without a QDRO, the plan administrator would not be able to release the assets to someone other than the account holder or plan participant.

From an income tax standpoint, the distribution to a spouse or former spouse is taxable as current income unless the distribution is rolled over to an IRA. If on the other hand, the distribution is made to a child or other dependent, the distribution is taxable to the plan participant. In the case of dividing an IRA, a QDRO is not needed, as a decree of divorce or other written instruments incident to divorce are satisfactory. In addition, the transfer will not be considered a taxable event to the participant or the recipient if properly structured. To avoid taxation as well as a potential 10% early withdrawal penalty for distributions made prior to age 59½, the spouse or former spouse must roll the funds into an IRA.

For the proper drafting of a QDRO, work with someone who has extensive experience and training in pension administration and the various regulations, such as an attorney or QDRO specialist. Keep in mind that not all attorneys have experience with qualified retirement plans. Many use a boiler plate type of document, known as a "model," which may not contain all the provisions critical to you and your specific situation. Since QDROs present unique problems for parties in domestic relations proceedings, be sure to do your homework. As with any legal work, determine up front what fees are involved. A QDRO can be simple, straightforward, and reasonably priced if it transfers interest in a defined-contribution plan, such as a profit-sharing or 401(k) plan. The QDRO for a defined-benefit plan (one that promises a future retirement benefit) can be challenging and often times prohibitively expensive. If the split of marital assets can be made without including a qualified retirement plan by using an IRA or other substantial investment assets, the procedure may prove to be more cost effective.

Remarriage Issues

As we've pointed out, for the majority of physicians, retirement plans represent their single largest investment holding. Upon retirement, qualified plan proceeds are typically rolled over into an individual retirement account (IRA), where distributions may begin at age 59½, and must begin by age 70½. Married individuals are allowed a unique tax savings strategy at the time of the IRA owners' death. If the spouse is named as the beneficiary of the IRA or qualified retirement plan, the spouse is allowed to roll over the proceeds into his or her own IRA and can continue to defer income taxes until age70 ½. Based on current tax law, only the spouse can roll over a retirement account and maintain the full tax benefits of the deferral.

While on the surface this may seem to be a "no-brainer," bear in mind that in the case of a second marriage, the new spouse, not the IRA owner's children, inherits the full value of the IRA account. Additionally, once the new spouse completes the rollover as the named beneficiary, he or she has the right to name the beneficiaries of the new IRA. With the original IRA owner deceased, the new owner has no legal obligation to name the stepchildren or any other family member as beneficiary. Therefore, it is possible that the original IRA owner's children will inherit nothing from this substantial asset.

Retirement plan issues are often brought to the forefront during prenuptial agreement discussions. However, based on current tax law, the new spouse's marital rights in qualified retirement plans cannot be waived in a prenuptial agreement. Those rights can be waived only by the new spouse after the marriage, so a prenuptial agreement is not applicable. If the IRA owner wishes to leave this asset to someone other than the spouse, such as adult children, he or she cannot defer distributions; thus any money will be received on a taxable basis at the beneficiaries' tax bracket.

CHAPTER 10

Risk Management

R isk management, in the context of a properly structured financial plan, focuses on the task of controlling that which cannot be controlled. Other than liability issues, it is important to protect against the two major hazards: death and disability. So much time and money are invested in so many different areas of insurance, from malpractice to health insurance to auto insurance and homeowners insurance. Unfortunately, very little time is spent protecting a physician's most important asset: the ability to earn income. Much of this lack of attention is due in part to the way life and disability insurance are usually purchased. Often times the insurance agent's job is to sell you the most amount of insurance that you will buy, with very little attention to the proper amount needed based on your specific goals and objectives. This is why it is common that purchases of life and disability insurance are rarely initiated by physicians; these are products that are sold to physicians. So, it is imperative for physicians to have a general understanding of how these unique insurance products can be used to meet the risk-protection needs of an overall financial plan.

Disability Insurance

Are you confident that your income is secure in the event of disability? The term *disability* can be defined in very different ways by the disability insurance company that is insuring the plan. Unfortunately, a great number of plans may provide benefits that are substantially less than you would expect.

Insurance carriers may have two definitions of disability. The first provides benefits if you are "unable to perform the important duties of your profession and specialty." On the surface this sounds great. This definition implies that if your occupation is limited to a recognized specialty, you will receive disability benefits, even if you can continue working in another aspect of the medical profession. But you must read the fine print, and in this case, read the sentence that may follow the first definition. Often times it may state: "After two years (or five years in some policies) you must not be able to perform the duties of any occupation." So, if you can work in any job at all, medically based or not, you will not be considered "disabled," and your benefit payments will be discontinued.

It should now be obvious to you why policies with this type of definition are less costly than those that provide monthly benefits for as long as you are unable to work in your chosen field or specialty; the insurance company is assuming less risk. But are these policies really less expensive? If you continually pay your premiums but are denied benefits due to the limited definition of "disability" in the policy, it can ultimately cost you and your family substantially more.

The definition dilemma can occur in all types of disability coverage—group and association, as well as individually owned polices. You should read the definition section of your current policy or any polices you may purchase in the future in order to guarantee that your definition of "disability" is the same as that of the insurance company providing the coverage.

Other than the specific disability definition used within the policy, there are other important features and provisions that need to be examined and compared. "Partial" or "residual" disability benefits may be paid in some policies when the specific disability impairment allows the insured to perform only a portion of his or her duties. This provision may also pay benefits in the event that the disability reduces the insured's income by a certain percentage amount, from the pre-disability levels. Another important provision deals with the ability to cancel and renew the policy. *Noncancelable* generally means that the insurance company cannot cancel the policy, change the policy provisions, or increase the premiums after the policy is issued if the premiums are made on time. *Guaranteed renewable* is similar in all aspects, except that the insurance company has the ability to increase the premium amount. Another provision, typically added as an additional cost rider, is the cost of living adjustment (COLA). This rider provides the benefit of an inflation-adjusted monthly benefit in the event of a disability claim.

Of course the more guaranteed provisions included in the policy, as part of the original policy or as a rider, the higher the premium cost. Fortunately there are a variety of ways to construct a policy so that you have greater control over the ultimate premium amount. The first is the monthly amount of the benefit. Unfortunately you are not able to replicate your income via a disability insurance policy. Generally you can purchase between 60% and 66% of your current income with a set dollar amount maximum, as the insurance companies do not want to give you an incentive to make a claim. Next is the waiting and elimination period, which controls how long you must be disabled prior to receiving benefits—similar to a deductible, but based on time, not dollars. Typical periods include 30, 60, 90, 180, and 360 days. Naturally, the longer the elimination period selected, the lower the premium payment amount will be. The key determinant here will be based on the individual's cash needs based on the amount of cash reserves being maintained and any other income sources available, such as a spouse's income, as well as the benefit period of any short-term disability program under which the physician may be covered. The other major cost factor is the benefit period. This decision will determine how long the benefits will be paid after the waiting or elimination period has been satisfied and the disability continues. Many companies offer lifetime benefits (the highest cost), benefits payable to age 65, benefits payable for five years, and shorter time frames of 24 months (the lowest cost). If you are a member of a small-group practice or a sole practitioner, you may also want to investigate the benefits of a disability business overhead expense policy. This unique type of insurance helps cover expenses such as staff salaries, office rent, malpractice insurance, and other expenses needed to keep your practice operating in the event of a physician's disability.

The following table is frequently used as a tool to identify the amount of income that would be required and available in the event of a disability:

Income Source	0–3 mos.	3–6 mos.	6–12 mos.	2–5 yrs.	5–10 yrs.	to age 65	Age 65 for life
Salary							
Disability Ins.							
Social Security							
Spouse's Salary							
Capital*							
Other							
TOTAL							

*Capital = depletion of investment and retirement assets through age 80 at 5% rate of return

Life Insurance

Many physicians recognize the benefits of an overall financial plan to meet their positive long-term objectives such as retirement planning, education planning, and generally meeting long-term savings goals and objectives. However, planning for the unexpected via life insurance is certainly less pleasant and also quite difficult. Understandably, no one likes to contemplate their own demise, and there are so many other important issues that seem to take precedence over the life insurance decision-making process. Whatever the reason, delaying this important part of the planning process can result in expensive and unintended tragic consequences. When planning for survivor income needs, you will need to consider the ongoing income needs of your survivors, as well as any immediate lump-sum needs. When considering future income needs, start by determining how much income will be needed for the surviving family. Is the desire to maintain the current standard of living of the family, or will the needs be less? Will the family be staying in the same home or moving to a different location? Will the surviving spouse be earning income, or do you want to provide sufficient income so the surviving spouse will not need to generate income? From a lump-sum standpoint, would you like to provide a lump-sum payment for the balance of your home's mortgage or other debt? With regard to college education funding, would you like to leave a lump-sum amount equal to the future college funding needs of your children? These decisions are difficult ones, but are important in quantifying life insurance needs. By completing this hypothetical thought process based on a worst case scenario—"what would I want for my family if I were to die today"—you will be in a much better forward planning situation. With this information, certain life insurance agents and financial planning professionals will be able to take your objectives and then combine various inflation factors and rate of return assumptions. By using insurance planning computer software programs, they can then determine the amount of life insurance needed to meet your objectives.

If you have sufficient investment assets to meet your survivor income objectives, there may not be a need for life insurance. People buy life insurance when they do not have sufficient assets to provide for their survivors. If you have sufficient assets, then you are considered to be self-insured. That is why a physician's greatest need for life insurance is often early in their career cycle, prior to having saved substantial investment assets. However, there are reasons other than purely survivor income needs to justify the purchase of life insurance. A life insurance policy can also create wealth that can be passed down to the next generation if that is the objective of the insured. This allows insured individuals to essentially spend their entire wealth during their lifetime with the peace of mind of knowing that they will still be leaving a substantial inheritance.

Other reasons for buying life insurance include funding retirement needs, creating liquidity as part of various estate-planning strategies, and using leveraged charitable gifting techniques. Many different types of life insurance products are available to meet the varying needs of physicians. Regardless of the reason you are buying life insurance, the key is to be certain that the specific life insurance product you purchase meets your unique objectives.

Once you have defined the qualitative and quantitative need for life insurance, you can begin to determine which specific product in the life insurance marketplace best meets your objectives. Begin by determining if your specific life insurance need is temporary or permanent. Temporary would imply that your needs are relatively short-term. A good example would be if you are trying to provide survivor income in the event you die prior to becoming self-insured. Once you have accumulated sufficient assets to provide for your surviving family, you may no longer need the life insurance for that particular exposure. Permanent insurance, on the other hand, is generally purchased with the understanding that the policy proceeds will be paid out at the time of your death, regardless when that occurs, even if you live beyond your expected mortality age.

Term Insurance

If your life insurance needs are temporary, then term insurance may be the most appropriate vehicle. Term insurance has no cash value or savings component attached to it. Quite simply, you pay your premium, and if you die during that policy year, the death benefit is paid to your beneficiary. Decreasing term insurance has a level premium, but a decreasing death benefit. It is generally used in conjunction with financial obligations that decrease over time, such as mortgages or other types of amortized loans. There are two types of term insurance that offer a level death benefit, but a differing premium paying structure. Annual renewable term insurance has a yearly increasing premium, which increases with the higher mortality cost associated with being a year older, and a year closer to your expected mortality age. It is primarily used for financial obligations that remain constant for a relatively short period of time. Level premium term insurance, on the other hand, offers a level premium payment amount over a fixed number of years, typically 5, 10, 15, or 20 years. This would be appropriate for needs that are finite in length, such as ensuring coverage until a young child has completed college, becoming self-insured through an increased net worth, or reaching retirement age with sufficient retirement income to meet your needs.

There are other differences that will be discovered when term policies are compared. The major areas impacting premium rates are policy provisions dealing with renewability and convertibility. Typically, renewable policies allow the policyholder the option of continuing term coverage after the stated period of time has expired. While the renewal will be at a higher premium rate than during the defined time period, new medical underwriting is not required. If during the term period you become ill in a manner that would deem you to be either uninsurable or insurable but with an added-on rating that would substantially increase premiums, you would at least have the option of continuing coverage with your current term carrier. A convertible policy, on the other hand, provides the insured with the option to convert the term policy to a permanent policy at some time in the future. Once again, this may be accomplished without proof of insurability or medical underwriting. Some term carriers will provide both renewable as well as convertible policy provisions with their contracts.

Other provisions, known as riders, can be added to certain policies for an additional cost. The waiver of premium rider allows you to stop making premium payments if you become disabled and are unable to work and earn an income. The accidental death rider obligates the insurance company to pay out to your beneficiary double or, in some cases, triple the stated death benefit if the insured dies in an accident. A newer rider that is starting to get a lot of attention is the accelerated death benefit. You may be able to receive a portion of your own death benefit while you are alive in the event that you have a major medical condition that is expected to lead to death within a short period of time. This rider will provide needed funds immediately to help with medical bills or other support issues during a terminal illness.

Permanent Insurance

Permanent insurance needs are met through varying types of whole life and universal life insurance policies designed to stay in force throughout one's lifetime. Unlike term insurance where premiums generally increase as the insured ages, most permanent life insurance premiums remain level. These policies combine the death benefit protection of term insurance with a savings element known as cash value. Life insurance cash values grow on a tax-deferred basis, thus creating a supplemental tax-advantaged savings vehicle. Unlike other tax-deferred vehicles such as IRAs, retirement plans, and annuities, life insurance cash values are not subject to the minimum penalty free withdrawal age of 59½. In addition, and of particular interest to physicians, is the fact that, in many states, life insurance cash values and the death benefits (assuming there is a named beneficiary) are shielded from creditors, creating an effective asset-protection strategy. The accumulated cash values form a reserve that enables the insurer to pay a policy's full death benefit while keeping premiums level. Depending on the specific life insurance company, cash values of permanent life insurance policies may be withdrawn or borrowed over the life of the policy. Cash-value loans or withdrawals can be used to supplement retirement income, fund college education costs, or for any other reason without restriction.

The main attribute of whole life insurance is the inherent guarantee that as long as premium payments are paid in a timely manner, the policy will remain in force regardless of changes in the insured's health.

Universal life insurance policies differ from whole life policies by separating the various components of the policy, such as cash value, mortality costs, and other expenses. This allows the insurance company to build a higher level of flexibility into the contract, which in turn provides the policyholder with the ability to make adjustments in response to changing needs and circumstances. This flexibility can include the amount and frequency of future premium payments, as well as the ability to reduce the amount of the death benefit as one's net worth increases.

Whether it is a traditional whole life or universal life insurance policy, it is important to understand the variables that impact the growth of your cash value over time. Most permanent insurance cash-value increases are due to either the dividend-paying ability of the insurance company (based on the company's earnings and profitability) or through the insurance company's own investment returns expressed as an interest rate percentage (interest rate sensitive insurance). In both cases, insurance companies offer a guaranteed minimum amount, or interest rate percentage, that they will credit to the policy. With interest rate sensitive policies, which are the most common type used in universal life, the insurance company invests their cash assets in relatively conservative investment vehicles such as government and high-grade corporate bonds, although they may also diversify into equities and real estate. The results of their investment strategy are passed to their policyholders via cash value additions at a specific interest rate.

Variable life insurance, whether it's a whole or universal life policy, actually allows the policyholder the ability to control the growth of his or her cash-value account. The policyholder can allocate a portion of each premium payment to one or more investment sub-accounts or separate investment options, based on their specific risk tolerance and long-term growth objective. Deductions for expenses and mortality charges are taken by the insurance company prior to the allocation to the specific sub-accounts. Most variable life policies offer the policyholder a wide range of investment options, including various stock and bond mutual funds. Depending on the specific insurance company, options may include index funds, real estate funds, foreign stock funds, small company, and other types of sector funds. Also included may be a fixed account option in which the insurer guarantees a fixed rate of return.

It is important to keep in mind that with most cash value life insurance policies, there may be substantial surrender charges associated with canceling or terminating the policy. These charges are generally highest in the early years of a policy and usually decline over time, typically from 7 to 15 years, depending on the specific insurance company. If your needs have changed since you purchased the policy, you do have options other than just surrendering the policy. Permanent insurance options may also include the ability to suspend premium payments while maintaining some level of coverage on a reduced basis. Based on the amount of cash value within the policy, life insurance illustrations can be prepared to determine the feasibility of actually lowering the face amount of the death benefit, and thus lowering the mortality cost within the contract.

This is accomplished by determining the amount of reduced benefit that can be supported by the current level of cash values. In this manner, you may still be able to take a partial withdrawal or loan against the policy, now or in the future, but avoid full surrender, thus eliminating any insurance company imposed surrender charges, and any potential income tax liability. If the desire is not to reduce the amount of the death benefit, then another option to explore is the feasibility of converting the permanent policy to a paid-up term insurance policy. Here, an analysis is completed that will determine how long the term coverage will remain in force, based on the mortality cost of the coverage. If this strategy is implemented, the cash value is used to pay for the paid-up term coverage, thus eliminating any future ability to access cash values in the future.

You can, however, access cash values without terminating a policy via cash-value withdrawals or through loans. Policy cash value loans allow the policyholder to borrow a portion of their cash-value account. The rate charged by the insurance company is typically lower than current market loan rates. The loan may not have to be repaid, but if there is an outstanding policy loan, the company will reduce the death benefit if the insured dies before the loan is repaid.

Long-Term Care Insurance

The aging of America has forced many senior citizens and their families to explore the myriad housing options available today. When faced with the difficult prospect of changing one's normal style of living, the major factors to consider are age, interests, finances, and of course, health issues and concerns. Elderly housing choices available include independent living, assisted living, nursing homes, continuing care communities, and staying at home.

Independent living housing is an attractive option for active seniors who can take care of themselves and prefer a social versus medical setting. The facility typically can accommodate a broad range of lifestyles. Often included are in-house activities and transportation to shopping and other outside events. Many also have dining rooms that serve daily meals, though most independent living facilities include a full kitchen within the resident's apartment or living unit.

Residents can enjoy daily activities without worrying about typical maintenance and repairs of individual home ownership. If ongoing medical care becomes a need, options include hiring a private aide (at the residents own cost) or moving to an assisted living or nursing home facility.

Assisted living facilities essentially are communities designed for seniors who have some level of difficulty living and managing on their own. They provide a moderate level of personal care, including assistance with bathing and administering medications. Individual living units, which are usually rented on a monthly basis, are often of the efficiency style, with very limited kitchens or no cooking facilities at all. Additional care may be available to residents at an additional cost. The assisted living option is a good choice for the elderly who can manage with some limited help from on-staff aides. Typically, assisted living facilities are less expensive but more comfortable than nursing homes.

Nursing homes offer a much more intense level of medical care and attention, usually under the supervision of a medical doctor. With so many other elderly care options available today, nursing homes have become geared toward dementia patients, limited rehabilitation stays, or patients near the end of their lives. Nursing homes can provide near-hospital-quality medical care for chronic illnesses, but at a lower cost. As opposed to monthly fees, nursing homes charge on a daily basis. Private rooms may be cost-prohibitive and difficult to find.

Continuing care communities, also known as life care communities, attempt to provide facilities for all stages of aging within the same housing complex, and include independent and assisted living, as well as nursing and rehabilitative care. Costs include substantial entry fees plus monthly payments. The major advantage here is the ease of movement between levels of care as the resident's condition changes. From a social standpoint, seniors may still maintain contact with friends as they move within the community.

Staying at home, with its familiar surroundings and proximity to friends and neighbors, remains the top choice for many seniors. By avoiding change, seniors can maintain an important sense of independence. Hired care can be tailored to specific situations, and the aides provide a more personal one-on-one care environment. The difficulty comes with transportation issues relative to shopping and other errands, as well as the relatively high level of turnover of home health aides.

WOMEN: A SPECIAL NEED FOR LONG-TERM CARE

More than any other socioeconomic group, women are disproportionately affected by long-term care, mainly because women live longer than men and thus are more likely to develop the functional ailments that require long-term care services. According to the U.S. Census Bureau, the average woman can expect to live as much as seven years longer than her male counterpart, all the while increasing her demand for vital long-term health care that ranges from help with day-to-day-activities to sophisticated therapy such as stroke rehabilitation.

For centuries, women have served as the primary caregivers of long-term health care. Today, women still bear the main responsibility of caring for their parents or loved ones when they need attention. The emotional strain and anguish that often arises when daughters, granddaughters, sisters, and nieces are faced with such decisions can have devastating effects, not just on the emotional health of the caregiver, but also on her financial well-being and productivity.

Not only are women viewed as caregivers, they also are more likely to require long-term care for themselves. The Health Care Finance Administration reports that three out of four nursing home facility residents are women. On average, married women live 15 years after the death of their husbands and therefore lack the spousal help at home that can prevent or delay the need for long-term health care. Along with the trauma of outliving one's spouse is the fear of outliving one's savings to meet future needs.

UNDERSTANDING POLICIES

The rising cost of nursing home care, combined with shrinking government assistance, has created the need to plan well in advance for long-term care expenses. With an aging population and advances in health care, which are improving mortality rates, it is estimated that 40% of Americans will require nursing home care at some point in their lives. Hence, it is critical to address long-term care issues in coordination with other risk management issues, as well as with your retirement and estate-planning strategies.

When shopping for long-term care insurance, you will find similarities between this exercise and how you compared different long-term disability policies. As with disability coverage, the benefits covered as well as the dollar limitations dictate the pricing of the policy. Begin by determining what levels of care you would like to insure against. Definitions within the policies may include the following:

1. *Skilled Care:* Physician-ordered daily nursing and possibly rehabilitation care under the supervision of licensed skilled registered nurses and other skilled medical personnel.

2. *Intermediate Care:* Same skilled personnel as above, except care is required only occasionally, not daily.

3. *Custodial Care:* Based on doctor's orders, assistance may be covered within the policy for help with daily activities such as bathing, eating, dressing, mobility issues, etc. The assistance generally does not need to be provided by skilled medical personnel.

Certain policies will also cover home health care coverage, either as part of the policy or as an added-on rider. Other determinants of premium pricing include: maximum allowable daily dollar limitations, inflation protection, guaranteed renewability, and a waiver of premium based on a specified number of days spent in a nursing home.

The funding of long-term care expenses, which include the cost of a nursing home as well as other care expenses, can come from personal savings and investments, retirement plan benefits, or from long-term care insurance. Long-term care insurance has become an attractive option due to tax incentives. The Health Insurance Portability and Accountability Act (HIPAA) allows some taxpayers to deduct (subject to limitations) long-term care insurance premiums and certain expenses associated with long-term care.

Qualifying medical expenses are deductible only if they exceed 7.5% of the taxpayer's adjusted gross income. Under prior law, it was very unclear if nonmedical nursing home costs were subject to the deduction. HIPAA clearly states that deductible medical expenses will include the cost of "qualified long-term care services." This definition by law includes "necessary diagnostic, preventive, therapeutic, curing, treatment, mitigating, rehabilitative services, and maintenance or personal care services."

The tax law also provides advantages when you assist others financially, such as parents, grandparents, or others who require nursing home care. In these situations, tax deductions are available to the payer as opposed to the recipient. As an example, perhaps your parent has limited taxable income, which translates into lower tax rates, thus making the deduction less advantageous. If you are in a higher bracket, you can directly pay the nursing home expenses. When providing more than 50% of their support, you can claim the parent as a dependent and be able to deduct the long-term care expenses to the extent they exceed 7.5% of your adjusted gross income.

In many situations, a parent may have substantial assets but relatively low income. The parent can gift assets to you, up to the annual $14,000 exclusion amount, which you can then use for their support while obtaining the deduction on your return. This gifting approach can be used to lower the value of the parent's estate, thus reducing their ultimate estate tax liability.

CHAPTER 11

Asset Protection

We live in a litigious society. Never before has there been such a propensity to bring legal actions against our fellow citizens. This situation is exasperated for members of any profession, and is especially intense for physicians. Given this environment, it makes sense to protect the assets you have accumulated during your professional life from frivolous actions by disgruntled employees, problem patients, and those who believe they have discovered a process for creating wealth at your expense.

In this chapter, we will examine our current litigious environment and identify commonly held and usually mistaken beliefs regarding asset-protection strategies. In addition, we will explore many of the common techniques that have been used to protect assets. Finally, we will conclude with a few case studies that will help enhance your understanding.

Background

More than 42% of physicians have been sued over the course of their careers. Before reaching the age of 40, more than half of obstetricians/gynecologists have already been sued. Ninety percent of general surgeons age 55 and over have been sued. (Source: American Medical Association survey, 2010, covering years 2007-2008).

If the jury finds for the physician, the plaintiff receives no compensation. However, if the jury finds for the plaintiff, the verdict may be separated into economic damages, noneconomic damages, and, rarely, punitive damages.

Economic damages, sometimes called special damages, can include lost wages and other income, medical care, custodial care, lost earnings, lost earning capacity, and funeral expenses if the injury resulted in death. Noneconomic damages can include awards for physical pain and suffering, mental distress, permanent impairment or loss of function, disfigurement, loss of the ability to enjoy life's pleasures, loss of consortium, and death. Punitive damages are awarded if the jury determines that the defendant's conduct was malicious, grossly negligent, or in total disregard of the patient's well-being, such as being under the influence of drugs or alcohol. Most insurance policies specifically exclude payment of punitive damages and the insured is usually personally liable for that award.

Fewer than 8% of medical malpractice cases ever reach a jury. About two-thirds of claims are dropped, dismissed, or withdrawn, while about 27% are settled. Physicians prevail in 80%–90% of cases that reach the trial stage. (Medscape.com)

In the past, malpractice coverage was viewed as the only necessary shield to protect assets. However, malpractice premiums can be a substantial expense for physicians. There are a number of reasons:

1. *Increased payments to plaintiffs.* Reported payments to plaintiffs in medical practice lawsuits have increased nearly 69% during the past decade, although the number of claims submitted to the National Practitioner Data Bank has remained about the same.

2. *Court settlements in medical malpractice cases.* Settlement amounts have seen a wide variance over recent years. The median malpractice jury award (made to plaintiffs) in 1996 was $473,000; in 2002 just over $1.01 million (*Wall Street Journal*, Thursday April 1, 2004). More recently median awards were $200,000 for settled claims and $375,000 for tried claims, according to an American Medical Association Survey that covered the years 2007–2008. The National Practitioner Data Bank, in their 2006 Annual Report (http://www.npdb-hipdb.hrsa.gov/resources/reports/2006NPDBAnnualReport.pdf) indicates that

the median medical malpractice award was $175,000 in 2006. Data from the Department of Justice's Bureau of Justice Statistics (BJS) paints a similar picture. BJS researchers examined medical malpractice insurance claims in select states and found median awards ranging from $107,000 in Missouri to $195,000 in Texas. As reported in their publication, Medical Negligence: The Role of America's Civil Justice System in Protecting Patients' Rights, between 5.5% (Florida) and 10.6% (Texas) of insurance payouts were for $1 million or more (http://www.justice.org/resources/ Medical_Negligence_Primer.pdf.) Of course, the relatively small percentage of payouts exceeding $1 million provides little comfort if you are the physician involved in the case!

3. *Loss of discounts.* Many premiums increased when insurance companies changed the criteria used to offer discounts, such as the number of years a physician has to go without a claim.

4. *Depletion of cash reserves of insurance companies.* Premiums in past years may have been kept low as a result of competition. In addition, insurance companies may have miscalculated the money needed to pay future claims. Thus, available cash reserves have been depleted by the higher claim costs. This issue is compounded by the loss of investment income that many insurance companies received in the past.

5. *Bankruptcy or voluntary withdrawal of insurance companies.* Occasionally, the economic realities force a company to close its doors permanently. Others attempt to manage their business by refusing to offer policies for certain specialties or geographical areas.

6. *Reinsurance company impact.* The aftermath of the 9/11 attacks on the World Trade Center placed a strain on the resources and reserves of these companies, who pass their costs on to the insurance carrier who issues the policy.

It is interesting to note that while malpractice premiums have increased rapidly, most physicians "win" the malpractice case brought against them. In their 2006 *New England Journal of Medicine* article, "Claims, Errors, and Compensation Payments in Medical Malpractice Litigation," Studdert, Mello, Gawande, and colleagues reported that "56% of the claims received compensation, at an average of

$485,348 (median, $206,400) per paid claim. Fifteen percent of the claims were decided by trial verdict. The awards in verdicts for the plaintiff on average were nearly twice the size of payments made outside of court ($799,365 vs. $462,099). However, plaintiffs rarely won damages at trial, prevailing in only 21% of verdicts as compared with 61% of claims resolved out of court. Administrative (or overhead) costs associated with defending the claims averaged $52,521 per claim, with the mean administrative costs for claims that were resolved by trial ($112,968) nearly three times those for claims resolved out of court ($42,015)" (page 2026).

What can physicians do? Is there relief from Congress? It appears unlikely. In April 2004, Congress rejected an attempt to cap non-economic damages at $250,000 in medical malpractice lawsuits involving emergency physicians and obstetrician-gynecologists. This was the third bill brought forward in the session of Congress by Republican lawmakers. Yet a slowly increasing number of states have passed such limits. Many physicians are disappointed that the latest round of health care legislation contains no meaningful attempt to address the malpractice issue.

Can you change your practice? Some physicians abandon high-risk procedures or specialties. Others may relocate to states that provide more physician-friendly legal environments. Others maintain their activities, but adopt more aggressive tactics to fend off possible lawsuits. Patients are being asked to sign forms and waivers promising not to sue for frivolous reasons, or in some cases for any reason whatsoever. These types of waivers have yet to be tested in court. In addition, some doctors are turning to countersuits when a suit is thrown out of court as frivolous.

Some consider "going bare" and eliminate malpractice coverage altogether. Before acting on this alternative, consider if this option is legal in your state, if you could maintain hospital privileges, or if you could remain on health plan panels. Of course, perhaps the biggest concern is whether you will be able to sleep at night knowing that you do not have a safety net of insurance coverage.

Given these relatively unattractive alternatives, it is obvious that every physician should be exploring strategies that can protect the assets they have accumulated.

General Concepts

A key element of asset protection is making access to your assets difficult, thus restricting liquidity. Your goal should not be to simply hide assets. Many plaintiff's attorneys operate under a "Hide and I'll find!" procedure. By making liquidity difficult, you frustrate the intent of the plaintiff who is interested in receiving a substantial windfall.

Another key element of asset protection is awareness of fraudulent transfers. Because most asset-protection planning involves a transfer of assets, it is important to understand the applicable fraudulent transfer laws as defined by the Uniform Fraudulent Transfer Act or the Uniform Fraudulent Conveyance Act. In general, the fraudulent transfer laws prevent transactions made with intent to defraud a particular creditor. If made with the intent to hinder a creditor, a transfer is fraudulent regardless of whether it also may have been motivated by nonfraudulent intentions. By failing to comply with the governing fraudulent transfer laws, an asset-protection planning transfer will be void and the individual making the transfer (and possibly his or her attorney or other advisors) may be exposed to civil and possibly criminal liability. In light of this potential liability, most professionals are willing to advise their clients about asset protection only if they are confident that neither a current claim nor a legitimate expectation of a future claim exists.

There are possible solutions for an individual who is faced with existing claims or creditors. A determining factor for a court in ascertaining whether a transfer was made with the intent to defraud a particular creditor is the solvency of the debtor. If the debtor became insolvent as a result of the transfer in question, there is a greater likelihood that transfer will be void. Thus, in instances where individuals have an existing creditor or claim, asset-protection plans often are structured for the benefit of protection against future creditors while ensuring the debtor remains solvent with regards to his or her current creditors.

Are You Worth It?

When we speak with a group of physicians, we usually ask what they believe is the goal of a plaintiff's attorney. Without exception, the response is, "All the money, as soon as possible!" Since it is most common for a plaintiff's attorney to work on a contingency basis (in which the attorney's fee is derived as a portion of the total settlement) the attorney will often apply a simple two-part test when considering taking a case: "What is the likelihood of obtaining a quick settlement or successful judgment?" and "Are there sufficient assets from insurance or otherwise available to satisfy the judgment?"

In considering the second aspect of this test, you should realize that before you are sued, somebody is going analyze your financial condition to see if you are worth the effort. Your assets and income will be investigated. County records can be checked to determine the amount of real estate you own, the date purchased, and approximate values of liabilities applied to the property. Once the lawsuit is started, additional discovery can take place to identify the history of your assets as it relates to amounts, dates transferred, and current ownership status. Not much privacy is available in these proceedings.

Common Misconceptions

It is helpful to identify the things you should not believe, tolerate, or implement when it comes to effective asset-protection strategies. By clearing up these misconceptions you will be ready to make the right choices for your plan.

1. *A revocable living trust protects assets.* A living trust can be an excellent estate-planning tool for many. However, a living trust does not provide you with any asset protection during your life. Because these trusts can be altered at any time during the life of the person who created them, the assets in the trust can be successfully attached in a lawsuit. Remember, something that is good for estate planning may not be worth much when it comes to asset protection.

2. *Malpractice insurance will pay for the judgment, thus, personal assets will not be touched.* Malpractice insurance can make sense. However, more and more judgment amounts exceed policy limits. Once that limit is exceeded, you are at risk!

3. *Assets can be safely transferred to children or others; once the case is closed the assets will be transferred back.* Remember the

concept of fraud. A transfer made once you are aware of the possibility of a lawsuit can be considered a fraudulent transfer. No protection there. In addition, even if you did transfer assets to children, those assets would then be at risk to any of the possible problems experienced by the children. It does not make sense to expose your assets to another's risks.

4. *Assets can be transferred to a spouse who does not have the same risk of being sued.* While true in general, many who follow this approach fail to make the necessary steps to complete these transfers so that a premature death of the spouse to whom the assets were transferred does not result in the loss of the protection that was available. In addition, counts may declare that transfers made to a spouse resulted in a "constructive trust" where your actions are deemed to have created (unintentionally) a trust for your own benefit, fully available to satisfy a judgment against you.

5. *A corporate structure will protect assets; thus, if your practice is organized as a corporation, your assets are safe.* A professional corporation will not protect you from your professional liability or from the liability you have in supervising employees in delivering heath care. In addition, any assets of the corporation are at risk. At best, the corporate structure may provide protection of the actions of your staff that are unrelated to the delivery of care.

Mistakes to Avoid

As a final comment on this topic: make certain you also avoid a couple of forms of ownership that generally create serious and long-lasting problems.

First, do as much as possible not to own any *non-exempt* assets in your own name. The key is the non-exempt aspect of the assets, which we will cover in much more detail. For now, remember that assets in your own name are easy pickings for the plaintiff's attorney.

Closely related is the ownership arrangement of jointly titled with rights of survivorship. Commonly abbreviated as JTWROS, this form of ownership provides an easy way to transfer ownership in the event of the death of one of the joint owners since joint property avoids the probate process at the death of a joint owner. However, in most states that recognize JTWROS, the property can be the subject of a lawsuit if *either* joint owner becomes involved in a lawsuit.

Finally, do as much as possible to avoid operating a business as a sole proprietor or general partnership. Operating a business as a sole proprietor occurs whenever an individual prefers not to go through the efforts of creating a corporation or other more formal business entity. Similarly, a general partnership exists when more than one person operates a business without going through the effort of organizing a corporation or other more formal business entity. The problem with these types of business arrangements is that you will have total responsibility for the debts of the business. Even worse in the general partnership setting, you will be liable for the debts of the entire partnership, not just for the activities that they were individually involved.

Positive Strategies to Consider

Throughout this chapter, we will refer to the high-risk or at-risk individual. This term refers to the individual who would most likely be the subject of a legal proceeding. For example, in the case of a married couple where the wife is a physician and the husband an artist, the wife would be considered to be the at-risk individual because of her professional activities.

INSURANCE

Properly used, insurance should play an important part of the financial and asset-protection plan for most physicians. We rarely meet a physician who likes to buy insurance of any kind, yet all physicians are interested in obtaining the benefits provided by appropriate insurance coverage. We will discuss additional insurance products later in this chapter. At this point, let's focus on the types of benefits provided by the general category of property and casualty insurance.

Property and casualty (P&C) is the term commonly used to describe insurance designed to protect an individual from loss or damage to the physical assets he or she owns. For example, a fire may seriously damage or even completely destroy a home. Without adequate homeowner's insurance to provide the funds to repair or rebuild, such a loss could be a financial disaster. Homeowner's policies can also provide protection for the home's contents, such as furniture, appliances, and other personal belongings. Many P&C policies also provide liability protection. For example, the owner of an automobile who causes an accident may be required by a court (be found liable) to pay others for repair of property damage, medical expenses, lost wages, or pain and suffering. The dollar amounts of such court decisions can be enormous.

As with any basic strategy, there are a number of limitations to the benefits of P&C coverage. These limitations should be understood in order to avoid placing too much reliance on this coverage. First, each policy has exclusions. Exclusions are the items or events that are not covered by the policy. Commonly referred to as the fine print of a policy, they deserve careful understanding. The second limitation is the limits of the policy. While coverage may be provided for certain items or events, the amount of coverage that is provided may be insufficient for the risk at hand. For example, home owner's coverage may be insufficient based on the appreciated value of the home. The third limitation could be the insurance company itself. Some companies may go out of business, rendering you in a position where no coverage is available. Many physicians have experienced this with the volatile aspects of the malpractice insurance marketplace.

There are numerous examples of P&C insurance such as automobile insurance, homeowners insurance, professional liability insurance, malpractice insurance, product liability insurance, and renter's insurance. Umbrella liability insurance is also a type of P&C coverage. Umbrella liability insurance acts as excess or catastrophic protection to the basic liability protection offered with most other P&C policies. The liability coverage offered by an umbrella policy begins where the coverage in a basic policy ends and, in some instances, offers broader protection. It usually makes sense to add this relatively inexpensive policy to your insurance portfolio.

GIFTS

Gifts of property to family members have long been part of an asset protection or estate plan. An outright gift to a spouse or family member not engaged in a high-risk profession has the advantage of removing the asset from claims of future creditors. In addition, a gift has the estate-planning advantage of removing assets from the transferor's taxable estate.

Any gifting program must consider gift tax consequences and maximize use of the exemptions available. Currently, an individual can gift up to $14,000 per year ($26,000 with the spouse's consent) to as many individuals as they like and avoid gift taxes. In addition, an individual can make a one-time total gift up to $5,120,000 and avoid gift taxation. A gift of this amount will reduce the amount that is available to pass free of estate taxation. Please see the Estate Planning chapter for a more thorough discussion of the gifting strategy.

Tenancy by the Entirety

As discussed, property held in joint tenancy with right of survivorship provides no asset protection. In fact, joint tenancy with right of survivorship exposes the property to the creditors of each joint tenant. Depending on your state of residence, there are several ways to hold the family domicile: joint tenants in common, land trust, solo (single) ownership, and tenancy by the entireties. Each of these methods has limitations and advantages. In most states, joint tenancy is the most common form of property ownership for married couples and generally, if no other form of ownership is specified, is the default method of ownership. In most states, there is another tenancy that deserves examination: tenancy by the entirety.

Tenancy by the entirety is a specific form of joint tenancy that can exist only between a husband and wife. Tenancy by the entirety is a popular, cost-effective form of ownership that often can protect a family's most valuable asset. Like joint tenancy with right of survivorship, upon the death of one spouse the entire property held in tenancy by the entirety will pass to the surviving spouse. However, in states that recognize tenancy by the entirety, the property is treated as being owned by the marriage and, therefore, the law prohibits a creditor of one spouse from executing upon property held in tenancy by the entirety to satisfy a judgment. In some states tenancy by the entirety can apply only to real estate or a primary residence; other states recognize tenancy by the entirety for real estate and personal property.

In states that recognize tenancy by the entirety for real estate only, a common strategy is to minimize any mortgage in an effort to maximize the equity of the protected asset. There is no gift tax consequence upon creation of a tenancy by the entirety if both spouses are U.S. citizens because of the unlimited marital deduction allowing tax-free transfers between spouses.

Tenancy by the entirety is routinely employed when both spouses are at risk of personal liability as a result of their professions. However, it is important to note the potential temporary nature of tenancy by the entirety. For example, the death of one spouse will immediately expose the property to the creditors of the surviving spouse. In instances where only one spouse is at risk, married individuals may transfer real estate and other assets to the spouse not at risk. Through the creation of a particular type of marital trust, the spouse's estate plan can provide for the residence to pass to a trust that will, in large part, protect the asset from the survivor's creditors. Divorce destroys tenancy by the entirety. The property reverts to tenancy in common, and the creditors of the debtor spouse can now reach the share of the property owned by the debtor.

The death of a spouse will result in a similar result, with the creditors of the surviving spouse being able to reach the property. This loss of protection from the creditors stems from the fact that the foundation of tenancy by the entirety is a valid marriage. Therefore, whatever destroys a valid marriage will destroy the tenancy by the entirety. Probate will be avoided with tenancy by the entirety.

The interest will automatically vest in the surviving spouse by rule of law outside of the probate court. The tenancy by the entirety is lost by the death and the surviving spouse will face probate for the properties previously held in tenancy by the entirety.

Personal bankruptcy results in three possible outcomes depending on your location.[1] First, the courts have decided that properties

---

1. States that recognize tenancy by the entirety include: Alaska, Arkansas, District of Columbia, Florida, Illinois, Indiana, Maryland, Massachusetts, Michigan, Missouri, New York, North Carolina, Pennsylvania and Virginia. New Hampshire does

held in tenancy by the entirety are not included in the bankruptcy estate.[2] Second, the courts concluded "that a debtor's interest is part of the estate but is exempt from the reach of all creditors."[3] Third, a majority of the courts have determined that a debtor's interest in the property passes over to the trustee and then can meet the claims of joint creditors. This decision flows from the idea that "it is entirety, while not transferable by either spouse acting individually, is nonetheless an interest and will be made part of the estate."[4]

Are there pitfalls? The document transferring the domicile to tenancy must be constructed properly. In a recent Illinois case, *Travelers Indemnity Company v. Engel, 81 F3d 711*, tenancy by the entirety failed because the document did not explicitly state the property was transferred by the Engels as "husband and wife." These are magic words that must be in the deed if it is to be a valid transfer.

Fraudulent conveyance law should not be forgotten. Generally, if one transfers property after the institution of a lawsuit, the property transfer will fail because it was made to beat the creditor out of his rightful share of the estate. A case on point is *United States of America v. Amos D. Jr. & Norma L. Davenport*. The Davenports, residents of Illinois, failed to pay U.S. income tax from 1980 to 1987 and owed the IRS a large amount of money. They transferred their domicile to tenancy by the entirety after the IRS had filed suit. The court said that the tenancy by the entirety failed because it was made after the suit started and the defendants knew that the IRS was assessing their domicile.

---

not recognize tenancy by the entirety, but rather joint tenancy with survivorship rights which is almost the same as tenancy by the entirety. Community property States such as, Arizona, California, Idaho, Louisiana, Nevada, New Mexico, Texas, Washington, and Wisconsin, do not recognize tenancy by the entireties. Community property states include some 80 million people.

2. 121 Bankr. 356 (Bankr. W.D.Mo. 1990) *cited in* Paul Wilson, "Fresh Start" or Head Start": *Missouri Courts Rethink the Role of Tenancy by the Entireties in Bankruptcy*, Mo. L. Rev. 817, 823 v.56 (1991) [hereinafter cited as Wilson].

3. 679 F2d 316, 312-22 (3rd Cir. 1982) supra 3. In 1985 the Court of Appeals for the Sixth Circuit adopted the reasoning of the *Napotnik* decision in *Liberty State Bank & Trust v. Grosslight*, 757 F2d 773, 776-77 (6th Cir. 1985).

4. supra 3 *id.*, 817, 825 v. 56 (1991).

DEBT SHIELDS

Besides the form of ownership, additional protection can be available by simply obtaining a mortgage against current home equity. The equity proceeds are then invested in an asset-protected manner, such as in exempt assets (see below) or as interests in family limited partnerships or limited liability companies. Before deciding to implement this strategy it is important to balance the cost of the anticipated interest expense against the expected earnings of the investment and the protection provided to the situation.

BANKRUPTCY EXEMPTIONS

An important goal of an individual's asset-protection planning is to maximize the equity in assets that are exempt from the bankruptcy estate. These exemptions are crucial because the threat of filing for bankruptcy by a debtor who owns substantial exempt assets may result in successful settlements without the need to file. Federal and state laws protect a wide variety of exemptions that are summarized below:

1. *Homestead.* Almost every state provides a debtor with a homestead exemption. Florida and Texas have unlimited homestead exemptions whereas the federal bankruptcy homestead exemption is limited to $21,625 (or $43,250 if filing jointly). If a state has a small homestead exemption, asset-protection planning should focus on whether tenancy by the entirety or a transfer to a nonworking spouse (either outright or in trust) is an option. Remember, such a transfer is best if coordinated with appropriate estate planning.

2. *Retirement Plans.* The most important of the retirement plan exemptions is the federal exempt status granted to retirement plans that are qualified under the Employee Retirement Income Security Act (ERISA), a body of federal law governing IRS-qualified retirement plans. Such plans include pension plans, defined-benefit and defined-contribution plans, profit-sharing plans, and 401K plans. In 1992, the Supreme Court provided conclusive protection for plans governed by ERISA and further provided that the federal law protecting these plans will prevail regardless of state law.

This protection is not absolute in all situations. The protection has been denied in at least one situation to a plan sponsored by a business where the plan covered only the owners and their spouses. It is therefore important to include other employees in such a plan. In addition, ERISA specifically provides an exception to the protective provisions in the case of qualified domestic orders obtained in connection with child support obligations, alimony payments, or marital rights. In many states, once an individual reaches an age at which he or she is forced to receive distributions from a qualified plan, any amounts distributed lose their exempt status. However, some states extend a level of protection to distributions from retirement plans.

3. *Individual Retirement Accounts.* Individual retirement accounts (IRAs) are established under the Internal Revenue Code and are not subject to ERISA. Until recently, their level of protection varied from state to state; however, the U.S. Supreme Court recently held that IRA accounts are exempt from a bankruptcy estate, thus providing these accounts with the same protection afforded ERISA plans (*Rousey et ux. v. Jacoway, 544 U.S. (2005)*).

4. *Roth IRAs.* At this time, it is unclear whether the protection provided to IRA accounts in the U.S. Supreme Court decision of *Rousey et ux. v. Jacoway* will be provided to Roth IRA accounts. Such regulations can vary from state to state. It is important to be aware of the protection provided in your current state and any state to which you may move during retirement. Individuals who have established a Roth IRA should be cautioned that a state exemption protecting traditional IRAs would not necessarily extend to a Roth IRA. This is because a different Internal Revenue Code section governs Roth IRAs and many statutes providing protection for traditional IRAs refer to plans under Section 408 of the Internal Revenue Code.

5. *Nonqualified Retirement Plans/Deferred Compensation Plans.* Because a nonqualified plan is not afforded ERISA's federal protection, a review of the governing state law is necessary. Once again, it is important to be aware of the protection provided in your current state and any state to which you may move during retirement.

6. *Annuity Contracts.* In recent years, annuity products have become increasingly popular for retirement planning. Exemptions for annuity contracts are available in many states and provide a valuable planning opportunity because a similar investment held outside of an annuity product (i.e., in an individual's name or jointly with a spouse) may be subject to creditor attachment. Florida exempts all annuity contract proceeds, whereas protection in other states depends on whether the named beneficiary is the debtor's spouse or dependents. The federal exemption extends only to an annuity contract to the extent reasonably necessary for the support of the debtor and dependents.

7. *Life Insurance Policies.* Exemptions for a debtor's interest in the cash value of a life insurance policy also allow an individual to accumulate investments in a product that is shielded from creditors. In some states, the protection also extends to the policy proceeds upon the death of the debtor. The federal exemption applies to all of the debtor's unmatured policies and the debtor/insured can continue to make premium payments on those polices without having the payments subject to the bankruptcy estate.

Like the protections for annuities, some state exemptions allow for protection of the entire cash surrender value of a life insurance policy and some limit that protection to when a dependent or spouse is named the beneficiary. In addition, life insurance proceeds payable to a spouse or dependent are also exempt from the debtor's creditors in many states.

TRANSFERS OR TRANSFERS IN TRUST: TO A SPOUSE OR CHILD

One of the most effective strategies to protect assets is not to own them if you are an at-risk individual. For many of our clients who have grown accustomed to controlling their financial matters, such a thought is nearly inconceivable. However, by efficient transfers to a spouse or children, you can protect substantial amounts of assets. Once again, keep in mind the importance of coordinating your estate plans with any use of the transfer strategies discussed in this section.

A key element to complete an effective and not-fraudulent transfer is to be certain that transfers are made without the intent to defraud a debtor and that the debtor received no equivalent value as a result of the transfer. Also be certain that no transfer is made after you become aware you are the subject of a lawsuit.

By far, the most common form of such arrangements is the spouse-to-spouse transfer. Since an individual can transfer an unlimited amount of property to a spouse and not pay any gift tax, such transfers are easy to accomplish. Therefore, it is often recommended that personal residences, personal investment accounts, and other property be owned by the spouse who is not at-risk. Such transfers can be effective even when these assets were acquired with property accumulated as a result the contributions of both members of a marriage and gifted to one individual at a later date. Be advised, such transfers will eliminate the "martial property" classification that is key to determining the assets available to divide in the event of divorce. Assets transferred become the sole property of the receiving spouse and usually are not included in the property to be divided between divorcing partners.

If transferring assets, additional care should be used to prevent the transfer from being classified as a "constructive trust" for the benefit of the transferor. Such can be the case if a court holds that assets transferred to a spouse were available for the support of the transferring spouse. To minimize this possible result, you would be well-served to consider any transfers made to a spouse be placed in the spouse's revocable trust. The possibility of independent use of the assets by the receiving spouse is an important element of such arrangements.

Transfers made for asset-protection purposes should also be balanced with the need to achieve your estate-planning goals. For example, we often see situations in which the spouse at-risk should transfer all assets, even those that would otherwise be available to use the unified estate and gift tax credit. Such an arrangement has the disadvantage of wasting the credit capable of saving an estate approximately $500,000 in estate taxes. However, especially for those who feel the likelihood of a lawsuit is greater than the likelihood of death, such an arrangement is useful.

One disadvantage of transferring assets to a spouse is the surrender of final control of the asset. After all, transferring assets to a spouse also transfers the right to leave the assets in question to whomever the spouse chooses. However, there is a method of controlling the final distribution of assets to a spouse that involves transferring assets via a trust with qualified terminable interest provisions (QTIP).

With such an arrangement, you transfer assets to an irrevocable trust that provides income benefits to your spouse for life. At the death of the spouse, remaining assets are distributed to the beneficiaries of your choice, rather than the choice of your spouse. Especially popular when couples have children from separate marriages, the QTIP arrangement is an effective technique to maintain control of final asset distribution while preserving the income produced by an asset and benefiting by the benefits of asset protection afforded by a spousal transfer.

Transfers can also be made to children. The use of various trust arrangements or state laws providing for uniform transfers or gifts to minors can be effective. The uniform transfer to minor laws of your state may be the easiest method to use for smaller amounts you wish to transfer. Keep in mind such arrangements should be completed such that the at-risk spouse is not appointed as custodian of the account. If completed in this way, a record of the gifts should be made that indicates that the transferor is not the custodian of the account. Transfers made by the custodian will be included in the estate of the custodian in the event the custodian dies during the term of the custodial account.

The major drawback of the uniform transfer arrangements is the age at which the custodial account terminates. In many states the age is 18 and in no state does the custodial arrangement extend beyond age 21. Given this relatively young age, you should carefully consider whether your child should receive complete control over the estimated assets you expect to have accumulated in the account.

An alternative to the uniform transfer option is to create a trust for the benefit of the child. Trusts known as 2503(c) trusts provide that trust assets be used for the nonessential support obligations of the child without being attachable by a creditor of the parent. Private schooling, music instruction, certain educational trips (also known as vacations) can all fall into this category. With the proper trust arrangements, you can have greater control over the use and age of distribution of trust property. Most importantly, the assets in such trusts are completely outside the scope of a successful plaintiff's settlement.

Finally, you can consider the use of transfers to irrevocable trusts. There is increased activity in certain states (most recently Alaska and Missouri) where individuals can establish a trust where the grantor is the income beneficiary yet prevent the creditors of the grantor from forcing the liquidation of the trust for the purposes of a lawsuit settlement in favor of the plaintiff. Such arrangements usually require the use of a trustee from the state offering such arrangements in order to be effective. Care should be used in this area, as the developments in these states are relatively recent and can be upset if tested in the federal courts.

In all areas where transfers to others are being considered, you must be certain that you are comfortable with the fact that these transfers are irrevocable. You should rarely consider the transfer of any asset you think may be needed to support your personal needs later in life.

TRUSTS

A trust is created when one person (the settlor or grantor) transfers to another person or corporation (the trustee) a property interest to be held for the benefit of himself or others (the beneficiaries).

In addition to their popularity in estate-planning, domestic trusts and offshore trusts are common asset-protection vehicles. A domestic trust is one that is governed by and administered under U.S. state laws. When viewed for its asset-protection abilities, the utility of a domestic trust generally centers on who created the trust (also known as the settlor), who is the beneficiary of the trust, and what rights are provided for the beneficiary or retained in the trust. Once again, please remember that a living trust or a self-settled trust will achieve no protection from creditors. Thus, the following discussion of the asset-protection benefits of protective trust provisions will only apply when an irrevocable trust has been created.

1. *Protective Trust Provisions.* Often an individual's most important estate-planning objective is to shield the inheritance of a

beneficiary from personal liabilities. So-called protective trust provisions are available to assist in this objective. For example, a discretionary trust is one in which the trustee has complete discretionary authority to distribute income or principal to a beneficiary. As you consider irrevocable trusts, keep in mind two important features that can be very beneficial for you: the spendthrift clause and the anti-alienation clause. A spendthrift clause allows the trustee to withhold income that otherwise would have been paid to the beneficiary if the trustee believes the income would be spent foolishly or attached by the beneficiary's creditors. This has the double benefit of preventing the beneficiary from wasting trust assets and protecting the beneficiary from creditors. The anti-alienation prevents the trustee from transferring assets to anyone other than the named beneficiary. Thus, this also allows additional protection for the beneficiary. Keep in mind that once a trustee distributes assets to a beneficiary, that distribution is subject to creditor attachment. However, distributions made for the benefit of the beneficiary, such as to an educational institution or medical provider, do not expose such distributions to creditors.

2. *Marital Trusts.* A simple and effective asset-protection strategy for a physician spouse and a nonworking spouse may center on the transfer of assets to the nonworking spouse (or a working spouse who is not at risk). It is equally important to address a situation where the nonworking spouse predeceases the physician spouse. If the physician spouse inherits assets directly (free of trust, in his or her individual name) from the nonworking spouse, such assets could be exposed to the physician's professional negligence claims.

3. *Additional Trust Planning.* More advanced trusts can also be considered. Such trusts are those in which the settlor makes an irrevocable gift of the trust property while retaining an interest in a portion of the trust property.

Because the settlor retains a portion of the trust assets, the IRS recognizes the gift is something less than the entire value of the property transferred and usually allows a settlor to obtain a discount on the value of the transfer. Examples include Qualified Personal

Residence Trusts (QPRTs), Grantor-Retained Annuity Trusts (GRATs), and Charitable Remainder Trusts (CRTs). Some experts recommend these types of trusts in place of an offshore or more obvious asset-protection trust as an attempt to counter fraudulent transfer claims. The argument is that since these trusts are commonly used in the estate-planning context, they are more likely to survive scrutiny in a fraudulent transfer setting than would, for example, an offshore trust. In addition to GRATs, QPRTs, and CRTs, an irrevocable life insurance trust, a routine estate-planning device, often is advisable to protect the cash value of a life insurance policy and its death benefit.

INCORPORATION

Business activity of any type can create an opportunity for a lawsuit. This possibility is compounded whenever a business employs more than one individual, since the actions of the individual performed in the completion of his or her employment duties is a potential for a lawsuit.

Many physicians may believe that incorporating their medical practice is unnecessary, since the professional liability issues are not protected through incorporation and since there are limited (if any) tax advantages. However, we need to be concerned about not only professional actions, but also of personal activities that can be actionable, and especially the activities of your employees that can create a problem. After all, what if an employee who is picking up a pizza for an upcoming staff lunch is involved in an accident resulting in fault being placed on the employee's actions? This liability will result in the practice being held liable for the accident. Such risks can be minimized through the effective use of incorporating.

Usually, any business activity should be incorporated. The day-to-day risks of the operations of a business require careful planning. However, not only should the business be incorporated, you must be careful to actually operate the business as a corporation. This can be accomplished by holding required shareholder meetings, holding regular board of directors meetings, issuing stock of the corporation, adopting corporate bylaws, maintaining appropriate accounting procedures, filing annual forms as required, etc. In this way, claims against the corporation can be insulated from your personal assets.

When a smaller corporation borrows money, personal guarantees are usually required by the officers of the company. Such guarantees result in your personal assets being placed at risk for the liability created by the corporation. Therefore, exercise caution when borrowing funds, as the likelihood is strong that your personal guarantee will be required for loan approval.

FAMILY LIMITED PARTNERSHIPS (FLP) AND LIMITED LIABILITY COMPANIES (LLC)

When the previously discussed strategies are not sufficient to provide adequate asset protection, it is time to become a bit more complicated. While more complicated to create, the following strategies should be relatively easy to understand and implement.

The Family Limited Partnership (FLP) and Limited Liability Company (LLC) have many similarities. Both are unique legal entities governed under the laws of the state in which they were created. Each also has two levels of ownership. One has relatively active characteristics in that the owners control the entity and any assets owned by the entity. For the FLP, this level is called the general partner, for the LLC this level is called the managing member. The other level of ownership is more passive, and is referred to as the *limited partner* in the FLP, and as *members* in the LLC. Each organization offers similar beneficial tax treatment of providing for pass-through taxation. In this manner the entity does not pay taxes, but the owners are responsible for the tax liability on any income. Each also has the benefit of allowing for various discounts to the valuation of the passive interests. This can be important for gifting these interests to family members. Finally, each offers the benefits of the charging order as it relates to claims made against the owners of the passive interests

There are a few important differences between these entities. The first is that only the LLC can be used for a single owner. The FLP requires at least two owners. This is important when the facts include a single individual. The second difference is that the general partner has liability for the FLP. Therefore, when owning dangerous assets (those types of assets that could result in a lawsuit) it may be best to consider the LLC structure rather than the FLP. To illustrate the benefits of these types of arrangements, let's take a closer look at the operation of a FLP.

The limited partnership concept has been available for some time. The FLP protects assets from outside creditors to the limit of capital contributed or agreed to contribute. A limited partnership interest is personal property, and claims against it are limited only to the distributive share of income from the partnership.

To create a limited partnership, or limited liability company, it is necessary that the state in which you wish to operate has a statute that allows for the creation of such an entity. Any actions of the entity must comply with the requirements of the statute. In addition, many state statutes allow for the creation of operating agreements that can supersede the statute-imposed operation of the entity. For example, you can allow for the transfer of entity interests, or for a specific time period in which the entity will operate.

The general partner interest is the interest that controls the operations of the limited partnership within the workings of the operating agreement. General partnership interests (usually owned by parents) can determine the amount of income distributions made by the partnership and make the basic decisions regarding the partnership operations. In addition, general partnership interests are fixed in value. Limited partnership interests share in the income distributions made by the partnership, and their values reflect a proportionate value of total partnership value (thus receive all appreciation of partnership assets) and are subject to a potential discount on transfer.

This potential discount is available to limited partnership interests because of the apparent lack of marketability of the interest (which can often be set in an operating agreement that prevents the sale of interests to nonpartners) and because of minority interest considerations. Given the fact that a limited partnership interest may not be able to be sold to a nonpartner and that the interest does not have control over the operations of the limited partnership, it is not unusual to see discounts of such interests range from 20% to 35% from market value.

These discounts can benefit you in two ways. First, when transferring interests to children, the values of the interest transferred can reflect the discounted value. This results in you being able to gift assets with a fair market value in excess of the annual exclusion gift amount ($14,000) without creating a gift-tax liability. This allows you to accelerate gifting to reduce your taxable estate. The second impact of the discount is in valuing the limited partnership interests that remain in your estate at the time of death. The same discount is available in valuing your assets, which will thus reduce the amount of estate taxation on these remaining assets.

In addition to the valuation discounts available, the impact of such a limited partnership arrangement can be most powerful. For example, let's assume a judgment has been entered against you and you have used a limited partnership as a means of holding assets. In such a case, the plaintiff will receive a charging order against the limited partner interest. Because of the personal nature of the limited partner interest, the charging order will have control only over the income that is produced from the limited partnership interest (unless the plaintiff is a creditor of the limited partnership). However, if the partnership is properly drafted, the partnership will have the ability to retain earnings for the benefit of the partnership for reasonable needs as determined by the general partners.

The charging order is the result of the judgment. With this in mind, consider the actions that a plaintiff *cannot* do:

1. The creditor cannot attach the assets of the partnership, thus assets transferred into the partnership are protected.
2. The creditor cannot remove you as general partner, thus allowing you to maintain operating control of the limited partnership.
3. The creditor has no vote nor management control, thus allowing the partnership to operate independently of the interests of a creditor.
4. The creditor cannot demand income from the partnership and receives only the income that is distributed by the general partners, thus allowing you the flexibility to retain income for partnership purposes and frustrate the intent of the creditor.
5. The creditor may receive "phantom income" from the partnership for income tax purposes without any cash distributions to pay

for the tax, thus creating the unenviable situation of receiving an item as settlement in a lawsuit only to discover that the supposed asset has actually generated a liability.

6. The creditor cannot force the partnership to unwind and require assets to be sold, thus allowing the partnership to continue operation as long as is served by your interests.

This list of restrictions will definitely result in a creditor being frustrated in attempting to collect substantial assets from you. The combination of valuation discounts and creditor frustration make this strategy most effective.

Because of the effectiveness, it is often appropriate to create multiple limited partnerships when you are working with various assets. For example, you may want to create a limited partnership for a rental property, another for an investment portfolio, and a third for a collection of antique cars. In the event a tenant of the rental property is successful in a lawsuit resulting from an accident on the real estate, your other property interests are protected as a result of the separate partnerships.

DOMESTIC ASSET-PROTECTION TRUSTS

As discussed earlier, an individual generally cannot create a trust for his or her benefit and protect the assets from creditors. However, in recent years, several states (Alaska and Delaware were among the first) have enacted legislation that purports to protect self-settled trusts from creditor attachment. These states have essentially set out to create what is achieved through an offshore trust arrangement.

Alaska's trust act provides that assets transferred to a trust containing spendthrift provisions are protected from creditors unless the intent was to defraud creditors or the transfer renders the settlor insolvent. Several other limitations are placed on these trusts: the settlor cannot retain the power to revoke or terminate all or part of the trust without the consent of a person who has an adverse interest in the trust; the transfer could not have been intended to hinder, delay, or defraud creditors; the trust cannot have a mandatory requirement that all or part of the trust income or principal be distributed to the settlor; and the settlor cannot be in default by 30 days or more in child support. For a trust to fall within the purview of Alaska's statute, the trust administration must occur in Alaska, meaning that part of the assets must be in an Alaskan account and the trustee must be an Alaska resident or an Alaska trust company or bank.

Unlike self-settled offshore trusts, the Alaska legislation attempts to make the transfer of property to a domestic asset protection trust result in a completed gift for federal gift tax purposes. If the transfer is deemed a completed gift, then the property is removed from the settlor's estate for estate tax purposes. The Alaska legislation theorizes that if the transferor's creditors cannot reach property, the transferor has effectively given up substantial control of the property.

If the transfer to the trust is a completed gift, the trust should be exempt from estate tax on the transferor's death. However, it is possible that the transferor's right to receive distributions may result in the trust assets being includable in the settlor's estate.

There is a question as to whether these protective trusts actually achieve their goals. The U.S. Constitution requires each state to give "full faith and credit" to judgments handed down by the courts of all states. Once the creditor receives a judgment order in any state, there is no need to relitigate the issues in the state where the assets are held. As of today, there has been no test case determining how the full faith and credit clause affects the enforcement of a judgment against these types of trusts.

OFFSHORE OR FOREIGN TRUSTS

An increasingly popular asset-protection planning device for physicians as well as other wealthy individuals and families is an offshore trust. Offshore trusts and foreign trusts generally refer to trusts that have a minimum of one trustee who is not a resident of the United States. Accordingly, an offshore trust is typically governed by the laws of a foreign country that is selected because of its favorable creditor protection legislation. Commonly utilized jurisdictions include the Isle of Man, the Cayman Islands, and the Cook Islands.

Foreign trusts are irrevocable but usually provide a third party with a power to amend and the settlor with controls over the trust. Such trusts almost always have one non-U.S. trustee acting at all times (regardless of whether the trust assets are situated in the

United States) and the foreign trustee holds the trust powers and in particular the power to distribute income and principal of the trust. Foreign trusts typically include provisions that allow the foreign trustee the power to change the situs (location) of the trust assets to another jurisdiction if the trust assets are under attack. Clauses known as "duress" provisions direct a foreign trustee to ignore an order of a U.S. trustee if given under duress such as a court order directing the trustee to turn over trust assets.

In recent years, foreign trusts have been heavily marketed by trust companies and financial institutions located in offshore jurisdictions largely for their ability to serve as a deterrent to a creditor or a creditor's attorney attempting to reach the assets of such a trust. For example, an attorney in the United States must confront the legal, geographical, procedural, and financial obstacles associated with the foreign jurisdiction. Obviously, the costs associated with attempting to seize assets of a foreign trust can be high, particularly since many foreign jurisdictions prohibit contingent-fee litigation.

In addition, unlike domestic trusts, certain foreign laws allow a settlor to effectively create an asset-protection trust for his or her own benefit, thereby giving the impression that a settlor can "have his cake and eat it, too." Other favorable aspects of offshore jurisdictions are their tendency toward "pro-debtor" fraudulent transfer laws that generally require a creditor to prove a fraudulent transfer beyond a reasonable doubt.

The perception surrounding foreign trusts often results in a misconception that they offer tax-avoidance advantages. Instead, foreign trusts are neutral for estate, gift, and income tax purposes for individuals residing in the United States.

A negative consequence of a foreign trust may arise in bankruptcy court. In particular, if a foreign trust is dated within one year of a bankruptcy filing, the bankruptcy court may deny a discharge of debts, thereby allowing creditors to pursue collection indefinitely. Other obvious disadvantages to offshore trusts include the cost, maintenance fees, political uncertainties of a particular foreign country, language and currency barriers, and conflict of law issues.

In spite of these disadvantages, creation of an offshore trust is perhaps the most advanced level of asset-protection planning.

Often the mere existence of such a trust will deter a creditor from pursuing collection of a claim. Overall, the foreign trust provides much greater asset protection than many domestic planning options mainly attributable to the expense, delay, and additional hurdles to be encountered when proceeding against assets held in such an entity.

It is important to keep in mind that an asset-protection plan can be as simple or as complex as required. While offshore trusts are appropriate for a select segment of our society, establishing conventional trusts for family members or transfers to a spouse faced with less professional exposure may be all that is needed for others.

DIVORCE AND ASSET PROTECTION

Divorce may be the most common risk to assets. Approximately 50% of all marriages end in divorce (higher for physicians, as we noted earlier), with an even higher percentage for second marriages. When considering this aspect of asset protection, we encourage our clients to not only consider the possibility of divorce in their marriage, but also consider the risks of divorce for their married children.

If the key to effective asset protection is to make liquidity difficult and not to hide assets, the key to effective asset protection for a possible divorce is to reach agreement regarding the division of assets in advance of the dissolution of the marriage, not to hide assets from a spouse. The best tool available for this asset-protection goal is the prenuptial agreement. If properly drafted, the prenuptial agreement will allow a court to require that assets be divided as previously agreed, rather than create a surprise during the divorce proceedings.

Careful attention must be paid to your state's laws regarding the requirements for a prenuptial agreement, but let's take a look at some of the basic requirements. First, the agreement must be in writing and signed by all parties. Notarizing is also a good practice. Second, there must be accurate disclosure of the assets of each party. Third, it is usually best that each party be advised by a separate attorney. Finally, the agreement should not be considered unreasonable or totally one-sided.

Many say that approaching the topic of a prenuptial agreement places an uncomfortable strain on a relationship. However, we generally recommend that the uncomfortable period be addressed to avoid the truly unpleasant emotions of a hotly contested divorce settlement.

Techniques That Do Not Work

In concluding this section on asset-protection planning strategies, it makes sense to be aware of the strategies that have not proven to be successful. In doing so you should be able to avoid these areas and focus your attention on the preferred and previously successful strategies.

The first and we hope the most obvious mistake would be to assume that a transfer made with the attempt to defraud a creditor will be successful. For instance, if you knowingly transfer assets to your spouse's name after you have been made aware of a pending lawsuit, you have committed a fraudulent transfer for asset-protection purposes. Such a transfer will be considered void, and the assets will be assumed to be under your control, thus available for attachment by your creditor. In addition, transferring assets to a creditor when you realize that the creditor will receive assets with no value is also considered a fraudulent transfer. The moral of this story is that once you have gotten in trouble, it is generally too late to do anything.

Another mistaken asset-protection strategy is to believe that assets transferred into a grantor trust will be protected. Remember, if you own or control the assets, chances are excellent that those assets will be part of your assets available for creditor attachment. Therefore, do not assume that a living trust will provide asset protection.

Oral agreements also result in the destruction of attempts at asset protection. Often, individuals do not believe they are liable for the debts of a business enterprise unless they have taken the steps to formally create the business. Please do not think that if your operating agreement is not committed to writing, that you are not liable for the company's actions. In these cases, liability is often found with individuals even though no formalized agreement was drafted.

Case Studies

As a way to illustrate the impact of the asset-protection strategies we have reviewed, let's consider the following:

Physician and spouse own the following assets:

Asset	Fair Market Value
Residence	$400,000
Investment Brokerage Account	$250,000
Summer Home	$125,000
Rental Property (Apartment Building)	$400,000
Miscellaneous Personal Property	$200,000
Cash Assets	$150,000
Total Joint Assets	$1,525,000

In addition, the physician owns the following assets:

Asset	Fair Market Value
Retirement Plan	$750,000
Farm	$300,000
Total	$1,050,000

Finally, the spouse owns the following assets:

Asset	Fair Market Value
Winter Home	$200,000
401(K) Account	$200,000
Business	$500,000
Total	$900,000

Based on these assumptions, the physician and spouse have approximately $2.5 million of assets. Of this amount, $1,825,000 is at risk, since the physician owns these assets directly, or they are owned jointly.

The physician can take the following steps to minimize the exposure of these assets:

1. Transfer assets from joint titled to the spouse's living trust. The residence, brokerage account, and cash assets would be perfect types of assets to transfer.
2. Transfer other joint assets into separate limited partnerships or limited liability companies. The summer home can be transferred into one partnership, the apartment building transferred into

another. In this way, the physician can transfer interests in one property independently of the other. In addition, any settlement resulting from a successful action brought as a result of an accident on the rental property will be limited to the value of the rental property. No other real estate assets need to be placed at risk.

3. Transfer the farm owned by the physician into a separate partnership. Once again, this allows for independent transfers of the property as well as the insulation of other assets in the event of a successful claim.

4. The spouse could also benefit from a number of strategies, namely transferring the winter home into a separate limited partnership (or perhaps the same partnership as the summer home) and making certain the business interest is incorporated.

The goal is to place these assets outside the reach of a successful plaintiff, while at the same time being able to enjoy these assets during one's lifetime.

Finally, it is crucial for physicians routinely exposed to professional liability to plan in advance of a claim. Such planning should not only involve a review of individual and family assets but also consideration of techniques that can shield a potential inheritance from creditor attachment.

CHAPTER 12

Estate Planning

W e have covered many different financial strategies that can increase your net worth. We have learned how to take advantage of income tax-planning strategies to increase after-tax income and how to maximize portfolio returns using modern portfolio theory. We have learned strategies to save for true financial independence as well as provide for children's college education. We have discussed risk management and the efficient use of insurance products to ensure future income in the event of disability or premature death. In the previous chapter, we reviewed the basic techniques for asset protection.

Up to this point, everything we have covered was with the long-term objective of accumulation or preservation of assets to guarantee future income. Now we need to look at ways to keep more of what we have accumulated for future generations or other potential beneficiaries. Equally important, we need to look at techniques that will coordinate the management and final distribution of assets you accumulate.

Estate tax planning is an important element of the financial planning process. Why work so hard to accumulate assets and then let the government take up to 40% in estate taxes? Why leave assets that were well-managed throughout your life in a state of confusion once you pass away?

The key objective of an estate plan is to maximize the available strategies in order to best preserve and manage your estate. Understand that estate tax planning is truly a selfless endeavor because while you may not receive a monetary benefit, others certainly can. Also keep in mind that for married couples, the estate tax is typically deferred until the second death. Estate tax planning is not just about strategies that will leave more of the estate to your spouse, though as you will see as we go further into estate planning, this can easily be accomplished.

We will review strategies that will ensure your children or other beneficiaries receive a greater portion of your estate while minimizing estate taxation and maximizing the benefits of a well-managed plan for distribution of assets

You must take the time necessary to develop an efficient and psychologically comfortable estate plan. Once again, this is a situation in which physicians procrastinate. Oftentimes they are forced to make a series of decisions without being able to take the time to consider the multitude of options that are available.

Goals

You can have numerous goals when you plan your estate. The first can be the effective distribution of your assets, making certain that your property is transferred to the individuals you wish at the time you believe is appropriate. Another can be providing needed income to surviving family members or other dependents. Another can be arranging for the needed management of assets for surviving family members, because chances are excellent that you made many of the financial decisions for your family while you were alive. Yet another goal often is avoiding the administrative headache of probate and the resulting fees.

However, for many physicians the primary common goal of estate tax planning has been the minimization of federal estate taxes. This is accomplished through the use of estate tax credits and available deductions. An efficient estate plan will utilize credits and deductions, but there is much more that can be done. You can have the finest trust documents drafted by a leading estate attorney, but if this is not coordinated with the titling of your assets, your expensive documents may prove worthless in terms of the purpose for which they were intended.

In spite of there being many reasons to create an effective estate plan, many physicians have not bothered to make any inroads in this important area. The excuses are numerous. First, they may believe they do not have enough money to worry about their estate. However, your estate tax is based on all assets you own or control, and when you add the value of all assets plus the death benefits of life insurance policies it is fairly easy to reach rather substantial numbers quickly. Or they may think they don't need to plan their estate because all assets are to be given to their spouse. Current tax laws make transfers between spouses quite tax-advantaged. However, while transferring all assets to a spouse may provide temporary tax relief, it usually increases the total tax liability over the long run. In addition, such a strategy often leaves the responsibility of distribution of assets and the timing of such distributions entirely on the surviving spouse's shoulders.

Second, some physicians claim they simply do not care what happens to their assets after their death. But would they be concerned if the government's share of their estate was the largest single distribution made when compared to the assets distributed to family? Are they willing to give up as much as 40% of their assets to the government in the form of estate taxes, not to mention income taxes from retirement plans?

Most commonly, physicians tell us they are just too busy to address these matters. We suggest they ask themselves if the few hours they spend getting their estate plan in order is worth the couple of hours they could have spent at the office. If two hours to get your estate plan in line can save your estate $1 million in taxes, that seems to be a reasonable pay back of time.

Estate tax planning attorneys tell us that the majority of plans they construct are done less than thoroughly due to their client's requested time frame for completion. They say that most successful people, physicians in particular, initiate estate plans from their death beds or, interestingly enough, right before they travel abroad. Curiously, while travel to Europe and other parts of the world is planned well in advance, the call to the attorney is usually placed within a week or two of the trip! This doesn't give you or the attorney enough time to do the job right. The result is usually a quick and supposedly temporary document that will be updated as soon as the physician returns from his or her travel. Is this the best document for the situation? It is simply a short-term solution for a long-term problem.

The Estate-Planning Process

Begin with the determination of beneficiaries. These are the people or organizations you care about. Very simply, who do you want to inherit your estate? If you are married, a logical choice (and in many states a legal requirement) is to include the spouse in this category. The primary beneficiary is the person first in line to inherit. You will also need to look beyond the primary beneficiary to the contingent beneficiary, which is the individual who will receive your property in the event your primary beneficiary predeceases you. At this point children, other relatives, friends, or charitable entities are often considered.

You will also need to give some thought to how your beneficiaries (or contingent beneficiaries) will receive assets at your death. For a spouse, a lump sum may be appropriate. For those other than a spouse, you could consider providing for income for a certain period, with distributions of principal at certain ages or after a certain number of years after your death. This "staggered" distribution arrangement allows a beneficiary the opportunity to acquire a greater degree of financial maturity before the entire estate is distributed. This is a most important decision that is oftentimes overlooked.

An actual case in point involves an individual we'll call John. Shortly after John completed his undergraduate work at the university, his father, a pediatrician, passed away suddenly. His mother had passed away only the year before, and John was an only child. Based on the instructions in his father's will, John was the sole beneficiary of the estate, valued at approximately $1.5 million. Estate taxes and other expenses totaled $500,000, leaving John with $1 million payable in a lump sum. At 22 years of age, John was devastated by the loss of his parents and faced many decisions regarding his own future. He decided to fulfill one of his dreams of owning a seat and trading commodities at the Chicago Mercantile Exchange. John used a portion of his inheritance to buy a membership which, at that time, was available for $327,500.

After a two-week training course, John began his commodity trading career in the volatile pork belly futures pit. Speculative commodity trading is a high-risk business where losses can exceed the original investment because of the high leverage nature of the business. Needless to say, John's trading career was short-lived. After just three weeks of excitement in the pits, he had incurred losses of $800,000. Since he didn't have the necessary liquid capital available, he was forced to sell his membership to settle his debt. Within just two months of his father's death, he had gone through more than 80% of what had been left to him.

Could this situation have been avoided? One option could have been limiting John's access to the funds. What if his father had divided up the lump sum over a period of years? A common approach is a one-third payment at death, one-third paid 5 years later, and the remainder paid 5 or 10 years after that. You must give serious consideration to such important decisions. Will the inheritance improve a child's situation or make his or her life more difficult?

Next, take an inventory of your assets. This inventory should include all your investment assets, retirement plans, the value of your home and other real estate, as well as personal property. Personal property includes jewelry, collectibles, furnishings, vehicles, and boats. You should also include the value of your practice as well as the death benefit of the life insurance policies you own.

Finally, your estate tally should include any asset that you control. For example, if your wealthy Uncle Harry left a trust for your benefit that allows you to distribute the trust assets to whomever you wish at your death, you have control over that asset and the value of that trust is in your estate.

Unfortunately, the total value of your estate includes more than hard assets or controlled trusts. You may need to consider income tax issues in addition to estate tax issues. Benjamin Franklin once pessimistically observed that, "In this world nothing is certain but death and taxes." While it is tempting to hope that the unfortunate occurrence of the former would put an end to payment of the latter, such is not the case. A tax provision referenced under Internal Revenue Code Section 691(a) known as Income in Respect of a Decedent (IRD) includes many circumstances hauntingly applicable to physicians.

IRD refers to amounts that the decedent was entitled to as gross income, but which were not included in his or her taxable income for the year of death. Included are situations where some form of income is distributed after the date of death that was technically earned by the physician during his or her working years. One example would be payment for services rendered before death or under a deferred compensation agreement, such as receivables from patients or the health insurance carriers. Also included would be any yet-unpaid salary or bonuses that were accrued but not yet distributed. Of great concern for most physicians is the treatment of qualified retirement accounts, including pension plans, profit-sharing plans, or other retirement accounts such as tax sheltered annuities (TSA) as well as individual retirement accounts (IRA). Not surprisingly, the IRS has determined that a distribution from a qualified retirement plan is includable as IRD unless a spousal beneficiary elects to treat the decedent's IRA as his or her own.

While the tax code details many technical situations, it's important for taxpayers to understand at least the basics in order to minimize confusion after the fact. When considering the complexity of Income in Respect of a Decedent, simplify it by considering that there are specific items for which income taxes must still be paid despite the death of the person who earned it. Consider two principals that will guide you through the provisions. First, most individuals pay taxes on income in the year it is received. This is known as the cash method of accounting. Second, a tax year ends on the date of death. Think of IRD as income that a decedent has earned or has a right to receive, but has not actually received. Simply stated, income taxes must still be paid on IRD items despite the death of the person who earned it. An IRA is considered IRD because it becomes automatically vested in the named beneficiaries at the time of the original IRA owner's death.

When preparing the tax return, you are allowed certain tax offsets that can reduce the impact of IRD. Generally IRD must be included in the gross income of the recipient; however, a deduction is normally permitted for estate and generation-skipping transfer taxes paid on the income. The amount of the deduction is determined by computing the federal estate tax with the IRD included and then recalculating the tax with the IRD excluded. The difference between the two equals the amount of the income tax deduction. When determining which entity must claim the gross income, Internal Revenue Code Section 691 spells out the following criteria:

1. The estate of the decedent, if the right to receive the amount is acquired by the decedent's estate from the decedent.
2. The person who, by reason of the death of the decedent, acquires the right to receive the amount, is not acquired by the decedent's estate from the decedent.
3. The person who acquires from the decedent the right to receive the amount by bequest, devise, or inheritance, if the amount is received after a distribution by the decedent's estate of such right.

In contrast to IRD is the taxation, or lack thereof, relative to appreciated assets. For example, if you were to sell a security prior to death with a lower basis than its current value, you would be subject to the capital gains tax. If, on the other hand, you were to die while still owning the security, your beneficiaries would receive a "stepped up" basis, which would be the value at the time of death. Then the security could be sold at the stepped up basis value without incurring capital gains taxation. This would allow the full amount to be distributed to the beneficiaries. Clearly, IRD can make a big difference to your heirs and should certainly be considered when preparing your estate plan.

Asset Titling

When listing the items in your inventory, you should designate the current owner of the property. It may be owned solely in your name, in joint tenancy, as tenants in common, as tenancy by the entirety or held in trust. Keep in mind that the titling of an asset can dictate the distribution of the property at the time of your death. So let's take a quick look at the different types of titling and how they work.

Solely titled assets have an individual owner. At the time of death, solely titled assets are distributed according to the will prepared by the individual, or via state laws if no will has been prepared (see the discussion of intestacy below).

Jointly titled assets have more than one owner. Joint tenancy with rights of survivorship property is technically 100% owned by each joint tenant. At the time of death, the property automatically passes to the remaining joint tenants, regardless of the direction provided in any will or trust document.

Tenants in common property also have more than one owner. Unlike joint tenants with rights of survivorship, tenants in common interests are specifically divisible, and these interests are distributed according to the will or trust of the owner.

Tenancy by the entirety is unique type of ownership that we also discussed in the Asset Protection chapter. It is a form of property ownership open **only** to a married couple. Tenancy by the entirety has one primary difference from joint tenancy with rights of survivorship: without the other spouse's consent, neither spouse is allowed to sell his or her ownership interest. Technically, the husband and wife convey their separate interests in their home to a third party, which is the tenancy by the entirety. Now the property is not owned by either the husband or the wife as individuals, but by the married couple as one ownership unit. It is important to understand that neither spouse can transfer their interest in the property to anyone except their spouse. However, they can undo this tenancy by divorce or mutual consent. In most states, the primary residence is the only property held in tenancy by the entirety.

Once you have prepared your personal inventory, take a good look at the bottom line—the amount of assets owned by you and your spouse minus any debt such as mortgages, student loans, or other personal liabilities. If that figure is greater than $5.25 million (the maximum amount you are allowed to pass tax-free to someone other than a spouse), there may be estate taxes due in the future. The amount you can distribute to someone other than your spouse is referred to as your estate exemption. The current exemption schedule is as follows:

Year	Estate and GST Exemption	Top Estate Tax Rate	Gift Tax Exemption	Top Gift Tax Rate
2013	$5,250,000	40%	$5,250,000	40%

These figures are referred to as the "exemption equivalent" or "exclusion equivalent." Be aware that the estate tax rates increase as the value of the estate increases. The easiest way to consider the application of the exemption is to think of it as a deduction applied against the lowest possible marginal estate tax rate. All transfers at death are subject to estate taxation, but the government gives each of us an exemption that reduces the taxable transfer. Further, married couples can combine their exemption amounts for a total of approximately $10.5 million.

Another commonly used estate-planning strategy, often used by default, is the unlimited marital deduction. This deduction provides the opportunity to leave as much as you wish to a spouse completely estate tax-free, be it $100 or $100,000,000. This is why we refer to estate planning as a selfless endeavor. Married individuals never need to pay estate taxes when they inherit from their spouse. Although this appears to be the greatest deduction the government can allow, it ultimately causes higher taxation when the surviving spouse dies.

The efficient use of the maximum available exemption equivalent or tax credit is also extremely important. Remember that this exemption is available to every U.S. citizen. This strategy allows a married couple to effectively use the exemption twice, thus allowing them to pass a total of $10.5 million (for 2013), completely free of federal estate taxes.

To take full advantage of both exemptions, the first person to die would have to leave the exemption equivalent of $5.25 million to someone other than the spouse. But most couples don't want to leave substantial assets to their children prior to their spouse's death. Most want to ensure financial security for their spouse, leaving all remaining assets to their children at the spouse's subsequent death. The key here is the ability to take advantage of the exemption without taking anything away from the spouse.

The utilization of trusts can accomplish this objective. A trust allows you to leave the then-current estate exemption ($5.25 million) to the children while still giving the spouse access to the funds during their lifetime. The children do not receive the inheritance from the first spouse's estate until the death of the second spouse. This is called an AB trust arrangement. Other common terms used to describe this technique are the *marital-non-marital trust*, the *credit trust*, the *family trust*, or the *by-pass trust*. Attorneys use these terms to describe the estate-planning strategy that allows married couples to take advantage of both the unlimited marital deduction as well as the exemption equivalent over both lives, thus allowing the maximum utilization of current estate tax law savings.

A trust is drawn that creates a division of assets at death. Using our previous example of an estate valued at $10.5 million, at the first death, $5.25 million of assets would pass to a trust in order to maximize the exemption equivalent. This is the amount that we are allowed to pass to someone other than a spouse.

The other part of the division involves the use of the unlimited marital deduction. In this situation, a trust is created at death for those assets that qualify for the marital deduction. If the estate was valued at $10.5 million, we know that only $5.25 million would pass in trust via the exemption equivalent. However, in this second arrangement, the remaining $5.25 million can pass to the marital deduction trust due to the unlimited funding allowed utilizing the marital deduction.

Going back to our example of the $10.5 million estate, some parameters are set to ensure that the couple's objectives are being met. First, the funds ($5.25 million) that flow to the exemption equivalent or B trust, need to be available in some manner to the surviving spouse. However, the government can make a strong argument that unlimited access to the trust's principal and interest by the surviving spouse indicates an intention by the first to die to leave all monies to the surviving spouse, thus this bequest was in effect made via the unlimited marital deduction, not the exemption equivalent. To qualify for the exemption, attorneys agree that the spouse's right of access should be limited to the interest, dividends or other income attributable to the B trust. For example, if the $5.25

million being held in trust is generating income of 7%, the spouse could receive $367,500 in annual income without jeopardizing the deduction.

In addition, estate tax law also allows the spouse to receive principal of the trust as long as it meets the ascertainable standard of health, education, maintenance, and welfare. The trustee is held responsible for these decisions with the understanding that their responsibility is to maintain the surviving spouse's standard of living while protecting the interest of the ultimate beneficiaries: the children. Prior to dipping into principal, the trustee will look at the surviving spouse's other sources of income, including personally owned assets and the value of the marital deduction trust in order to effectively perform their fiduciary responsibilities.

Interestingly, if the goal is to maximize the value of the inheritance to the next generation, as is often the case, the B trust holds a unique planning advantage that can increase over time. Once the exemption equivalent is maximized and maintained within the B trust, the future growth of the trust is sheltered from estate taxation upon the subsequent death of the second spouse. The $5.25 million held in trust can certainly grow if properly invested. If the value of the trust at the survivor's death has appreciated to $12 million, the entire amount passes to the children completely estate tax-free. That is why many times a B trust may be invested with a growth objective, as long as it is still consistent with a surviving spouse's income requirements, or lack thereof.

Care should be taken when making investments within a trust, since trust income tax rates for 2013 are higher than individual income tax rates, as the following chart illustrates:

Base Taxable Income	Marginal Tax Rate
$0-$2,450	15%
$2,451-$5,700	25%
$5,701-$8,750	28%
$8,751-$11,950	33%
$11,951 & up	39.6%

The key here will be for the trustee to invest the assets of the B trust in a manner that ensures adequate income for the needs of the spouse. Once the income is distributed to the spouse, the trust is not liable for the taxation since the liability is transferred to the recipient. If only a minimal income is required, a greater portion of the trust may be invested for longer-term growth. In this way, the trustee can shelter the growth of the trust for the next generation. An awareness of the survivor's income needs allows the trust's portfolio to be allocated efficiently, providing income needs using bonds, CDs, etc., while also providing growth through the use of stocks, mutual funds, real estate, etc.

The other side of the trust, commonly referred to as the A trust, or marital trust, is comprised of those assets that pass via the unlimited marital deduction. In this trust, the spouse has access to both the interest as well as the principal.

Situations can exist that necessitate placing limitations on the spouse's access to the A trust. Perhaps there is a concern that the surviving spouse may not use the funds responsibly, or that the surviving spouse may remarry and use the funds to enhance his or her new family's lifestyle. Another common concern is the surviving spouse who has children from a previous marriage. Assets can be withdrawn from the A trust and gifted to those children or a bequest can be made to them at death.

There is an estate-planning technique used to control the final disposition of that part of the trust estate which qualifies for the marital deduction. This can be accomplished through the use of a qualified terminable interest property trust, commonly called a QTIP trust. During the surviving spouse's lifetime, this additional trust provision allows distribution of A trust income and limited access to the principal under certain predefined conditions. This gives the deceased spouse control over the ultimate disposition of the property.

Utilization of the AB trust strategy requires proper funding. The time spent developing an estate plan using an AB trust is wasted if it is not coordinated with proper asset titling.

Distribution Strategies

Now we are ready to study the various strategies that control the distribution of your assets. The distribution of your assets can be accomplished by any of three possible arrangements: by titling of the asset, by beneficiary designation, or by the directives spelled out by various estate planning documents such as your will or trusts.

Let's look at each of these in more depth, taking that which could control the least amount of assets first.

WILLS

Many physicians are surprised to learn that a will may be the least important element in their estate plan. A valid will provides directions to those who survive you as to how you would like to have your assets distributed at your death. Think of your will simply as a note you are writing to a judge requesting that certain things be completed. The drawback to using a will as your only estate-planning tool is that the will only controls the distribution of solely titled assets (or beneficiary-designated assets that are paid to the estate). In addition, all assets that are distributed through a will must be probated, which may be something to be avoided as we will discuss shortly. Finally, a will controls asset distribution if it is found to be a valid will. Remember Howard Hughes? As you may recall, the will contests regarding his estate were front page news!

Most wills are written so that all assets are transferred to the surviving spouse (or to the children if there is no surviving spouse). This is often referred to as an "I love you" will, since the availability of all assets is provided to the survivor. While such an arrangement will make all assets available, it does so in a manner that maximizes the ultimate estate tax liability on the assets.

TRUSTS

Despite their apparent complexity, trusts can be most useful in many aspects of estate planning.

To understand trusts, you need to know who the players are and what they do.

First, there's the *grantor*. This is the individual who transferred funds into the trust. Next is the *trustee*. This is a manager's job. The trustee is supposed to make certain that the terms of the trust, as outlined by the grantor, are carried out. Finally there is the *beneficiary*. This is the fun job. The beneficiary is the person (or individuals) for whom the trust has been created. Often a minor, the beneficiary can also be a surviving spouse, adult child, or any individual who is in need of financial assistance (or supervision) after the death of the grantor.

Knowing these basics, we can quickly examine a couple of different type of trusts often used for estate-planning purposes. The first is a testamentary trust. This trust is usually part of a will and comes into existence after death. With a testamentary trust, assets are passed through probate before being managed by the trust. The trust can then help divide assets for each beneficiary, manage assets, or distribute assets as required by the directions of the trust.

A living trust may also be known as an *inter vivos* trust. Basically, this trust is created during the life of the grantor. Assets are transferred into the trust and will thus avoid probate at the time of death. As an added benefit, living trusts will provide benefits during life, particularly in the event of the incompetency of the grantor. A living trust will identify a list of contingent trustees that are able to assume the role of trustee in the event the original trustee (usually the grantor) is unable to perform their duties. Such forethought will avoid the excessive legal costs required if a grantor is declared incompetent, since in such cases annual accountings to the court are required.

A trust can be an excellent method of controlling the management and distribution of assets. However, a trust only works to the extent that assets have been transferred into the trust. Often, we see physicians who have spent hours in their attorney's office creating what they hope will be the trust arrangement for their estate. Unfortunately, they never get around to transferring their assets into the trust so the trust never really controls anything! Remember, if you bother to create a trust for your estate plan, make certain that your assets are titled in the way necessary for the trust to work!

BENEFICIARY DESIGNATION AND ASSET TITLING

Asset titling and beneficiary designation take precedence over the directives of your will or trust. Too often we see a physician with a substantial retirement account naming the surviving spouse as beneficiary, a large life insurance policy naming the surviving spouse as beneficiary, a residence and summer home jointly titled with the spouse, and various investment accounts that are jointly titled with the spouse. To control the distribution of these assets, the physician has paid handsomely for trust documents that provide management assistance for the surviving spouse, and require the attainment of carefully thought-out ages before the distribution of assets to the children.

Unfortunately, the physician and spouse could have saved the money spent to produce the trust. The trust will not make any difference to their plans since all the assets will be distributed in a manner other than as the trust directs. In this case, all assets will be transferred to the surviving spouse. Whatever plans the survivor has made (or may make) will be the controlling factor for all assets.

Distribution - In General

How assets are distributed depends on the titling:

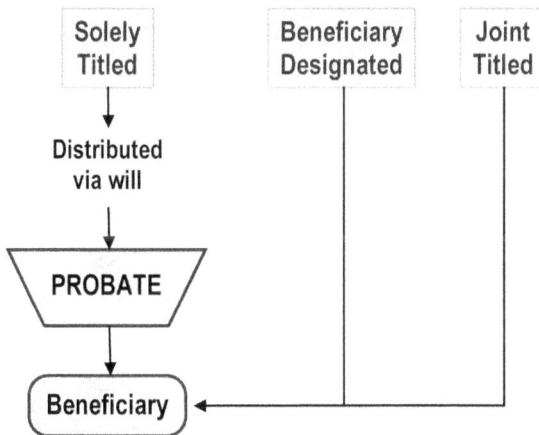

```
┌──────────┐      ┌──────────────┐    ┌─────────┐
│ Solely   │      │ Beneficiary  │    │ Joint   │
│ Titled   │      │ Designated   │    │ Titled  │
└──────────┘      └──────────────┘    └─────────┘
     │                    │                 │
     ▼                    │                 │
 Distributed             │                 │
  via will               │                 │
     │                    │                 │
     ▼                    │                 │
  ╲ PROBATE ╱             │                 │
     │                    │                 │
     ▼                    │                 │
 ( Beneficiary ) ◄────────┴─────────────────┘
```

Now that we understand the relative power of different tools of distribution, let's take a closer look at the various legal arrangements or legal documents that typically have been thought of as ways for arranging the distribution of your assets.

Intestacy

If you don't have an estate plan, don't worry! The state in which you live or own property has one for you! Don't get too excited, since it is probably not the estate plan you had in mind.

For those who die without a valid will, the intestacy laws apply. Most states follow the Uniform Probate Code, which generally provides for the distribution as follows:

1. If you are married and have children: half of your estate to your spouse, the other half to your children. Assets for the children are distributed at their age 18 (which many of our clients agree is not really the age of financial wisdom).

2. If you are married with no children: all assets to your spouse.

3. If you are single: your estate is divided into shares, with one share for each of your parents (if one of your parents is deceased the surviving parent receives a double share) and one share for each sibling.

There are many other "what ifs" that are part of intestacy laws. If you are really interested in learning about something that you shouldn't have to know about, call your state capital and request a copy of the law. Your time is certainly better spent doing your estate plan the right way.

Probate

No discussion of asset distribution would be complete without an explanation of the probate process. Historically, probate existed to provide a forum for creditors of a decedent or for those who had evidence of improprieties regarding the will submitted to the probate court. From this rather simple beginning, probate can produce quite a bit of red tape and expense.

If you have ever attended a seminar regarding living trusts, you have certainly heard many supposed horror stories regarding the probate process. Let's look at the just facts:

1. Survivors don't have access to most of the property or assets that are a part of the probate process. This lack of access lasts during the probate periods, which could extend 16 months or longer. At best, this can be an inconvenience for the surviving family; at worst, it could result in additional legal fees as the attorney works to have assets released by the judge.

2. The cost of court fees, attorney fees, executor fees, accounting fees, and appraisals average 5% of the value of the estate, based

on a national average. The costs in your state can be significantly lower or higher.

3. Probate files are open to the public in most states. Let's face it, most of us like a reasonable degree of privacy. This does not exist if your assets pass though the probate process.

ADVANTAGES OF PROBATE

There are actually some potential benefits of the probate process. This can be especially important for physicians who are concerned about possible judgments resulting from lawsuits. These benefits are outlined in *It's Easy to Avoid Probate and Guardianships*, by Barbara R. Stock:

1. In many states, a probate proceeding closes the window of possible claims made against the estate as a result of a successful lawsuit. The window may close as soon as a few months after the conclusion of the probate process. If this window did not close in this manner, the estate could be liable for the entire statute of limitations period as in existence in your state.

2. Probate provides for the distribution of your assets exactly as you wanted (assuming you leave a valid will).

3. Probate usually limits the amount of time someone can challenge the will. This provides the degree of certainty required to allow for distributions to be made without concern of future claims.

4. Probate also limits the amount of time during which creditors can make claims on the estate (in the same spirit as mentioned in #3).

5. Probate provides that the executor's activities are supervised by the court. This degree of oversight will assist in the distribution of assets in the manner originally desired by the decedent.

Taxes

The next step in the estate-planning process is to calculate the approximate amount of taxes that would be due on your estate. Keep in mind that the federal tax structure has undergone substantial and beneficial change for most individuals. However, each state can have a separate state estate (or inheritance) tax. Please be certain to obtain an understanding of the potential liabilities that can occur from your state of residence.

Power of Appointment Trust

The tax law specifically provides that property passing to the surviving spouse under a trust which meets the following requirements will qualify for the marital deduction: the surviving spouse must be entitled for life to all the income, such income must be payable at least annually, the surviving spouse must have power to appoint the trust property to his/herself or to his/her estate, the power (whether exercisable during life or by will) must be exercisable by the spouse alone, and no other person must have a power to appoint someone other than the surviving spouse. A specific portion of the trust can qualify if all requirements are met with respect to that specific portion. IRC Secs. 2056(b)(5), 2056(b)(10).

Estate Trusts

Under an estate trust the income is either distributed to the surviving spouse or accumulated during their lifetime, and the principal and accumulated income, if any, is payable to their estate.

Special Rule Charitable Remainder Trust

If the surviving spouse is the only non-charitable beneficiary of a qualified charitable remainder trust created by the decedent, the spouse's interest is not considered a nondeductible terminable interest and the value of such interest will qualify for the marital deduction. A qualified charitable remainder trust means a charitable remainder annuity trust or a charitable remainder uni-trust.

Qualified Domestic Trust

In general, a marital deduction is not available for a transfer to a surviving spouse who is not a United States citizen unless the transfer is to a qualified domestic trust (QDOT) for which the executor has made an election. A QDOT must qualify for the marital deduction as well as meet the following requirements:

1. At least one trustee of the QDOT must be a United States citizen or a domestic corporation.

2. No distribution (other than a distribution of income) may be made from the trust unless that trustee has the right to withhold any additional gift or estate tax imposed on the trust.

Additional gift tax is due on any distribution while the surviving spouse is still alive (other than a distribution to the surviving spouse of income or on account of hardship). Additional estate tax is due on any property remaining in the QDOT at the death of the surviving spouse (or at the time the trust ceases to qualify as a QDOT, if earlier). The additional gift or estate tax is calculated as if any property subject to the tax had been included in the taxable estate of the first spouse to die.

How To Reduce Taxes

Now that you have the basics of the estate-planning rules and have an idea of calculating the amount of tax on your estate, we can begin to look at ways to reduce your tax liability. In general, there are three ways to reduce your estate tax liability.

1. Drafting the appropriate documents
2. Gifting assets
3. Giving to charity

DRAFTING THE APPROPRIATE DOCUMENTS

The best way to make effective use of documents is to effectively utilize the marital deduction and estate tax credit. The example below illustrates the effective use of the credit explained earlier.

GIFTING ASSETS

Gifting can play a crucial role in a physician's estate tax plan. An effective gift strategy can accomplish the goal to support your preferred religious, educational, or professional organization. In addition, gifting can help distribute assets to family members or friends who may be in need of an additional financial boost to support their needs. Finally, a gift strategy can reduce your estate tax liability.

Effective in January 2013, the estate exemption is $5,250,000, and the gift exemption will increase to $5,250,000. This eliminates the previous dissimilar treatment of estate tax compared to gift tax.

An efficient estate plan can be utilized to take advantage of the current law, which effectively allows a married couple to pass a total of $10.5 million (in 2013) free of federal estate taxes. Assets in excess of the exemption begin to incur estate taxation at the 40% rate. For estates larger than this, various gifting strategies should be considered as an effective way of reducing the tax liability of the estate.

Once you determine that a gifting strategy is appropriate for you, the next step is to determine whether your situation would benefit most by gifting large amounts to quickly transfer assets or if a series of smaller gifts made over a number of years would better serve your needs.

To qualify for the annual gift tax exclusion, the gift must be available immediately to the person receiving it. This definition, in the government's terms, is known as a gift of present interest. By following a consistent program of annual maximum gifts to children, grandchildren, etc., a health care professional with an estate larger than the combined exemption can dramatically reduce the future size of the estate and ultimately lower the estate tax liability.

Many professionals are wary of making gifts of this size and frequency to their children for unrestricted use. Perhaps the children or grandchildren are too young, or the parents may feel that current gifting may inhibit their child's motivation to work hard to earn income.

One alternative that addresses these concerns is the use of an irrevocable trust. An irrevocable trust can be structured so that annual gifts are made to the trust, thus reducing the taxable estate while at the same time placing restrictions on when the funds can be withdrawn by the recipient. The most common time frame for withdrawal is after the donor's death. Here, the gifted assets within the trust are removed from the donor's taxable estate due to the irrevocable nature of the trust. The beneficiaries then receive the trust assets on an estate-tax-free basis.

However, this strategy involves the gifting of future interest, which is in direct conflict with the rule of present interest spelled out in the tax law. Remember that if the gift is of present interest, it qualified for the annual exclusion, while future interest gifts certainly do not qualify. To make the gifts to the trust eligible for gift-tax exclusion, you need to allow the beneficiaries a limited power to withdraw the gift shortly after it is made to the irrevocable trust. This technique is known as *Crummey Power*, named after the actual case that decided the validity of such a gift (*Crummey vs. U.S., 397 F.2nd 82 (CA-9, 1968)*). Mr. Crummey argued that the gifts made to his irrevocable trust did indeed qualify for the annual exclusion since the beneficiaries, his children, had 13 days each year to withdraw the trust contributions. After years of arguments and testing, Crummey Powers are now widely used to qualify seemingly future interest gifts as gifts of present interest.

Several steps should be taken to avoid potential problems relative to the irrevocable trust. The most important is to send a letter to the trust beneficiaries notifying them of this withdrawal right. The hope is that beneficiaries will *not* exercise this right of withdrawal. Your intent in using this estate-tax technique should be discussed with them in order to avoid any surprises. It is also a good idea to document all of the withdrawal notices by having the beneficiaries sign an acknowledgement that they have waived their right to withdraw the contribution. Additionally, the trust should include language that states how the beneficiaries will be notified of the gift, especially if they are minor children. The beneficiaries should also keep copies with the irrevocable trust document. If the Crummey trust rules aren't followed to the letter, the IRS will be in an excellent position to deem the gifts taxable.

When implementing a life insurance strategy, much thought and time are usually given to the nuts and bolts of the purchase—the type of policy that best meets the insured's objectives and the dollar amount of required death benefit.

Often neglected in the process are the estate-tax consequences associated with the ownership and ultimate pay out of the insurance policy. In the majority of cases, the policy tends to be owned by the insured party, with the death benefit beneficiary being the spouse, the insured's children, or a revocable trust. While life insurance death proceeds are received by beneficiaries on an income tax-free basis, the death benefit is included in the owner-insured's estate upon his death.

Life insurance policy owners in this type of situation may want to consider an alternative ownership and beneficiary strategy that completely excludes death benefit proceeds from the insured's as well as the beneficiary's estate. Further, this arrangement guarantees that the distribution arrangements are satisfied regardless of which spouse may die first. The vehicle used to achieve this goal is an irrevocable life insurance trust. When properly structured, the irrevocable insurance trust can be both the owner as well as the beneficiary of a life insurance policy, without being estate taxable at any time in the future. The trust escapes estate taxation since the insured has given up ownership, including the ability to control the policy, which becomes the duty of the trustee. Due to this inherent lack of control, term insurance is often the product of choice when funding the trust. Because term insurance has no cash value, it is purchased for the death benefit only as opposed to any investment advantages that other types of policies offer.

If a current policy is transferred to an irrevocable trust, the original policy owner must outlive the transfer by at least three years in order to avoid gifting-in-contemplation-of-death rules, which would nullify the tax advantages of the trust (IRC Sec. 2035). If, on the other hand, the insurance is owned initially by the irrevocable trust, the three-year rule does not apply. Due to this rule, the better alternative would be to have the trust drafted and implemented prior to applying for the insurance coverage.

For owners of life insurance policies interested in this estate tax-saving strategy, there are many more issues that need to be discussed with legal and financial planning professionals prior to implementation. These include the proper use of the recently increased $14,000 annual gift exclusion, the income needs of beneficiaries, and transfer limitation rules. These issues should be addressed prior to the insurance purchase in order to fully take advantage of the unique estate tax treatment associated with a properly structured irrevocable life insurance trust.

As a word of caution, make sure your estate plan is being coordinated properly with your legal and insurance advisors. To make this strategy successful, all parties should be made aware of the importance of structuring the estate plan efficiently to avoid inclusion of gifts and trust proceeds within the taxable estate.

In addition, the proper use of family limited partnerships or limited liability companies can also leverage the impact of your gifts by utilizing various discount techniques. Please reference the chapter on asset protection for additional details.

Finally, keep in mind that when you gift, at least the value of those gifts will not generate additional estate tax on your estate.

A unique form of gifting also exists that we refer to as *controlled gifting*. Using this strategy, you transfer assets into a trust that for the purpose of paying your estate tax liability at the time of your death. In this way, relatively small gifts can be leveraged in an impressive manner to pay your estate tax liability in full. This strategy makes use of a "last-to-die" life insurance policy. Please reference the section on how estate taxes can be paid for more details.

CHARITABLE GIFTS

The final basic strategy of estate planning is the effective use of charitable gifts. We could write another book on the variety of possible charitable gifting strategies. Our efforts will focus on just a few different aspects of this strategy.

The first alternative is to make a direct bequest of assets from your estate to the charity of choice. This simple method will allow you to control the assets during your life and change the charitable beneficiary whenever you believe necessary. Assets you leave to charity are not included in your taxable estate, assuming the charity you chose is considered a qualified charity by the IRS. Check with the charity in question or with your advisor if you have any doubt. Lists of such organizations are on file with the IRS.

Another alternative is to use a charitable remainder or charitable lead trust. Either of these trusts recognizes the fact that all assets are made up of two distinct interests: a present interest (which allows you to enjoy property during your life) and a remainder interest (which allows you to bequeath assets at death). While we usually and unknowingly own both interests whenever we own a piece of property, we can separate these interests. You can sell or give away either one and retain the other. Interests that are given to charity qualify for a tax deduction.

Charitable remainder trusts are created by transferring assets into the trust. The income generated by the trust is paid to you (or you and your spouse) for some predetermined time period or for life. After that period, the assets remaining in the trust are paid to the charity as identified in the trust. Charitable lead trusts work similarly, however, the income is paid to charity and the remainder is distributed to individuals after the income time period.

Once again, the benefits of these trusts are to exclude assets from your taxable estate while maintaining the benefit of these assets during life and generating some amount of tax deduction. Another benefit of these trusts is that you can shelter appreciated property from capital gains tax. If appreciated assets are transferred into the trust, the subsequent sale of these assets produces no taxable gain. Therefore, you are able to allow the full value of your capital to produce income for you rather than an amount reduced by the tax.

Charitable arrangements are usually best for those situations where you have a real need to benefit a particular organization or group of organizations. Rarely does it make sense to use one of these techniques for the possible tax advantages only.

Paying Estate Taxes

Once you have done all that is possible to reduce your estate tax liability, it comes time to identify the most appropriate asset to pay the liability that remains. In this regard, we find there are three methods of paying your taxes: use cash dollars, use borrowed dollars, or use discounted dollars. Let's look at each.

Cash dollars implies that as part of your estate, there is a money market account equal to the total tax liability. For example, if total estate taxes are $1,000,000 and your children have a money market valued at the same amount, all they have to do is write a check for $1,000,000 and send it to the government. For every dollar due in taxes, they paid 100 cents.

The next alternative is to use borrowed dollars. In this case, you may not have the $1,000,000 sitting in a money market account, but own real estate valued at $1,000,000. Your heirs could sell the property (but property sales under forced conditions rarely produce the best value for the seller). As an alternative, the children could borrow the needed cash by using the property as collateral. Once you factor in interest payments, you have a total cost running from 150 to 180 cents for every dollar.

Discounted dollars provide a different approach. When you use discounted dollars you can pay estate tax liabilities with pennies on the dollar. How does this work? Very simply. Estate taxes are usually due at the death of the surviving spouse. Discounted dollars makes use of a last-to-die life insurance policy, usually owned by an irrevocable trust or by your children. At the time of the death of the survivor of you and your spouse, the death benefit is paid creating the needed cash for estate-tax payment. Cash available on an estate tax-free basis!

Second-to-die life insurance is used to provide the liquidity to pay the ultimate estate tax. It provides insurance coverage for two individuals, typically a husband and wife, but doesn't pay a death benefit until both have died. This fits in well with estate tax planning, since the estate tax is almost always deferred until the second death. Once again, with the insurance owned by and paid to the irrevocable trust, the proceeds are received income and estate tax-free. The beneficiary children can use the insurance proceeds to pay the tax, thus avoiding the liquidation of other estate assets. The Crummey provisions are utilized to ensure that premium payments made to the irrevocable trust are deemed gifts of present interest, thus qualifying for the annual gift tax exclusion.

The discount comes into play when you compare the sum of the premiums needed to purchase the policy. For example, assuming a 65-year-old male and 65-year-old female, the annual premiums for a last-to-die policy would be approximately $16,000 for a benefit of $1,000,000 policy. (Actual costs will vary depending on the health of each individual insured.)

The net benefit is that instead of your estate being reduced by approximately 30% to 40% from estate taxes, you can transfer amounts for the last-to-die policy that may result in a total of 1% to 12%. This can be an excellent way to preserve your estate assets for children or grandchildren. Please reference the following diagram:

Discounted Dollars

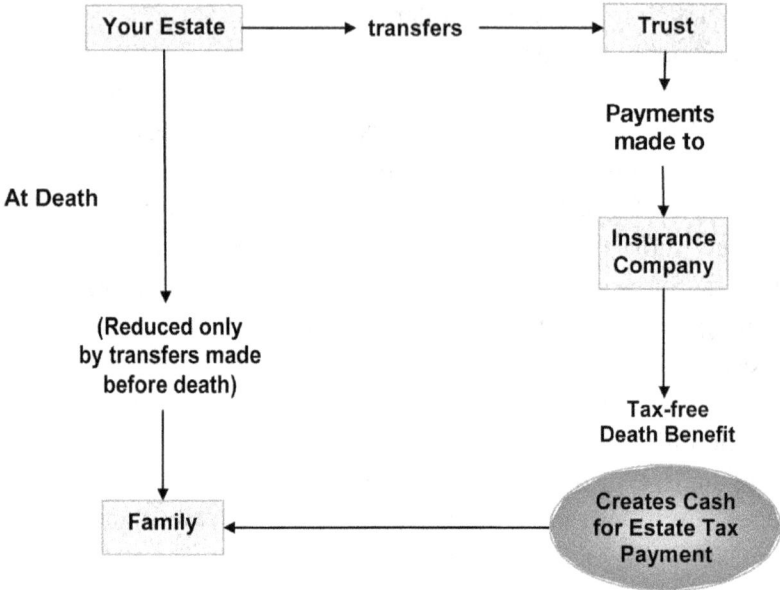

Summary

The most effective estate plan is the one that uses a variety of strategies. By combining the proper documents, gifting strategies, and charitable strategies along with an efficient manner of paying estate taxes, you are in the best position to accomplish all of your estate-planning objectives for the appropriate distribution, efficient administration, and necessary management of your estate assets. In addition, you can be certain that you have done as much as possible to position your assets at the time of your death for maximum income generation for surviving family as well as the preservation of your estate assets from the impact of estate taxation.

CHAPTER 13

Conclusion

N ow that you have learned the key principles and strategies involved in structuring an efficient, as well as a successful financial plan, it is now time to act . . . to implement. The best financial planning knowledge is worthless without taking the proper steps to improve your situation. Remember, most physicians don't plan to fail; they simply fail to plan . . . and then fail to follow through and actually implement those plans. You are now in a position to select those advisors who will assist you in reaching those long-term goals. If you have always done your own planning but are now considering working with a financial advisor, be sure that you work with an individual whom you are comfortable with.

The relationship with one's financial advisor is a true partnership, where both parties are working toward a common goal: your financial stability and financial independence.

A financial advisor may help manage your investments, evaluate portfolios, and serve as an educator to ensure a greater understanding of the investment environment. To be sure you are receiving the full benefit of such a relationship, you should take the following proactive steps to ensure that both you and your advisor are working together, as partners, to meet your current and future financial goals.

- *Evaluate your portfolio at least annually.* Even if you work with an out-of-town advisor, it is still important to put aside time on the phone or in person to review past performance and to discuss changes in goals or other life circumstances that may affect your future investing habits. Perhaps you have become more conservative and you want your portfolio to be realigned to better mirror your new risk tolerance. Any major changes could have tax implications. Before any portfolio change is made, your advisor should be able to determine its tax ramification.

- *Be specific.* When communicating with your advisor about your financial goals, be open to constructive input. The best way to guarantee that your portfolio continues to support your objectives is to talk openly and frankly to your advisor about your objectives. Let your advisor know exactly what you expect from your investments as well as from your advisor, and make sure you are comfortable with your choices.
- *Read your mail.* Don't discount investment materials as junk mail. Many of these materials provide valuable information that impacts your portfolio. The more you read, the more you'll learn about your investments as well as other investment options. If you have questions about the materials, speak with your advisor.
- *Ask your advisor questions.* If you read or hear something you don't understand—ask. It's your responsibility to let the advisor know what you need.
- *Expect the market to continue to fluctuate.* Advisors cannot eliminate market fluctuations but they can design and implement strategies to minimize volatility.

In addition to investment advisors, there are a number of other finance-based advisors who may be in a position to assist you in many of the financial planning areas. The following list of professionals, as well as their industry-focused professional designations and educational requirements, should guide you in your search for advice:

- *Accredited Asset Management Specialist (AAMS).* Twelve module, self-study course, followed by a comprehensive exam. Modules cover asset management, investment policy, risk, return, performance, asset allocation, investment strategies, tax issues, retirement planning, insurance products, estate planning, ethics, and legal and regulatory issues.

- *Accredited Tax Advisor (ATA)*. Self-study program includes six courses. This is a graduate-level course that requires a bachelor's degree, five years professional experience, a description of goals, and tax-planning experience.
- *Accredited Tax Preparer (ATP)*. Course provides basic background on tax preparation issues for individuals and sole proprietorships. Candidates must have three years of work experience in tax preparation and pass the ATP examination.
- *Chartered Financial Analyst (CFA)*. This program has three levels and can take between two and five years to complete. At the culmination of each level, there is a six-hour exam. Prerequisites for the designation include a bachelor's degree or minimum four years work experience.
- *Certified Financial Planner (CFP™)*. The Certified Financial Planner Board of Standards is a regulatory organization for financial planners. It awards the CFP designation to individuals who meet its requirements. The curriculum covers insurance, income taxation, retirement planning, investments, and estate planning. In addition to self-study programs, there are classroom instruction programs offered at colleges and universities across the country. The board requires a bachelor's degree, three years of work experience, and a passing score on the exam.
- *Certified Investment Management Analyst (CIMA)*. Three years of investment management consulting experience and completion of a preliminary exam are prerequisites for the course. Candidates must attend a one-week executive education class onsite at one of two registered education providers of the CIMA certification curriculum, The University of Chicago Booth School of Business, and The Wharton School, University of Pennsylvania. The program covers due diligence, asset allocation, risk management, and other investment management consulting concepts. Following the education component, candidates must pass a comprehensive certification examination.
- *Certified Investment Management Consultant (CIMC)*. CIMC certification is a two-level, self-study course that covers investment management consulting. It also addresses asset allocation,

formalizing investment policy, and active versus passive investment performance evaluation.

- *Certified Specialist in Tax Sheltered Accounts (CSTSA).* The CSTSA
  self-study program is for advisors who work with 403(b) plans.
  There are six courses required in the program.
- *Chartered Life Underwriter (CLU).* The CLU self-study curriculum is
  comprised of eight or more comprehensive college-level courses
  covering all aspects of insurance planning, estate and retirement
  issues, taxation, business insurance, and risk management. Three
  years of business experience and client service in the financial
  field are prerequisites for the course.
- *Chartered Financial Consultant (CHFC).* The CHFC self-study
  program includes 10 courses—9 required and 1 elective. Three
  years business experience and client service in the financial field
  are required.
- *Chartered Mutual Fund Counselor (CMFC).* This nine-module
  self-study course is a primer on mutual funds.
- *Chartered Retirement Planning Counselor (CRPC).* The CRPC
  program is an 11-module self-study program for advisors who
  provide retirement planning for individuals. Applicants gain
  indepth knowledge of individuals' needs both before and after
  retirement. The study program to become a CRPC covers the
  entire retirement planning process, including meeting multiple
  financial objectives, sources of retirement income, personal savings, employer-sponsored retirement plans, income taxes, retirement cash flow, asset management, estate planning, and more.
- *Chartered Retirement Plans Specialist (CRPS).* The CRPS program
  is targeted at advisors who work with qualified and nonqualified
  retirement plans.
- *Master of Science/Financial Planning Concentration.* This graduate-level program focuses on financial planning, wealth management, tax planning, retirement planning and estate planning.
  Participants must have a bachelor's degree to enroll and complete
  12 courses for 36 credits.

As is the case with all professional designations, just because you
have one does not necessarily mean you are good at what you do.
Word of mouth, through referrals made by friends and colleagues, is

an excellent way to meet potential advisors. Even though they may come highly recommended, it is always a good idea to interview a number of advisors to determine compatibility. Only in this manner will you be able to determine who you are most comfortable partnering with in guiding you towards, reaching, and ultimately maintaining true financial independence and long-term security.

Index

Page numbers followed by "f" indicate figures; those followed by "t" indicate tables.

A